THE VEIL

ROSEMARY ARGENTE

First edition 2011

Revised second edition 2017

Editor: Ann-Marie Budyn

Publishers: Asaina Books

Website: www.asainabooks.co.uk

Email: rosa@asainabooks.co.uk

Books by the same author:

Blantyre and Yawo Women
The Veil
The Promised Land – Companion to The
Veil
Praying Mantis
Broken Temple
Praying Mantis
Difference
Share the Ride
Home From Home
Essays and Poetry
The Place Beyond
Caesar and Mapanga Homestead

Novels:
All Mine to Have
Farewell Sophomore
The Stream of Memory
A British Throne Scandal

Science Fiction:
Farewell to the Aeroplane

Booklets:
Journey of Discovery
Enduring Fountain – Health and Well-
being
Katherine of the Wheel
Cooking With Asaina

ACKNOWLEDGEMENTS

My sincere thanks are due to Ann-Marie Budyn, for editing the manuscript and for our general discussions; to Dona Gondwe for her constructive comments; to Ian Upton, David Duddle, Brian Sherman, and Mark Sherman for their invaluable help on technology; and also to persons too numerous to mention, transcending faiths and cultures, for giving me much of their time in our discussions to share their personal views on life, death, and immortality.

Author' note:

The Hebraic Yeshua and Jesus Christ in Christianity, are interchangeably applied in the text.

Rosemary Argente

Dumfries, 2017

In memory of the infant siblings
Basil, Joseph, and Natalie
and their cousin Yusof

CONTENTS

THE VEIL

PART ONE

1 THE HOLY BIBLE

"A closed Bible is just an ordinary book.

A read Bible is a mind-opener."

Fatima Sale Moreira [1]

The Bible is about Jesus from Genesis to Revelation, according to the Christian interpretation. He is depicted and prophesied about in each of the 66 Bible books as in numerous typology (types) in the lives of different characters in the Bible. Genesis 3:15: *"...Between your seed and her seed"* (God speaking to the serpent); and Luke 1:34-35: *"...who is to be born will be called the son of God"* (angel speaking to Mary). Revelation 1:17, 22:13: *"The Alpha and Omega", the First and the Last."*

The Bible is a continuous story of mankind. There is nothing that has taken or takes place on this earth up to modern times that the Bible does not reflect universally, touching on life temporal and spiritual. The Bible is also a learning institution, a legal document, and a covenant document. To some the Bible contains entertaining fables while to Abraham Lincoln: *"The Bible is the best gift God has given to man."*

The two sections of the Bible are referred to as "Testaments", Old and New. Where there is a testament there is a testator whose testament only takes effect after the testator's death in favour of a named beneficiary or beneficiaries:

> *"For a testament is in force after men are dead, since it has no*
>
> *power at all while the testator lives.* [1a]
>
> *Though only man's covenant confirmed none can amend."* [2]

Notes, references, and comments:

1 Sister of the author. 1a Hebrews 9:17. 2 Galatians 3:15, origin Latin: *testamentum* equivalent of *testa(ri)* to bear witness. It may be said that the meaning of Testament, in welcoming the 'open mind' but without imposing upon that mind: the Revelation of Yeshua Messiah = Jesus Christ. The Apocalypse stands in the closest affinity to the Gospel of John: *"The Son has everything the Father has and yet has nothing but what He has of the Father."* This clearly indicates that Jesus is 'the son' of God, as we all are children of God. God is the ultimate testator but we look to Emmanuel, *God with us, Child of God,* who lived an exemplary life; for Yeshua, by his teachings, is the incarnate answer to the cry for a tangible God, such as we are so far removed from the spiritual side of ourselves, as Yoga teaches but based on Jesus. The Testament took force after the death of Yeshua: the *Beneficiary* is the *child of the promise,* and the *Bible* is the *witness* document prepared and recorded by those who possessed the art of writing. The difference between the testament by a human, whereby the beneficiary benefits during life on Earth but after the death of the testator; and, the Testament of the Bible is that the *Beneficiary* benefits only after his or her own death; for Yeshua, as the messenger of the testator's message of redemption dies, symbolising the human testator and as the way to God.

A testament can also mean *witness* in the form of a document containing information witnessed by someone. These pose some questions:

> *The Bible as a testament, who is the testator?*
> *Who is the beneficiary or beneficiaries?*
> *As a witness document, who is the witness?*
> *What does the document witness?*

The New Testament was written after the death of one who was understood to be a *redeemer,* though the New Testament connects to the Old Testament as containing one continuous message.

The first five books of the Bible collectively are the *Ten Commandments* containing (the Pentateuch) the law of YAHWEH (God) as revealed to Moses on Mount Sinai.

The Pentateuch is the Mosaic law:

Genesis: Recording genealogy and origin of man, from creation to Joseph in Egypt;

Exodus: The Israelite going out of Egyptian bondage and building of God's Tabernacle;

Leviticus: Ritual rules for Levite priests;

Numbers: Census, counting the people and forty years of wandering in the desert; and

Deuteronomy :`second law', a mistranslation in Greek, containing the speech of Moses to the Israelite before he dies and before entry into Canaan, the Promised Land.

The Mosaic Law is in three parts:

One: The moral law summarising the requirements of the infinitely holy God for the Almighty's redeemed people;

Two: The civil law conditioning the social life of Israel; and

Three: The ceremonial law governing the religious life of Israel, to be abolished in the era of the end time when a *redeemer* for all was to manifest.

These laws refer to the Israelite, the land they live in, the meaning of which is indicated in a *tabernacle* yet to be constructed by Moses. The Bible contains a number of discrepancies. At the beginning of the Old Testament, it is stated that mankind was, at first, only two people, Adam and Eve. They had three children, Cain, Abel, and Seth, and yet it goes on to say that:

> *"After he begot Seth, the days of Adam were eight hundred years;*
>
> *and he had sons and daughters."* [3]

Notes, references and comments:

3 Genesis 5:4.

But the Bible does not give us the names of the daughters or tell us who were the wives of Cain, Abel or Seth. Were they excluded because of the masculine mindset of the writers? Are we to assume that they married their sisters? But such assumptions are forbidden in the same Bible:

> *"None of you shall approach anyone who is near of kin to him,*
>
> *to uncover his nakedness: I am the Lord.":* [4]

The King James Translation of the Holy Bible known as the King James, or Authorised Version of the Bible was commissioned by King James V1 of Scotland, who became James 1 of England, in 1570 from the Hebrew and Greek languages. It is the most widely published text in the English language and has been called the *"noblest monument of English prose"* recognised for centuries as both a religious and literary classic. Translation of the Bible into national languages enables readers to understand its message in a language familiar to them but the short comings of translation leave much to be desired. If a tutor were to ask a class of any number to write an essay on the same subject each would produce an *own mindset* version of the same thing – though a pupil may pass the test if the 'gist' of the matter is captured in the essay (but also according to the mind-set of the tutor; tutors hold absolute discretion). This is well-demonstrated by the poet Du Bartas:[5a]

"Bring me, quoth one, a trowel, quickly-quick.
One brings him up a hammer; then this brick,
Another bids, and then they cleave a tree;
Make fast this rope, and then they let it flee.
One calls for planks; another mortar lacks;
They bare the first a stave – the last an axe.
One would have spikes, and him a spade they give;
Thus crossly crost, they prate and prate in vain;
What one hath made, another mars again."

Some sections of the Old Testament make alarming and unpleasant reading, such as the draconian prescriptions on issues of morality which reflect a male-dominated society of Biblical days and ways.[5b]

Notes, references and comments:

4 Leviticus 18:6-18, Proverbs 30:6 "Do not add to His words, lest He rebuke you, and you be found a liar." What is the answer to this? Though Matthew, Mark and Luke describe the same miracles they are not entirely similar, while John's account is lengthy. An example is the Parable of the Vineyard, also known as Parable of the Wicked Tenants: Matthew 21:33-46; Mark 12:1-12; Luke 20:9-19, with Matthew's account being the most complete; in the accounts of the others there are additions. The vineyard = God's earth; tenant farmer = mankind; servants = Old Testament prophets; and the son = Jesus. 5a: Guillaume de Salluste, seigneur Du Bartas (1544-1590), an ardent Huguenot who sought to use poetic techniques for Protestant views [henceforth the *Du Bartas syndrome*]. 5b continued below...

Covenants successive to the Mosaic Covenant manifesting the Tabernacle refer to and are in conjunction with the message in the Tabernacle.[6a] The Old Testament Pentateuch[6b] contains the earliest dispensations, [6c] as revealed to Moses at Mount Sinai, much related to the Tabernacle.

Three-Act Human Drama: [7]

Act One - From Creation to Jesus, Calvary Hill. The Old Testament is a Hebraic sacred anthology on God. All about the law recording to God's direction through Israel as a way back to the Creator after Adam and Eve had lost fellowship with God. Unlike their contemporaries, Egyptians and Babylonians who wrote on religion, legal codes, legends, prophesies, proverbs and poetry. Those chosen to lead the people during the Eras of Dispensation believed that the Hebrew were God's "chosen people" set apart from other races in developing their identity. But sadly, the Israelite themselves lacked that belief; nonetheless, the leaders did not deify their forebears, a quality that makes the Old Testament a truly *human record.*[8]

Notes, references and comments:

5b continued from above: There is some degree of discord amongst Christians as others believe that the male-dominated characteristic of the writers of the Old Testament does not devalue the truth of the Bible. Others believe that it does detract from its truthfulness but even the writers of the New Testament exhibit a degree of male-domination contrary to the teachings of Yeshua Subordination of women: Genesis 3:16, pain and anguish in childbirth; Levititus 21:9: "...the daughter of a priest as a whore...she shall be burned with fire"; and Genesis 38.24: "...Tamar...has played the harlot... 'bring her out and let her be burned'." But the men those women liaised with are not mentionedl. Deuteronomy 25:11, 12, wife in defence of husband, if her hand fell on the genitals of the other...cut off her hand; Leviticus 12:2: woman considered unclean after giving birth: purification ritual 7 days for a male baby; and Leviticus 12:5, 14 Continued below...Continued from above: days for a female baby, despite that woman was the nurturer of the human being at the first stage of entry into the world and the male child is also born through woman. The NT writers also exhibit some degree of male chauvenism despite Jesus' liberal attitude towards women. Christians live under a *new covenant* and most know that where the OT exhibits male chauvinism the choice is clear: as the NT asserts that there is neither Jew nor Gentile, neither slave nor free, nor is there male nor female, for all are one in Christ Jesus. Yeshua brought the new era of love, peace, and charity. 6a A covenant (Latin origin = *con venire,* meaning coming together) is a contract or agreement between two or more parties. Biblical covenant is how God has chosen to communicate and to redeem man and to guarantee eternal life in Jesus, not only according to Christian interpretation of the Bible, but also those non-Christians who have and follow the teachings of Jesus.   6b First five books of the Holy Bible, the *Ten Commandments* collectively; said to have been written by Moses.   6c Dispensation, in tandem with covenant, is a method of interpreting history that divides God's work towards mankind into different periods of time. 7 According to William Neil, *One Volume Bible Commentary.* 8 William Neil, ditto.

Act Two - Is about a redeemer who pacifies the people, breaking down a middle veil that separated them, and Jesus' new apostles breaking the barriers that kept humans from God and separated them from one another. In the Old Testament are prophesies on the coming of a Messiah who fits the description of Yeshua, the Hebrew, Saviour of Jews and Gentiles, according to Christianity:

"For he [Jesus] is our peace, who hath made both one, and hath broken down the middle wall of partition between us." 9

Act Three - Covers the period from Calvary Hill *to the Ascension*, the second coming of Jesus and is about God's grace in human redemption through Jesus followed by God's divine eternal government.

How the Bible was written

For over 300 years dissenting opinions were debating about exactly what should be considered scripture and what should not, followed by a few early councils that decided what should and should not be included as scripture. Translations of documents written during these councils had an inclusive, though not exhaustive, list of seventy-three books considered valid scripture, leaving room for potential additions later. For another 1200 years, the list was considered scripture, at this point the Orthodox leaders decided more books belonged in the Bible. Dissent increased on exactly what belonged in the bible. Martin Luther wanted not just the seven books called "deuterocanon" or "apocrypha", which were not considered scripture to be removed, including Daniel and Revelation. The Church held another council where it officially declared and settled the matter on what was, and was not to belong in the bible. For a time afterward the seven books were still included in the bible, plus protestant ones - in a separate section labelled "apocrypha",10 and were included in the 1611 King James versions but later the apocrypha was excluded. The early Christian groups were much influenced by the Roman legacy and it was a chaos of contending beliefs. Some believed that there was not one God but several, while others claimed that the world had been created by a lesser deity and not by God: all of whom maintained the teachings of Jesus and his apostles, based on writings as evidence of their claims, such as books reputedly produced by the followers of Jesus.

Notes, references and comments:

9 Ephesians 2:14, Proverbs 27:10; *The Good News,* November-December 2009. 10 Apocrypha (hidden) or Deuterocanonical (second canon) books were written in the time between the Old and New Testaments, the *Canon of Scripture* by F F Bruce and *Logos Bible.* The content of the Bible is according to 'personal perception'. Faith is belief in something that is not supported by evidence. Each one of us is a potential Melchizedech, priest or prophet of our own destiny. Our actions are the basis of the prophesy of our own making, in the second place, as legacy plays a vital role in our lives. Peter 3:15, 16). Some of the NT books were being circulated among the churches (Colossians 4:16; 1 Thessalonians 5:27). Clement of Rome mentioned at least eight NT books (AD 95). Ignatius of Antioch acknowledged about 7 books (AD 115). Polycarp, a disciple of John the apostle, acknowledged 15 books (AD 108). Later, Irenaeus mentioned 21 books (AD 185). Hippolytus recognised 22 books (AD 170-235). The NT books receiving the most controversy were Hebrews, James, 2 Peter, 2 John, and 3 John.

Ehrman offers his fascinating study of these early forms of Christianity and shows how they came to be suppressed, reformed, or forgotten. Ehrman's discussion covers various "lost scriptures", including forged gospels supposedly written by Simon Peter, Jesus' closest disciple, and Judas, Thomas, Jesus' alleged twin brother; to the different beliefs of the Jewish-Christian Ebionites, the anti-Jewish Marcionites, and a variety of "Gnostic". Ehrman examines in depth the battles that raged between "proto-orthodox Christians", who eventually compiled the canonical books of the New Testament, and standardised Christian belief, and the groups they denounced as heretics and ultimately overcame by the winners. [11]

The Masoretic Text is one of the many Translations of the Bible [12] and is the authoritative Hebrew language text of the Jewish Bible regarded almost universally as the official version known as the Masorah. The Torah, Mosaic law from the Pentateuch has been interpreted by Gentiles into the Old and New Testaments as a highly specialised full-time Christian occupational profession.

The Codex Sinaiticus is a fourth century version of the Bible said to be the oldest Greek language Bible, the prominent language of the early Christian era since Emperor Constantine.

The Bible we have today is said to be an accurate copy of the original Bible of the first century and the earlier Bible from which it was copied was lost and current texts are copies of copies.[13] The oldest is not necessarily the most accurate. The Bible battles commenced after Constantine had adopted Christianity apparent in the emergence of various Christian denominations.

The Douay-Rheims Translation of the Roman Catholic church had its own difficult passage through history, following the forced conversion of England to Protestantism. At the subsequent persecution and martyrdom of Catholics, a good number of the English fled to the Continent, and the need for a new English translation of Scripture arose.

The first English Version Translation used by the Roman Catholic Church since AD 1582 with the words of Jesus in red, was translated from the Latin Vulgate. The New Testament was first published by the English College at Rheims, France. The Old Testament was first published by the English College at Douay, France, an English translation of the Vulgate – principal Latin version of the Bible, prepared mainly by St Jerome (late 4th century, revised 1592, adopted as the official text for the Roman Catholic Church. The principal Latin version of the Bible, was prepared mainly by St Jerome in the late 4th century (revised in 1592) and

Notes, references and comments:

11 Bart D Ehrman, leading Bible scholar, analyses the formation and history of Christianity, *Lost Christianities, Books That Did Not Make It Into The New Testament.* Recent scholarship has explored many fascinating bypaths of Early Christianity. Paul considered Luke's writings to be as authoritative as the OT (1 Timothy 5:18: Deuteronomy 25:4 and Luke10:7). Peter recognised Paul's writings as Scripture.12 *The Good News* ditto. 13 Here the *Du Bartas syndrom* is most applicable. *The Good News* ditto page 3 says: "*The Interpreter's Dictionary of the Bible* states: 'The text about the three heavenly witnesses (1 John 5:7 KJV) is not an authentic part of the NT.'"

adopted as the official text for the Roman Catholic Church. The whole Revised Version had diligently been compared with the Latin Vulgate by Bishop Richard Challoner, AD 1749-1752. Published with the approbation of James Cardinal Gibbons, Archbishop of Baltimore (1843-1921). Translations were carried out by Roman Catholic scholars, and the Old and New Testaments comprised in the Douay-Rheims.

Other records show that the original texts of the Bible were written by various authors sometime after c. AD 45 and gradually collected into a single volume.14 Christians differ as to the works included in the New Testament but the majority of scholars are settled on the same twenty-seven book canon: four gospels, narratives, on the life and death of

Jesus; a narrative of the Apostles' ministries in the early church; the epistles, twenty-one early letters,

in biblical context, by various authors and consisting mostly of Christian counsel and instruction; and an Apocalyptic prophesy. Until the 1300s clergy were the ultimate Biblical authority for the average person, particularly given that the Bible was only available in the Latin version (The Vulgate). [15]

In John 8:38 Jesus says:

"I speak what I have seen with my Father..."

In 1 Corinthians 2:14:

"But the natural man does not receive the things of the spirit of God, for they are foolishness unto him...never can he know them, because they are spiritually discerned.

The Bible as also a legal document and the *law of constant prayer* is part of the law of reciprocity:

"Therefore I say to you whatever things you ask when you pray, believe that you receive them and you will have them ...but forgive to be forgiven...to see miracles there must be forgiveness and love." 16

Notes, references and comments:

14 Walter Veith, Battle of the Bible, Changing the Word, Cds Parts 1, 2 and 3; See Part 4, Chapter 9, Assumed Divine Mandate. The inspiration and authenticity of the Bible is said to be the testimony of Scriptures and original copies of autographs inspired by God. Many of Jesus' sayings would have been written down at the time, according to Christian belief. 15 1 Corinthians 2:14, 2 Corinthians 4:4 and Matthew 7:7, 8; these are lessons for those who do not believe. 16 Matthew 6:14, 15, Psalms 103:12, Hebrews 9:14. 1 Matthew 28:18-20, 10:2-4, Acts 1:8, 20:26, Luke 6:13-16. Matthew's relationship to the Gospels of Mark and Luke remains an open question known as the "synoptic problem:" they may have copied from each other or all copied from a common single source, written in Greek or Aramaic though this is uncertain; *The Good News,* ditto. *The Good News,* November-December 2009.

The Gospels

Christian theology teaches that after His resurrection and ascension,

Jesus sent the disciples out to be His witnesses and He called them "Apostles".[17] The Synoptic Gospels of Matthew, Mark and Luke are similar in a number of ways, such as wording, sequence, and episodes, which largely differ from John. Excluded from the four gospels is the Gospel of Thomas, which radically differs from gospels accepted by most Churches.[18] A sixth-century manuscript was translated from the ancient language of Syriac into a book: *The Lost Gospel*. For the first time, the book is credited with finally explaining about the life of Jesus during the decades before he appeared in the Bible.

The manuscript dates back to 1,450 AD, and was found in the British Library, London; and the book claims that Jesus' sexuality was whitewashed from history by prudish early Christians, who also downplayed the importance of Mary Magdalene, his wife and mother of his two children. Further, that she is a co-deity, a co-redeemer, and she is called 'Daughter of God' as he's called 'Son of God,' [19] According to Simcha Jacobovici:

"We think of Christianity as sexless, this [Gospel] says that sex is sacred."

The Church of England dismissed the claim comparing it to the work of Dan Brown.[20]

Absent from the Gospel, unlike the canonical Gospels, are: resurrection, a God named Jesus, physical miracles by Jesus, fulfilment of prophesy, apocalyptic kingdom that would disrupt the world order, Jesus dies for no one's sins; Yeshua critiques religious piety, and offers a way to salvation: Most Christians believe that most probably these are the reasons for excluding the Gospel of Thomas from the New Testament. The sayings of Yeshua in the

Notes, references and comments:

17 Matthew 10:1-42, Jesus chose 12 disciples before he died: Luke 6:13; Acts 9:15 and Galatians 1:11,12. The New Testament tells of the fate of only two of the apostles: Judas, who betrayed Jesus and then went out and hanged himself, and James the son of Zebedee, who was exeuted by Herod about 44 AD, Acts 12:2. 18 Elaine Pagels (one of the students at Harvard), *Beyond Belief*, pages 29, 34, *The Coptic Gospel of Thomas* (the Gospel); was discovered in 1945 amongst other unheard of secrets, written in the first century many of them contain Biblical events, sayings, rituals, and dialogues attributed to Yeshua and his disciples. It has been described as "one of the world's best loved sacred texts": Tau Malachi, *The Gnostic Gospel of St Thomas, Mediation on Mystical Teachings* (2004). 19 The *Lost Gospel: Decoding the Sacred Text That Reveals Jesus' Marriage to Mary Magdalene* (12/11/14), by Barry Wilson and Simcha Jacobovici. *The Daily Mail,* 09/11/14; indeed sex is sacred, it is through sex we

are conceived; sex beomes dirty by those who abuase it. 20 Dan Brown, *The da Vinci Code.* No where does the Bible mention that Mary Magdalene was ever an Apostle. The only authority quoted for this is said to be 'apocryphal'. The question is "Who said so?" Does it matter whether Jesus was husband and father? Is it not that the most important point is the value of the message he delivered to humanity? Some read the Bible literally with a closed mind, others claim that their understanding of the Bible is best and only they hold the key to heaven, as they pontificate: *"This is the word of God..."* But Jesus said: *"...according to the grace of God which was given to me...as builder I have laid the foundation...another builds on it. But let each one take heed [how] he builds on it."* 1 Corinthians 3:9-15, 1 Peter 2:24, 2 Corinthians 5:10, Ephesians 2:8-10, John 3:16, 36, 5:24, Romans 1:16, 5:1.

Gospel also lead to questions on Canonical Christianity in the Virgin Birth, the Trinity, the nature of God in relation to Yeshua and humans, and Punishment after life as taught by canonical Christianity, Tau Malachi, The Gnostic Gospel of St Thomas, Mediation on Mystical. Teachings (2004). The Gospel is conserved at the Coptic Museum in Old Cairo, Egypt; and papyrus Oxyrhynchus 1,654 and 655 are preserved in the Bodleian Library at Oxford University, the British Library in London, and Houghton Library at Harvard University. Gospel of Thomas is comprised 114 of The Secret Sayings of the Living Jesus, within and behind your heart. Thomas also held a prominent place in Syrian Christianity where his memory was respected.

Subordination of Women and Jesus is featured in many passages of the Bible. In scripture women are not called disciples despite that the New Testament indicating that women were closely identified with Jesus and his disciples. Particularly in the epistles, are mentioned a number of women who were followers of Jesus are mentioned: Mary Magdalene; Mary, the mother of James and Joses and others. 21

Paul thanking the churches at Colosi of the Gentiles tells Phoebe, servant of the Church in Cenicherea, to greet Priscilla and Salome, fellow workers in Jesus; 22 sisters Mary and Martha; Tabitha Dorcas; widow of Nai; the sick woman who Jesus healed on Sabbath at the Synagogue; 23 the poor widow who gave "two copper coins" to the Temple treasury; 24 the unnamed sisters of Jesus; 25 wife of Simon Cephas, also known as Peter; the wives of Jesus' brothers, Joseph, James (Jacob), Simon and Jude; wives of the apostles other than Paul and Barnabas; 26 the woman who was stoned for adultery; the woman who anointed the feet of Jesus 27 and the Samaria woman at the well 28 and many others.

Women were reported to be first witnesses to the resurrection, chiefly

Mary Magdalene, who was witness and messenger of the risen Jesus. The apostles had little regard for her witness and of the other women, saying they "seemed as idle tales." [29]

Between 1975 and 2005, the worldwide Catholic population increased by 57 percent, from 709.6 million to 1.13 billion, while the number of priests remained about the same with an increase of only 0.4 percent (Centre for Applied Research in the Apostolate). The Second

Notes, references and comments:

21 Matthew 27:55-56. The Old Testament highlights major roles played by various women, names over a hundred Women, a host of others unnamed, prominent queens, prophetesses, judges such as Deborah and military leaders, such as Jael. 22 Romans 16:3. 23 Mark 16:1. 24 Mark 12:41-44, the famous *widow's mite.* 25 Matthew 13:55. 26 1 Corinthians 9:5. 27 Luke 7:44-50. 28 John 4:5-28. Continued from above: 29 Luke 24:11.Some believe that the roles of women were severely restricted and they were treated as inferior to men in the ancient world, consequently men featured prominently in the writing of the Bible though these views have been debated. Women most probably became apostles. Continued below...29 Continued: after Jesus' death and resurrection, but more likely than not, the patriarchal stance would not permit this to be included in the Bible. Karen L. King, *The Gospel of Mary of Magdala: Jesus and the First Woman Apostle.* The Bible contains many passages indicating women as leaders in early Christianity: "*I commend to you our sister Phoebe, a deacon of the church Cenchreae*", Romans 16:1.

Vatican Council called for all discrimination to be removed: Every type of discrimination based on gender is to be eradicated as contrary to God's intent.[30]

In 1976, the Pontifical Biblical Commission determined that there was no biblical reason to prohibit women's ordination. December 28, 1970, Bishop Felix Davidek ordained Ludmilla Javorova a priest in the underground church of Communist Czechoslovakia. In 1991, Cardinal Miloslav Vlk of Prague confirmed that five other women were also ordained as priests during that time. Archaeological discoveries indicate evidence that women served as deacons, priests, and bishops in early Christianity. [31]

2 The Covenants

Introduction

Covenant theology is based on the theory that God has only one covenant with humans, the covenant of grace, and only one people, represented by the Old Testament and the New Testament saints – one people, one church and one plan for all.[1] The meaning is the "way" is open to all. However, "all" is qualified, those who are or have become by choice the *children of Israel*; and the choice is by repentance and belief in Jesus who is the "way" to God.

A covenant in scripture is not the same as a covenant between humans. God cannot enter into an agreement with human, as fellow humans would. And, human cannot enter into an agreement with God, because the two parties to the covenant are not equals. A covenant in scripture is peculiar and unique, a solemnly declared purpose, *dispensation* or promise of God with corresponding obligations on humans. For example, the ark was commanded to be made; the requirement on the part of Noah was faith and obedience. Dispensation is a system of theology with two distinctions: a consistently literal interpretation of Scripture, especially Bible prophecy, and a distinction between Israel and the Church in God's program.[2]

The Covenants of Scripture are several within the historical context of the Old and New Testaments and each relates to the moral and spiritual history of humans on earth. In the narrative of "human redemption", a *Covenant* is a specific revelation of God's will for humans

Notes, references and comments:

30 *Vatican II, Gaudiumet Spes, #29.* 31 www.womenpriests.org, Genesis 1:27: *"Humankind was created as God's reflection: in the divine image God created them, female and male."* Has the interpretation by the Church fathers (so-called), and leaders, served Yeshua well? Has the Church followed the teachings of Jesus? Women are mentioned in the Bible but not honoured as men have been. However, it is not only male priests, or even men in general, undermine women or object to the ordination of women, but also an appreciable number of women. And, it was not until close to 2,000 years after the death of Jesus, despite his liberal attitude towards women, that the liberation of women emerged.

2 The Covenants: 1. The Moody Handbook of Theology by Paul Enns. 2. Page 16, Holy Bible, King James Authorised Version. References 3, 4, 5, and 6 continued beloe...in a relationship of responsibility; which covers a time period called an *era, economy, dispensation or*

administration. God monitors the response of each one of us to the divinely-revealed Covenant for the duration of each of such time. A new administration is introduced in each covenant which has a time element and expires at its given period.[3]

Because God and human are not equals, covenant required animal sacrifice. By symbolic ritual of dividing an animal goes back to the ancient idea that the life of an animal is in the blood.[4] The sacrifice was for some dedicated purpose whereby the two parties pass between the dismembered animal.[5] The parties are thus bound by the third unifying factor, the liberated life of the consecrated victim into which they enter. Variations of the basic idea lie at the root of all sacrifices in the Old Testament, purified in the New Testament teaching as the meaning of the sacrifice of Jesus, by whom God and human are bound together in a deeper covenant relationship[6] but only God passes symbolically between the sacrificial victims. It is God's own act of grace to bind the people to the Almighty. In the symbolic rite God is represented as a smocking furnace and a burning lamp.[7]

The Abrahamic Covenant, perhaps of all covenants, has the most controversial interpretation, particularly on the point of "the promised land". Each of the three monotheistic religions claims to be the true descendant of Abraham: Judaism (Isaac), Christianity (Jesus), and Islam (Ishmael). According to Christian theology, the Abrahamic Covenant was made with Abram (before his name was changed to Abraham) and confirmed to Isaac and Jacob, in the Administration of Promise of the "Redeemer" for the entire race in Adam. [1]

Judaism claims YAHWEH gave the holy land of Canaan, modern day Palestine, to the Israelite as an ever-lasting possession when God said to Joshua:

"Every place on which the sole of your foot treads shall be yours..." [2]

History shows much of `every place' to have fallen into a succession of non-Israelite, whether individual or national ownership.

Islam claims that the only true religion is the religion of Abraham, that Islam is the religion of Abraham through Ishmael, Abraham's first-born son.[3] In the same vein, the Christian church holds itself as the heir of salvation, promised to all who believe in the *one true God* and that Israel shall accept the Messiah at the second coming of Jesus.[4]

Notes, references and comments:

2 The Covenants references continued:

16

3. *Unger's Survey of the Bible.* 4. Genesis 9:4-6. 5. Jeremiah 34:18. 6. Hebrews 9:15-22. 7. Exodus 13:21-

The Abrahamic Covenant: 1 Deuteronomy 11:24, Joshua 1:3. Abram was a Semetic Gentile who was saved in the Mesopotamian city of Ur during the Third Dynasty of the Sumero-Akkadian Empire under King Ur-Nammu. 2 Genesis 26:1-5, 15:6. see Chapter 11: Palestinian Covenant on Messianic Administration. 3 Imran N Hosein, *The Religion of Abraham & The State of Israel.* 4 Galatians 3:16,28,29.,The irony is that the leaders of Judaism condemned to death one of its own, Yeshua. Judaism in the majority rejects the claim that Jesus is the redeemer, except those Jews who follow the Messianic sect, who are in the minority comparatively. Islam rejects the Judaism claim but accepts Jesus as a prophet and awaits his second coming.

Those who bless Abraham's descendants are blessed and those who curse them are cursed. According to the Bible, all the three claimants have a legitimate claim as the descendants of Abraham, founder and believer of the one true God. Abram was told to leave and go to a place where God would later direct him,[5] the divide between Jews and Gentiles had not existed then. As a specific period of testing, the Administration of Promise in Abram ended with Israelite acceptance of the law in the Mosaic Covenant at Sinai.[6]

The Christian church (Gentiles) holds that the nation Israel in Abraham's "seed" is privileged to provide the Messiah[7] and to inherit a specific territory for ever.[8] Israelite, Jews and Hebrews are said to be God's chosen people:

"For you are a holy people to the Lord your God [who] has chosen

you to be a people for Himself, a special treasure above all the

peoples on the face of the earth." [9]

On Judaism Pope John Paul II says:

"Origins of the Church's faith and election are already found in

the Patriarchs, Moses and the Prophets...neither can the Church

forget that it received the revelation of the Old Testament with

whom [Hebrews] God made the Ancient Covenant nor can the

Church forget that it draws sustenance from the root of that good

olive tree onto which have been grafted the...Gentiles." [10]

The Israelite as a race had been a unit until the call of Abram, with the vision of the one true God, after the Edenic, Adamic, and Noahic covenants, covering the three eras of God's disappointment in the human race, according to to Christian theology.

The Edenic Covenant dealt with Administration of Innocence and was given to Adam and Eve after Creation, according to Christian theology. The first narration is said to be the *non-subordinating view of woman* declaring God's purpose before division of the sexes:

> *"And God said, Let us make man In our image, according to our likeness...*
>
> *let them have dominion over the fish of the sea, over the birds of the air, and*
>
> *over the cattle, over ...all ...that creeps on the earth..." 1*

Notes, references and comments:

5 Genesis 12:1-3; God's covenant for Abram, father of many nations, Genesis 12:1-3. 6 See Mosaic Covenant. The conditions of which span over all succeeding ages, like those of the previous covenants: Administration of Innocence (Edenic), Administration of Conscience and Moral Responsibility (Adamic), and Administration of Human Government (Noahic). 7 Galatians 3:16, 28, 29, *Unger's Survey of the Bible.* NT word for seed is sperma: W E Vine's An Expository Dictionary of Biblical Words, pp.1010-11. 8 Genesis 12:2. 9 Deuteronomy 7:6. 10 *Crossing The Threshold of Hope.* The Covenant of Abram continued below after Noah...

Edenic Covenant: 1 Genesis 1:26-27, as these passages are in the plural who was God speaking to, Yeshua, angels, and others in Heaven? *Unger's Survey of the Bible,* Hebrew "Adam" was made from *adamah,* earth male and female. Cross references Mark 10:6-8 says "into one flesh", Matthew 19:5 says "God created male and female".

The second narration in the New Testament says:

"...a man shall leave his father and mother and be joined to his

wife, and they shall become one flesh...2

God gave the human pair joint responsibility and "ruler-ship" over the Almighty's creation:

"Then God blessed them and said be fruitful and multiply fill the

earth and subdue it. Have dominion over the fish and the sea,

over birds of the air and over every living thing that moves on

the earth [including vegetation]." 3

he Edenic Covenant was composed of the following conditions:

1. *Populate the earth with Adam and Eve's offspring.*

2 *Control nature and earth to human needs.*

3. *Have dominion over animals.*

4. *Live on a vegetable diet.*

5. *Engage in delightful light work in the garden.*

6. *Not to eat of the tree of knowledge of good and evil. 4*

Although Eve has been blamed for the fall of man for following the serpent's trickery to eat fruit from the forbidden tree, Adam lacked the conviction to say `No'. Breaking the last tenet of the covenant, ended their fellowship with God and were subjected to threefold death: *immediate spiritual death*; *gradual physical death* (the toll of the years to old age) and *eventual eternal death* in Gehenna. The so-called Eve's sin found full expression in the Middle Ages.[5]

The Edenic Covenant was annulled and followed by the Adamic Covenant and Administration of Conscience and Moral Responsibility. [6]

Adam, Eve and descendants were delivered from instant eternal spiritual death by God's grace through Christ's redemptive work. By faith we understand and believe that the worlds were framed by the word of God, so that things which are seen were made not of things which appear apparent to the eye[7] and humans of all nations were made of one blood to dwell on the face of the earth. [8]

Notes, references and comments:

2 Genesis 2:24. Also known as covenant of life, Romans 5:12-21. 3 Genesis 1:28, God gave the human pair joint responsibility over the Almighty's creation, Psalm 8:3-9. 4 Genesis 2:7. Adam lived on for 930 Jeremiah 33:20-26 (*cf.* 31:35, 36) compares the covenant with David to God's covenant with day, night, life and statutes of heaven and earth. 5 The subject in John Milton's classic epic *Paradise Lost,* and for centuries the unmarried woman, blessed by the maternal covenant, took the blame but never the man she shared the experience with. Has the masculine mindset writing and interpretation of the Bible been fair to women? Or should we put the shortcomings to the writers of the Bible? 6 *Unger' Survey of the Bible.* Genesis 2:15-17, 29, 30. 7 Hebrews 11:3. 8 Acts 17:26.

Creation or Evolution?

"The aim of science is not to open the door to infinite wisdom but to set a

limit to infinite error." [9]

Before the Bible story was there life then? Some believe that the world could not have begun with the incomparable Biblical story of Adam and Eve because there are many fossils, some mysterious and others un-ravelled, of human habitation in structures around the world. Sometimes humanity may lack due respect for the possibility that there may have been far more superior technology to what we have today, albeit of a different nature. Most knowledge is based on the legacy of written history, which is a written form of oral testimony, though the value of oral testimony rests within the living, until put in writing.

Science and religion compete with each other on the origin of life. Darwin's publication of *The Origin of Species* on the theory of evolution opened the floodgates to the freedom of scientists and philosophers to pursue the theory of evolution which had been suppressed by Christian orthodoxy for centuries.

Creation and Evolution are not in disagreement that humans were created last, each arriving at that conclusion through different paths.

Dawkins, demonstrating on a piano keyboard as a yardstick, explains that from the bottom of the keyboard to the last but a few keys was the period without humans on earth. In chronological terms, human existence covered only the last few keys on the piano keyboard.[10] Scientists speculate that 15 billion years ago the Universe was non-existent. There was no life, but a great void of a cold and dark solar system; and life began by a cosmos explosion, the *Big Bang* [11] expanding from nothing to 1.25 billion, billion miles. Within a second after the Big Bang four major events took place: T*he central event of creation, the cosmos, space-time,* and interdependent *mass and gravity*. The *building substance of all matter* was created: the planets; Earth's basic bacteria pulsated and commenced to evolve along with the Earth itself. Methane, carbon dioxide, ammonia and water in the atmosphere and seas of the young Earth, along with ultraviolet radiation or lightning, *could have* combined the chemicals into amino acids, the building blocks of protein of all living things.

Chemists have placed similar substances into a flask to imitate chemical conditions of the young Earth; and seven days later a brown 'primeval soup' with large numbers of molecules, building blocks, claimed to be DNA itself, the original replicator of life have been found.[12] So say the Evolutionists.

Evolution works on probabilities in Darwinian terms of the origin of species. In the Bible are many facts for Faith in Creation such as the fact that all living things are reproduced after their own kind as in the Old Testament:

Notes, references and comments:

9 Bertolt Brecht, *The Life of Galileo.* 10 Richard Dawkins, *The Genius of Darwin, The Origin of Species,* published 24/11/1859. 11 Readers Digest, the phrase 'Big Bang' was coined by Fred Hoyle, astronomer who regarded the theory as similar to the Biblical notion of creation. 12 Richard Dawkins, *The Genius of Darwin.*

"So God created great sea creatures and every living thing that

moves, with which the waters abounded, according to their

kind, and every winged bird according to its kind..." [13]

The human body is programmed to evolve from a dot at conception, through different stages over the span of life, to death and beyond. This is *evolution* and all living things are programmed in the same way. The human body may die but the seed and that of the flower, genetically, will produce more flowers.

Omar Khayyam *says:*

"The flower that has once blown forever dies". [14]

Evolution can also be applied to things such as society, ideals, concepts and situations that *change* from their current order to give birth to new ideals. All things are governed by two major inextricable components: Lineal Time and Evolution, the natural order which motivates irreversible change in almost everything. However, the theory of evolution as held by evolutionists is mystifying as to why the chimpanzee never continued to evolve but remained as such:

"The chimpanzee and the human share about 99.5 per cent of their evolutionary

history and yet most human thinkers regard the Chimp as a

malformed,

irrelevant oddity while seeing themselves as stepping stones to the Almighty. [15]

According to scientists:

"The lives of Genes are measured in millions of years unlike the bodies they inhabit. A gene is defined as any portion of potential chromosomal material not in any way physically differentiated from the rest of the chromosomes." [16]

From the science and Biblical writers it would seem that when God created the world the *universal orbit commenced on an infinite journey in linear time.* One way street, incidentally, as we recede into the past. The notion of Darwin's origin of species claims to be scientifically proven. Those scientists who reject the existence of God as the Creator demean the power and usefulness of science. Creation and Science share the same author, God, though some creationists tend to place importance on the human alone but the universe is 'holistic' and everything in it is inter-related.

Notes, references and comments:

13 Genesis 1:24-25. 14 *The Rubaiyat of Omar Khayyam.*15 Robert L Trivers in his foreword to the book *The Selfish Gene* by Richard Dawkins. Some do not share the Evolutionists' view of physical evolution from non-human organisms to the Homo Sapiens (modern man). Others keep an open mind to other theories or hypotheses.16 Richard Dawkins, *The Selfish Gene,* pages 35, 36 and 37.Scientific hypothesis demonstrates how the process of Creation may have taken place. In Christianity, life begun with the Bible as most knowledge has been built upon legacy: *"...were you the first person born...were you made before the hills... were you there when I laid the foundations of the earth?"* Job 15:7, 12:7. Archaeology tells a different story, and the question "Who said so?" will always arise: The Almighty is our God of variety and creation is a secret that belongs to God alone but man will endeavour to probe into God's secret.

Mitochondrial DNA has enabled science, archaeology and other related disciplines to look into the existence and migration of humans. The existence of humans before the Bible story is based on scientific research and on mitochondrial DNA. Mitochondrial Eve mothered an unbroken line of females to the present, according to the *"Out of Africa theory."* [17] She lived in the Kalahari Desert about 200,000 years ago. Scientists embrace the *Out of Africa* or *recent African origin hypothesis* on modern humans (Homo sapiens) which states that modern humans arose in Africa and migrated out of the continent around (50,000) to (100,000) years ago, replacing populations Homo erectus and Neanderthals in Europe.

It is also said that Y-chromosomal Adam, fathered an unbroken line of males who are forebears of all the men on earth, traced to half of Mitochondrial Eve's length of time.

"Eve" and "Adam" are taken from the *Creation* story in the *Book of Genesis* in the *Holy Bible.* Out of Africa second major dispersal of humans from sub-Sahara areas were: by boat to Australia 50,000; Western Pacific Islands (33,000); Americas (4,500), expansion into Arctic as continual ice retreat and extending to New Zealand (1,200).[18]

The *Out of Africa theory* competes with the *Multiregional hypothesis* that human evolution from the beginning of the Pleistocene 2.5 million years to the present day has been within a single continuous human evolving worldwide to modern Homo sapiens.[19] Seven Daughters of Eve, major mitochondrial lineages for modern Europeans, is on the theory of Human mitochondrial genetics on the principles of human evolution.[20]

Sykes explains that Mitochondrial Eve had seven daughters, named from the alphabetical character of the Haplogroup:

Ursula: corresponds to Haplogroup U

Xenia:	"	Haplogroup X
Helena:	"	Haplogroup H
Velda:	"	Haplogroup V
Tara:	"	Haplogroup T
Katrine:	"	Haplogroup K
Jasmine	"	Haplogroup J

Notes, references and comments:

17 Rebecca Cann et al, first upright man in the theory of evolution. 18 1,000 years before the voyages of Captain Cook; *The Times History of the World;* Genesis 11:6: *"Indeed the people are one and they will have one language, and this is what they begin to do...nothing that they propose to do will be withheld from them and 1:28: "...be fruitful and multiply." ."* 19 Byran Sykes, *The Seven*

Daughters of Eve. and analysis of ancient DNA genetically linking to Prehistoric ancestors to modern humans. 20 Sykes ditto. Sykes describes the use of mitochondrial DNA in identifying the remains of Czar Nicholas II, last Tzar of Russia, who was murdered with his entire family by the Bolcheviks in 1918; and currently (2009) the same methods are being used to identify the nine "clan mothers" of Japanese ancestry, different from the seven European equivalents. Darwin in his theory of evolution strengthened the view that black people were inferior because they had not fully evolved into proper humans. A legacy that overshadowed modern European thought, undermined the value of imperialism, and demeaned the sanctity of the human being.

According to the theory of human mitochondrial genetics, there were seven major mitochondrial lineages for modern Europeans, though Sykes later wrote with the additional data from Scandanavia and Eastern Europe. He also wrote that an eighth, named Ulrike, could have been promoted to be the clan mother for Europe.

The seven clan mothers mentioned by Sykes (above) each correspond to one or more human mitochondrial haplogroups. Sykes traces back human migrations by following the developments of mitochondrial genetics.

Sykes refutes Thor Heyerdahl's theory of the Peruvian origin of the Polynesians. Heyerdahl (Norwegian, 1914-2002), with a scientific background in zoology, on his Kon-Tiki expedition found oral testimony evidence from Easter Island people. Suggesting that seagoing war canoes similar to Viking ships had brought Stone Age Northwest American Indians to Polynesia (1100 CE); who had mingled with tiki's people. [21]

Separation is inevitable in all of its various heart-rending forms. In addition to the separation that takes place after clinical death there are other situations that refer to separation as a mode of conduct and represent the human side of sanctification. The Old Testament illustrates Abram's separation from idolatry and Israel's separation from Egypt by Exodus. According to Christianity, the believer has been separated from the old position of sin in Adam by the redemptive work of Christ.[22] Some who belong to other faiths, also believe that death is not the ultimate end of life.

Christianity teaches that believers are expected to separate themselves from unholy alliances of any kind; that God's people ought to distance themselves from every sinful or defiling action; and that separation from all sin must be followed by joining one-self actively to God in dedicated service;[23] and one should seek to separate from embracing false views.[24] Separation in Scripture in the ethically bad aspect of the present world system is twofold: The underlying principle is that in a moral universe it is impossible for God fully to bless those who advocate evil. Separation from evil implies separation from the worldly aspects of desire, motive, evil acts, and separation from false teachers, who are the means to dishonour. [25] Separation is not from contact with evil but *from complicity with and conformity to it.* [26]

Notes, references and comments:

21 Multiregional Hypothesis, a "Scientific modelling" of human evolution proposed by Milford H Wolpoff in 1988. It is important to keep an open mind on various theories presented by researchers because it would not be reasonable to assume that everything is cast iron fact. 22 Romans 8:12, 6:23. Prevailing circumstances influences separation: an unhappy marriage; oppressive regime; from neighbours by house move, among many others and that of death on earth. 23 2 Timothy 2:20, 21; John 1:9-11, Romans 12:1, 2. 24 Romans 12:2. 25 2 John 9-11, 16:23, similar to *dhammapada* in Buddhism. 26 1 Corinthians 15:55, Hosea 13:14.

Death

> "O death, where is thy sting? O grave, where is thy victory?" [27]

According to the Bible, physical death is the separation of the soul from the body, and spiritual death is the separation of the soul from God.

> "For the wages of sin is death." [28]

Sin entered the world by Adam and death by sin, and so death passed upon all humans, for all have sinned according to the Bible.[29] God warned Adam that the penalty for disobedience would be death.[30] When Adam disobeyed he realised he was naked and he hid from God in the foliage of the garden; and experienced immediate spiritual death, and later he experienced physical death.[31]

Christian theology teaches that Gehenna is the ultimate separation from God for the hopeless and is said to be associated with the "lake of fire". That Jesus showed his power over death and sin by rising from the dead on the third day after his death and because of this death is a defeated foe. For the unsaved, death brings to an end the chance to accept God's gracious offer of salvation. It is appointed unto humans to die followed by judgment, and death ushers the saved into the presence of Jesus. So real is the promise of the believer's resurrection that the physical death of a Christian is called sleep, looking forward to that time when there shall be no more death. Gehenna is derived from the polluted Valley of Hinnom. It is a real garbage dump in existence since long before the birth of Jesus. It is located below the southern wall of ancient Jerusalem, on the south side of Mount Zion. It stretches from the foot of Mount Zion eastwards to Kidron Valley. [32] Gehenna is the ultimate separation from God, for the hopeless, [33] and is viewed in different ways. In Rabbinical Jewish and Christian writings, Gehenna is not the same as Sheol,the place of the dead. In the Hebrew Bible Gai Ben-Hinnom refers to a valley outside of the city of Jerusalem where the bodies of criminals, carcasses of animals, and garbage are cast. [34]

The valley was defiled by Topeth who burned children in the fire as sacrificial to the pagan god Molech, a practice outlawed by King Josiah, for which God condemned the Israelites. The Book of Revelation describes the final destination of Hades as the Lake of Fire, which many Christians interpret as Gehenna. [35]

In the King James Version of the Bible "Valley of Hinnom" appears thirteen times in eleven different verses and as "valley of the son of Hinnom" or "valley of the children of Hinnom.

Notes, references and comments:

27 Romans 6:23. 28 Romans 5:12. 29 Genesis 2:17, 3:8, Revelation 20:11-15. 30 Matthew 27:50. 31 Joshua18:16, 15:8, cross references 2 Kings 23:10, 2 Chronicles 28:3, 33:6; Jeremiah 7:31-32, 19:2 and 6, 32:35; Metzger & Coogan (1993) *Oxford Companion to the Bible"*, p.243.

32 Oral testimony of Daniel and Mary Marne, Jehovah Witnesses who visited the place in 1986. The New Testament cites Gehenna as the place where evil will be destroyed. It lends its name to Islam's Jahannam, a place of torment for sinners.33 Revelation 20:11-15, 20:14: "...whosoever was not found written in the book of life was cast into the lake of fire", Matthew 25:41, Gehenna outer darkness, Mark 9:43-48, Matthew 8:12, Separation from God. 34 Until today, it remains a garbage dump. 35 1 Corinthians 15:22, 33; 1 Thessalonians 4:13-17; Revelation 20:4-6, 12, 13.

Resurrection, Judgment and Eternal life are inter-related and the Death and Resurrection of Jesus symbolises the death and resurrection of the redeemed, in the first and the second resurrections, according to Christian theology.

The first is the resurrection of the new and heavenly body and its reunion with the redeemed soul and spirit.[36] There is the first and second resurrection, taking place in stages and eventually apply to all of God's elect saints from Adam to the end of the Kingdom Age; [37] and the names of the elect shall appear in the Book of Life. [38]

The second resurrection refers to the resurrection of condemnation. It constitutes the Great White Throne of Judgment and includes every unsaved person from the fall of Adam to the creation of the New Heaven and New Earth.

The unsaved shall be judged according to their obedience to the moral law of God; the punishment shall be imposed in degrees, commensurate to the quality of deeds; and the worst of the punishment is separation from fellowship with God.[39]

By careful inductive study of God's Word, the scriptures in the long-held concept of a single general judgment cannot be sustained,[40] the scriptures contain eight well defined and separate judgments.

When Jesus died He bore all the sin and guilt of every believer.[41] When He was lifted up on the cross the justification of every believer was secured[42] and the world was judged and Satan was defeated.[43]This is referred to as God's judgment of sin. A believer must confess to sins committed to avoid chastisement by the heavenly Father.[44]

Christ's judgment of the believer's work does not apply to the salvation of the believer but reward for Christian service which[45] takes place immediately after Christ's coming for His own.[46] The judgment of all unsaved is called the Great White Throne Judgment and involves every person that has ever lived.[47] The unsaved are judged on the basis of their works. Those whose names are not written in the Book of Life are cast into the lake of fire, Gehenna.[48] The Judgment of the nation takes place at the second coming of Christ to establish God's Kingdom.[49]

Notes, references and comments:

36 Revelation 20:12, 13. 37 Yeshua instituted the first fruits of the first resurrection 1 Corinthians 15:23. 38 John 5:28, 29; Revelation 20:11-15, Matthew 23:31-33, 25:-34-36. 39 Revelation 19:20, 20:10. 40 *Unger's Survey of the Bible.* 41 1 Corinthians 15:3; Hebrews 9:26-28. 42 John 5:24; Romans 5:9; 8:1; 2 Corinthians 5:21; Galatians 3:3. 43 John 12:31. Corinthians 5:10; 1 Corinthians 3:11-15, 4:1; 2 Timothy 4:8; 1 Corinthians 3:15. 44 Hebrews 12:17; 1 Corinthians 11:31, 32, 1 Corinthians 11:32; 5:5. Does punishment exist in two realms, the material or spiritual or both in varying degrees? Some people, including leaders, do atrocious acts upon others and continue to live in trouble-free world until they leave the material world. Does greater punishment await them in the world hereafter? 45 Romans 14:10; 2 2:24; 3:18. 46 Revelation 20:15. 47 Revelation 20:11, Matthew 23:31-33, 25:-34-36. 48 Luke 24:36. 49 Matthew 28:10.

Jesus gave an assurance in the statement "*Be not afraid*" to the apostles and to the women after His resurrection. This was *said to all people* to conquer fear in the present world situation:

> *"As much in the East as in the West, as much in the North as in the South… Have no fear of that which you yourselves have created…of all that man has produced, and that every day is becoming more dangerous for him! Finally, have no fear of yourselves!"* [50]

The Adamic Covenant was given to Adam and Eve and their descendants after their fall.[1] The covenant governed Administration of Conscience and Moral Responsibility. Despite the loss of innocence they were given the grace to honour the Creator by observing moral law written in their heart and conscience. Their ability to adhere to moral law in token would satisfy God's holiness; and by animal sacrificial approach to God[2] in appealing to the Almighty's grace, was eventually to be replaced by the atoning death of Jesus. The Covenant operates for as long as the fallen race is on earth and spans all succeeding administrative covenants.

The curse was four-fold decreed by God's wrath after the fall of Adam and Eve: a curse upon the Serpent, the Woman, the Man and the Earth and remains operative throughout the Administration of the *Adamic Covenant.*

The Serpent: Satan's agent in temptation, changed from an exquisite, vertical, intelligent creature to an abominable crawling reptile.

The Woman: her position altered in three ways: multiplied conception as a young race productive to fill the earth; sorrowful in motherhood, peril, pain, anguish in childbirth, loss of equality with the man which Eve had by creation because she caused man's fall.[3]

The Man: While he was created to cultivate the garden in delight changed to living on soil by sweat and toil for livelihood, become physically exhausted by the passage of time followed by physical death.[4]

The Earth: God caused difficulties such as thorns, thistles, weeds, blight, drought, and all the things that make the earth almost insurmountable by

man.[5]

The Promise: As there were no conditions to the covenant, a promise was embodied into it to offset the curse: Glorious prediction "the seed of the woman" would give virgin-birth to a Messiah who would bruise the

Serpent's head and redeem from sin fallen humans from Satan's power, death and hell;[6] and would overcome evil in all its force and concentration.

Notes, references and comments:

50 As quoted by Pope John Paul II, *Crossing the Threshold of Hope*, page 219. This was the covenant of *innocence*.

Adamic Covenant: 1 Genesis 3:14-19. Genesis 3:15, shows redeeming care clothing the pair in garments of skin. 2 Genesis 3:21. 3 Paul in 1 Timothy 2:12-15, "... I suffer not a woman to teach nor to usurp authority over the man, but to be in silence". 4 Genesis 3:17-21. 5 Genesis 3:18. This was the covenant of *grace*. 6 Genesis 3:15.

Enmity was imposed between Eve and the Serpent, and between their respective seed.[7] The way to the tree of life was open and the glory pointed to it to awaken hope, protected by the *flaming rotating sword* and two *cherubims* symbolic of mercy. Now through faith in Jesus the redeemed can eat of that tree and live for ever, according to Christianity.[8]

Christian theology interprets that the first proclamation of the Messiah's coming is contained in Genesis,[9] by his death and resurrection:

"Be clothed in Christ rather than our good works"

Notes, references and comments:

Adamic Covenant: 7 Genesis 3:14, 15, 16, Unger's Survey of the Bible, p 26. 8 Genesis 3:21-4. 9 Genesis 3:15, Galatians 3:27, Hebrews 9:12, Matthew 26:28: If clothed in Christ one cannot fail but engage in good works. This was the covenant of *grace*.

The Noahic Covenant - Noah was six hundred years old when the Almighty chose him to build an ark for himself and his family and to collect every creature of the earth male and female. The intention was to cleanse humanity by divine retribution through a universal flood. Noah had never seen rain only a mist that went up from the earth to irrigate and moisturise vegetation on the whole face of the ground.[1]

He lived hundreds of miles away from the nearest sea and could not visualise how the ark would float. How he would round up all the animals presented a further dilemma but he soldiered on placing complete trust in God.[2] Only Noah, his wife, three sons and three daughters-in-law, along with the selected animals, survived the flood in the Ark.[3]

The Noahic Covenant (the covenant) was made despite that by the

Adamic Covenant God had introduced the Administration of Conscience and Moral Responsibility. In Noah's day humans had become so depraved, selfishness abounded, and they lacked morality to maintain piety and prudence. There was only one man, Noah, who faithfully abided by the acts that pleased God:

> "... love God supremely...trust God completely...obey God whole-
>
> heartedly, to thank God continually; and to use one's abilities." 4

After the flood the covenant and the *Administration of Human Government* was established, which extended to the entire race from Noah.5 The Gentiles were chosen to govern for God Jew and Gentile alike in 'human government'. For the purpose of establishing order, punishing offences and promoting justice; for the protection of the sanctity of human life to the extent of the administration meting out capital punishment for taking life. Like the Adamic Covenant, which it overlaps, the covenant is operative as long as unglorified mankind exists.

Notes, references and comments:

1 Genesis 2:5-6, Hebrews 11:7 shows Noah's faith in God, Deuteronomy 6:5 directs love for God, cross reference Genesis 6:22, 7:6. *Unger's Survey of the Bible*, page 27. 2 Hebrews 11:1-40, lists Biblical heroes of faith. Noah built the ark from gopher wood, of cypress tree, a hard-odorous durable wood, which later Egyptians used for coverings of mummies and the Greeks for coffins. 3 Genesis 7:13. 4 Hebrews 11:7. 5 Genesis 9:1-17.

Noah was blessed to be fruitful and to multiply. This change took the form of the confusion of languages at Babel but with freedom to people to expand and build.6 The covenant indicated that the administration was successive, not exclusive, overlaps other administrations in a number of cases; and continues in force despite successive covenants to introduce new administrations. The failure to observe them resulted in hostility against scriptural time distinctions.7

The covenant spans all succeeding ages in time till the creation of the *New Heaven* and *New Earth* where the righteous shall dwell and covers three aspects: The universal catastrophe was supernatural and is never to be repeated. This will continue till renovation of earth by fire in preparation for eternity. The sign of the covenant is the rainbow, symbol of the orderly on going of nature.8 All must submit to the governing authorities and those who rebel against government will bring judgment on themselves.

Noah and his sons, Shem, Ham and Japheth were told to replenish, possess and rule a new world with benediction nearly as that bestowed on Adam. God also added the prerogative for man to eat meat. The prohibition on meat applied to eating of the "flesh with the life thereof", the blood. Noah built an altar to God with burnt offerings. [9] The failure to observe them produces hostility against scriptural time distinctions.[10]

The Pharisees sent one of their disciples to ask Jesus whether or not it was lawful to give tribute to Caesar. Jesus asked whose image was on the monetary coin and they replied it was Caesar's image. Then Jesus said:

"Render therefore unto Caesar the things which are Caesar's...

and unto God the things that are God's." [11]

Is there a time when we should intentionally disobey the laws of the land? If citizens are deprived of their liberty, the civil government loses its authority from God; if government keeps within its proper line of jurisdiction, then it becomes disrespectful to disregard authority; and citizens are justly condemned to suffer temporal punishment. Then the judge becomes the minister of God to chastise the disobedient.

Notes, references and comments:

6 Genesis 11: 1-9: *"Indeed the people are one and they will have one language, and this is what they begin to do...nothing that they propose to do will be withheld from them".* The purpose of causing confusion in the languages was because men had become immersed in self-importance, unrestrained imagination, and there was need for intervention, a device to lessen freedom. *Unger's Survey of the Bible.* Since the early nineteenth century the flood became the subject of conflicts between scientists, geologists, Christians and others before Darwin's birth. Some believed it to be the most complete act of genocide ever performed, others said the Genesis account on Noah's flood was a myth or may have been influenced by cataclysmic events that occurred in different parts of the world. 7 *Unger's Survey of the Bible.* 8 Genesis 9:11-13-16. 9 Genesis 9:20-21, but to eat meat is to eat blood. 10 *Unger's Survey of the Bible.* 11 Matthew 22:19-21.

When the apostles were brought before the Sanhedrin high priest to answer why they had disobeyed orders that they should not preach in the name of Jesus, they replied that they should obey God rather than man.[12] If members of government break the law and they place themselves above the law, they provoke public anger:

"It is good neither to eat nor to drink anything whereby others are

offended or made weak." [13]

The Blessing of Animals

"Animals are such agreeable friends – they ask no questions,
they pass no criticisms."   George Eliot.

Animals are saved in Noah's ark because we co-exist and are attuned to the natural world. Ever since Adam and Eve, domestic animals have held an important place in the history of humans. When God said have dominion over all animals the meaning was not to treat them with cruelty or callousness. [14] Animals had been sacrificed since the fall of Adam until Jesus died as the ultimate offering for the remission of sin.[15] The sacrifice was vicarious, voluntary redemptive, reconciliatory, efficacious and revelatory.[16]

Job 12:7-9 says:

"The beasts and the fowls shall teach you...the birds of the air,

...will tell you, or speak to the earth. The earth it will teach you;

and the fishes of the sea will tell you. Who among all these

does not know that the hand of the Lord has done this?

Notes, references and comments:

12 Acts 5:28-32, 5:40-42, and in obeying God they were martyred. 13 Romans 14:21. Do not fear the power of governments, respect them, they are sanctioned by God to govern but not as *rulers.* Whether or not they govern with fairness and compassion is a matter between them and God. 14 Animals lost their lives in the futile exercise of remission for man's sins under the Hebrews. 15 Hebrews 9:7, 22, Exodus 29:16, 30:10, Leviticus 1:5, Ephesians 1:7, Colossians 1:20, 1 Peter 1:2, Revelation 1:5. 16 *Unger's Survey of the Bible*, p 18. Ancient literature of Greeks, Egyptians, Chinese, Hindu, and traditions of many races are agreed that first humans brought animals to represent or substitute for them in their worship of God. Exodus 12:3-14, Deuteronomy 14:4-8, 22:10, for meat but only those that chewed the cud and had split hoofs considered clean/fit for consumption under the Mosaic law. On animals: Who hails the carrier pigeons sent as couriers into enemy territory during the Second World War? They saved many human lives but ended their own. The cat is not mentioned in the Bible but once in the book of Baruch, also referred to as 1 Baruch, under the reference

Bar., vi, 21. Cattle were known as "migrels", meaning "property"; the mule is a breed between horse and donkey. According to Christian theology, the Bible indicates that on forgiveness of sin animals have played a vital role. In the Old Testament period sins "covered" anticipation of a Redeemer's coming as sacrifice; Acts 13:38, 39, John 3:18, 5:14, Colossians 2:13: In the New Testament era, there is forgiveness for placing faith in Jesus. In the herd of elephants a matriarch is the pillar of their social organisation. The list is endless.

The Abrahamic Covenant (the covenant) was revived through Abram, and his descendants, when the race was utterly lost in idolatry (2000 BC). God had called the descendants of Shem, first son of Noah and progeny of Adam, to form a separate people, Israel, to become a witness to all other nations for the blessing and serving the one true God and to expect the promised redeemer.

Abram and descendants were chosen in order to ensure obedience, order, harmony, and to prevent universal idolatry as the end of all law given to Moses who urged the people to follow and be faithful to the only one true God.[11] To demonstrate and to receive, preserve and transmit the written word of God. According to Christian theology, Israel is now set aside in its election, to be re-gathered and restored to national favour at the second coming of Jesus.[12] During the test period of the Administration of Promise a warning is included, as working on individuals and nations and appears in the entire span of the Administration. The covenant is said to be exclusive and everlasting to Abraham and his spiritual descendants.[13] Elements of the twelve tribes integrated with the Judeans or "Jews". This was viewed as a fulfilment of God's faithful covenants and promises made to the nation Israel. [14]

As used in the Bible the term "Jew" in the pre-exile era referred to citizens of the southern state of Judah and post exilic the name denoted the people of Israel in contrast to the Gentiles. In the New Testament the term applied to those who were Jewish by both nationality and religion. In a few cases, in the era of Christ, Jewish Christians were also called Jews.[15] In the Scriptures *Hebrew* pertains to Heber which is the name as Eber, meaning: `beyond' or from the other side as having crossed over. However, Abram means `father is exalted' and he is eighth generation from Shem, the eldest son of Noah.[16]

Israelites fitted the category of nomads. Not all Habiru were Israelites.[17] New Testament Hebrew was Jew who spoke Hebrew or Aramaic language – distinguished from Jews who spoke Greek and were called Grecians. "A Hebrew of the Hebrews" was a thorough-going Hebrew in language, parentage, and religious custom.[18]

Notes, references and comments:

11 Joshua 24:2,3, Genesis 12:1, 3. 12 Isaiah 11, 12. *Unger's Survey of the Bible.* Theologians give different date on Abraham's birth: 352 years from the Deluge c. 2018 BCE, some say c.2161 BC, and that he entered Canaan at age 75, c.2086 BC.13 Genesis 17:7; accepted by faith not works 15:6, ensign of Abrahamic Covenant was the establishment of circumcision, acceptance was by performance 17:10, but it has to be matched by internal change: the circumcision of the heart Jeremiah 4:4. According to Paul, those who have faith are children of Abraham Galatians 3:7. The mixed Jews in turn adopted the broader term of "Israelites". Their prophets foresaw a congregation of representatives from every tribe and the establishment of the converted and blessed nation under the Messiah-Saviour in the End Time. 14 Zachariah 12:1-14:21. 15 John 8:31; Acts 21:39; Galatians 2:13. 16 Genesis 14:13 10:21-31; 11:14-16; derived from the name "Eber". Some scholars think it means nomads of Euphrates, or "Habiru" of antiquity. Habiru are prominent in Tellel Amarna Letters, who invaded Palestine. The Letters say. Abdi-Heba of Jerusalem appealed to the Egyptian Pharaoh Akhenaton (1375 BC) in the invasion corresponding by and to Joshua, successor of Moses in the search for the Promised Land. 17 Genesis 12:5;Joshua 24:2, 3. 18 Acts 6:1; Philippians 3:5.

The story of Sarai and Hagar indicates that since the dawn of time man-made barriers of rank have separated people but humans are brought into this world under a variety of circumstances, some of which disregard barriers of rank. An indication of the equality of birth. Abram is saddened that he has no heir, his wife Sarai is childless but shares his sadness. She offers Hagar, her Egyptian slave handmaid, to her husband so as to produce an heir, for them an heir is the crowning glory of a family. Hagar is blessed by the *Maternal Covenant* and she becomes elevated, that she had a quality which her mistress lacked and she demeans Sarai, by the inevitable characteristic of human relations `friction' between the two women follows.

Women slaves constitute part of the private patrimony of a wife and she could dispose of them as she pleased, including the produce of their labour and their children. Abram passes the responsibility back to Sarah to deal with Hagar. Sarai does just that and Hagar flees into the wilderness. At a fountain she met an angel who told her to return to her mistress and that her seed would be multiplied exceedingly. When Hagar returns she has a son whom Abram calls Ishmael meaning `God hears' because God heard Hagar's prayers before she was invited back into Abraham's household. When Abram is forty-six years of age, God changes his name to "Abraham", meaning Father of a Multitude. God also changes "Sarai" to "Sarah", that she shall be the mother of nations and was made co-ruler with her husband.[19] God said Sarah shall have a son who shall be called Isaac and the Almighty would establish a covenant with him and his seed. Abraham pleads for Ishmael as his first born and God blessed Ishmael:

"...as for Ishmael, I have heard you...I will make him fruitful, and will multiply him exceedingly. He shall beget twelve princes and I will make him a great nation." [20]

Notes, references and comments:

19 Genesis 17:16, 18.20 Genesis 17:19, 20, 21, 23-27. Genesis 17:19. Genesis 21:5 says Abraham was 100 years old when Isaac was born to him. Isaac was weaned at 3, like most children of that era when celebration was made. Sarah caught Ishmael mocking Isaac, Genesis 21:9; Sarah demanded that Ishmael be cast out, Genesis 21:12, 13. This was the first point of conflict between Ishmael, the father of the Arab nations, and Isaac, the divinely chosen line of the Jewish people, according to Christian theology. That same hostility rages to the first quarter of the twenty-first century. Galatians 4:29 "He who was born according to the flesh [Ishmael] persecuted him who was born according to spirit Isaac in Genesis 21:9. Shall there be a peace treaty between the Jews and Arabs? Islam claims Muhammad to be a descendant of Ishmael, the first son of Abraham, and the named prophet. According to Sheikh Ahmed Deedat: "these are not hard facts but beliefs & that Muhammad was illiterate yet he wrote the Qur'an": Holy Qur'an 7:158:3-5.

21 Hebrews 11:17-19: In the Old Testament Scriptures: Saul 1 Samuel 10:10, 11:6 on Saul; and 1 Samuel 16:13 on David regarding prophesy.

Abraham and Sarah were doubtful about the promised son due to their advanced age but God's promise endured and they were blessed with a son whom they called Isaac. [21] God passed over Ishmael and made Isaac leader of his generation:

"I will make you exceedingly fruitful and I will make nations of you, and

kings shall come from you."

As Isaac grows, Abraham is faced with the most difficult test of his faith when God commands him to sacrifice Isaac as a blood burnt offering. Abraham builds an altar in the mountains of Moriah, places wood upon it, literally binds Isaac, and lays him upon the wood. At the last moment an angel appears to halt the sacrifice.

The sacrifice of Isaac symbolises two things: the making of the *first altar* as the origin of an altar to be made in a *Tabernacle* yet to be revealed. [22] The second symbol is the slaughter of the final lamb yet to be revealed, a blood sacrifice as the *Way* to the *inner chamber* of the *Tabernacle,* in a new Passover for the whole of mankind. The identity of the lamb, the *lead player* in the human drama, is hidden though is in existence through the ages of dispensation, from the Old to the New Testament. [23]

The Mosaic Covenant (the covenant) replaced the *Abrahamic Covenant* at Sinai with Israelites' acceptance of law in exchange for grace, also referred to as the Old Covenant. The covenant is conditional made between God and the nation Israel through Moses. It introduced the administration of law and the legal economy; and revealed to the people their sinful ways and their need for a saviour. [1, 2, 3]

Notes, references and comments:

22 Genesis 22: Isaac, the sacrificed son. Islam holds that God sent a lamb to be sacrificed in place of Isaac. Abraham is not shocked by his God's request for the blood of Isaac. This indicates a powerful God, much like a bully, who demeans man to the level of extreme fear based on loyalty. Some may ask "is this a God of love and compassion? To others, since God decreed that the end of man's journey on earth is death, it would not be shocking at all. According to Christianity, Jews and Gentiles together form the Israel of God in which Abraham was the founder. 23 Genesis,19:24, the genealogy of Jesus, at the point of Isaac, is interrupted by the destruction of Sodom and Gomorrah, two cities which were part of five cities, upon which God rained brimstone and fire, turned them to ashes as an example of punishment to the ungodly. Note: The age of Isaac when he was about to be sacrificed is uncleare in the Bible; he oculd have been in his teens or 36 years.

The Mosaic Covenant references: 1 Exodus 19:24. The Mosaic Covenant is connected to two infants, each in his own era, saved from ruthless despots for the good of humanity: Moses, the child in the ark in the bulrushes, was unwittingly mothered by the Pharaoh's daughter Hebrews 11:23-25, circumstances of the birth of Moses & rejection of a princely life. 2 Yeshua, the child in the manger, was saved by his parents, Mary and Joseph, from Herod, Matthew 2:12-16, Luke 2:7. 3 Exodus 19-24, 2 Corinthians 3:14, Hebrews 8:6,13, cross reference Exodus 19:5, 6, 8: "All that the Lord has spoken we will do." 3 Hebrews 8:8-10 9:15, 12:24,13:16, 9:1: New Covenant, Jesus as mediator.

The covenant remains in force from Sinai (Moses) to Calvary (Jesus), it is a *"learning institution"* as the way to the coming of Jesus. It was made when Israel was in Moab, distinctive from the one made in Horeb, not dependent on Israel's obedience, and to be completely fulfilled in the millennial reign of the second coming of Jesus.[4] The Mosaic law is in three parts: the moral law summarising God's requirements; the civil law conditioning the social life of Israel; [5] and the ceremonial law governing the religious life of Israel, the latter was abolished when Jesus died in fulfilment of its prescriptions: [6]

> *"Your faith should not be in the wisdom of men but in the power of God...[7] our gospel did not come to you in word only but also in power... we speak wisdom among those who are mature...not of those who are coming to nothing... [8] the law was our tutor to bring us to Christ, that we must be justified by faith.[9] Christ is the end of the law for righteousness to every believer".[10] He will sit on the throne of glory". [11]*

Ten Commandments

The Tabernacle, under the covenant, indicated that a redeemer of the New Covenant was within the Old and the New Testament.[12] Israel the *elect* through Abraham[13] and as a people redeemed out of Egypt, were manifestly before all the nations of the world as witness to the fact of the need for a saviour. [14] The condition was that they were to observe God's eternal moral law summarised in the Ten Commandments.[15]

Our Relationship to God

1.Thou shalt not have other gods before Me:

Christianity, Judaism and Islam recognise one true God, but material progress and governmental *laissez faire* attitude towards commerce overrides this commandment as some choose to worship Mammon in a free market. This has become increasingly so in the first quarter of the twenty-first century.

Notes, references and comments:

4 Exodus 20:1-7, the deliverer: Exodus 12, John 1:29, 36. 5 Exodus 21:2-49. 6 24:12, 31-18, 20:1-7 and *Unger's Survey of the Bible*, pp. 30-31. 7 1 Corinthians 2:5. 8 1 Thessalonian 1:5. 9 1 Corinthians 2:6. 10 Galatians 3:24, Romans 10:4, Matthew 25:31-46. 11 2 Corinthians 5:10, cross references: Genesis 12:3; Isaiah 60:3-5, the Gentiles bless Zion.12 *Unger's Survey of the Bible*, Hebrews 10:1-4, 8:8-13, 9:15, 12:24; Luke 22:20; Jeremiah 31:31-34, new covenant, 1 Corinthians 11:25. 13 Galatians 3:16-18. 14 Exodus 15:13.15 Decalogue: Greek meaning "ten words"; Exodus 20:3-17, Revelation 20:11-15, Deuteronomy 10:1. Mostly the Ten Commandments are apparent in human government, though other offences

are left to the moral law written in the heart and conscience and so far not legislated. Continued from above: It was once said: *"...you cannot legislate to make people good"* but the passage of the *Anti-Social Behaviour Act* by the United Kingdom Westminster Parliament in 2003 is close to making people good by legislation. Evolution of society proves itself as an influencing factor for repealing old or passing new laws.

2.Thou shalt not make unto thee any graven image:

Hebrews lived in a world where every tribe made idols and images of various items because of the need to visualise the image of YAHWEH.[16] Christianity is no different, particularly Roman Catholic, other churches or temples which are adorned with images. Though some regard them as an appreciation of aesthetic art.

3.Thou shalt not take the name of the Lord thy God in vain:

If one regards oneself `perfect' there could be no reason to know God save as a means for cursing others.[17]

4.Remember the Sabbath day to keep it holy: 18

The Sabbath is a unique feature of the moral law in its Mosaic form and is part and parcel of the Passover; the ensign of the *Mosaic Covenant* and was imposed only upon the un-fallen. The Sabbath was in recognition of observation of the completion of God's perfect work in six days, as day of complete rest. Failure to keep this tenet resulted in the death sentence under the draconian laws of the Old Testament. Sabbath is for Judaism and Sunday for Roman Christianity.

Our Relationship to Fellow Beings

5.Honour thy father and thy mother: 19

According to Deuteronomy this tenet imposes a death sentence to those who disobey it. Jews in Judaism have had, and have to the present day, a strong sense of family obligation and values. Generally *parental* influence of any home is the root of various beliefs. Humans from infancy are largely the product of legacy through parents or those in authority. Some dishonour or kill their parents, and some parents kill their children.

Notes, references and comments:

16 Romans 1:20-25, Deuteronomy 4:16-19, Not unlike other societies in worshipping idols, rivers, mountains, celebrities and other things; see Part 4, Chapter 12, God of People. 17 Romans 3:23. 18 Exodus 20:8 and Leviticus 25:2, Genesis 2:2-4, John 5:16-17, God gave the two tablets of the Ten

Commandments to Moses after instruction on the Sabbath. The Sabbath and the Sunday worship in Christianity are two totally different things. Sabbath keeping is Mosaic, legalistic and is the logo of the Mosaic Covenant. The commandment of Sabbath keeping represents the moral law of God only as adapted as a requirement of the Mosaic Covenant and elect nation Israel. It has no direct relevance to Church or Christianity. Sunday worship is traced to the Roman emperor Constantine who worshiped the Sun-god. He issued a Sunday-keeping edict in the year 323 AD, and it was not done in honour of Christ but to venerate a day of the Sun-god and its origins are Pagan, Encyclopaedia Britannica, Eleventh edition, Vol. 14, p. 273. Luke 22:20; 1 Corinthians 11:25; 2 Corinthians 3:6; Hebrews 8:8, 8:13, 9:15, 12, 24. See chapter on *Divine Mandate*. The Mosaic Covenant was replaced by the New Covenant in Christ[16]and it fulfills the promises or predictions made by Jeremiah 31:312-34.[17]as quoted in Hebrews. See chapter on *New Covenant and Administration of Fullness Times*. 8.[18]Judaism places emphasis on the Sabbath, Luke 4:4. Psalm 66:4; 67:4;10.Genesis 49:28 "...for God blessed the seventh day and made it holy" Leviticus 23.42, Genesis 2:3. 19 Luke 7:10-13, cross reference Deuteronomy 21:18-21, Exodus 21:15. 20 An example is the "Death Row" in the United States.

6.Thou shalt not kill:

The seriousness of this offence may depend upon a type of government. Killing by some
governments is regarded as `lawful' by them. [20]

7.Thou shalt not commit adultery:

This tenet means lust in any form [21] and over the centuries the least heeded. In earlier
times adultery was a ground for divorce but with the widespread notion of 'free love'
adultery as a ground for divorce has lost its potency.

8.Thou shalt not steal: [22]

Disregard of this tenet abounds in its many different forms: theft by servant, public or
private; inflated allowances; tax evasion; the insurance claim; the payment of wages
not commensurate with the labours of an employee; making employees redundant and
expecting those not made redundant to do extra work; employees working overtime
without pay; knowingly short-changing anyone. The list goes on. These are ill-
acquired gains or wealth. Though latent, it does not mean they are not forms of theft but

God knows everything.

9.Thou shalt not bear false witness:

In the Biblical sense false witness includes slander and gossip of a malicious nature.

How many witnesses hold the Bible in court and swear to tell the truth but tell untruths

and commit perjury when discovered? How many knowingly and intentionally give false

witness to condemn another to prison or to death?

10.Thou shalt not covet:

Yeshua said:
"Out of the heart proceeds evil thoughts, murders, adulteries, fornications, thefts, false witnesses, blasphemies. These are the things which defile a man, but to eat with unwashed hands does not defile a man...[23] "every kind of beast and bird, or reptile and creatures of the sea, is tamed and has been tamed by mankind...but no man can tame the tongue. It is an unruly evil, full of deadly poison... with it we bless our God...and with it we curse men who have been made in the similitude of God." [24]

The Passover is part of the Exodus and is celebrated with the Feast of the Unleavened Bread.[25] In Judaism the Passover began in Egyptian darkness in the bondage of the Israelites under the Egyptian Pharaohs. God's vengeance on Egypt was the killing of every first-born in Egypt including animals. Egyptian homes suffered loss but all of the Israelites

Notes, references and comments:

21 Matthew 5:27-28. 22 A thief is a thief `only' when caught, some get caught and do time but God sees all and denies us nothing, but sooner or later, we have to take the consequences of our actions.

23 Matthew 15:19, James 5:15, earthly sensual, demonic. 24 Sermon on the Mount, Matthew 5:30, 15:17-20, James 3:7-13: "the horse is controlled by bits put in its mouth." 25 Leviticus 23:5, Exodus 13:4. The first of four Spring Feasts symbolic remembrances of seven annual festivals in the Holy Walk from the day after Passover continuing for seven days. listed in Leviticus 23:1-44, Exodus 23:14-17, as directed by God through Moses. See chapter 9, *Assumed Divine Mandate*.

were spared. Prior to which, on the tenth day of the month God called Abib and ordered each household to select a perfect year-old male lamb from the flock, small households would join larger ones.[26]

The lamb was slain on the fourteenth day at twilight and its blood splashed on the sides and top of their door frames to protect the Israelites:

> *"Now the blood shall be a sign on the houses ... when I see the blood I shall*
> **pass over** *you; and the plague shall not ...destroy you when I strike the land*
> *of Egypt.* [27]

> *"Remember this day in which you went out of Egypt, out of the house of bondage:*
>
> *for by strength of the hand of the Lord brought you out of this place. No leavened*
>
> *bread shall be eaten".* [28]

The Tabernacle

What began with Abraham in the first altar for Isaac, God took forty days to instruct Moses to build the Tabernacle for worship during the Exodus, as a Tent of Meeting, symbolising the whole world what the Almighty God's six-day creation of the world. In accordance with his prophetic vision on Mount Sinai, Moses faithfully carried out God's command, with the help and willingness of the people.[29] It took Moses and the people six days in the actual building of the tabernacle.The Tabernacle also symbolises the human body on its earthly sojourn:

"Do you not know that you are the temple of God and that the Spirit of God dwells in you?" [30]

Notes, references and comments:

26 Abib or Nisan, fourteenth day of the Hebrew calendar, Leviticus 23:5. 27 Exodus 12:13,14 & John 1:29, 36: a day of memorial; Jesus the Passover Lamb is typified in the life of Moses, the deliverer. Prophets and psalmists regard the Exodus as the most significant moment in the real beginning of Israel's history. The New Testament writers see it as an act of God having an affinity with the death and resurrection of Jesus; symbolising a saviour as the innocent lamb to the slaughter. 28 Exodus 13:3, 23:14-17; Sabbath and Annual Feasts, Matthew 26:2-5; 26:57, 58, Unleavened Bread signifies two things: while on the move the Israelites could not wait for bread dough to rise; unleavened is `unpuffed',

without `pride': *humility* in righteousness. Cross reference with Part 3, Chapter 7, Ministry of Yeshua. The Exodus is "going out" of Egyptian bondage by the Pharaohs, under forced labour for the construction of schemes on the Delta; as fugitives the Israelites carried with them the destiny of Israel to bring the whole world to the knowledge and service of the *one true God* as symbolised by the *Tabernacle.* 29 Exodus 25:10-16, 36:8-39-43, 25:1-40, structure of Tabernacle, 26:34; Exodus 35:1-35, 26:31, instructions for the Veil,   Leviticus 1:1-17, instructions for Aaron as first priest and his two sons: the Levites, eternally sanctified priests; Leviticus 1:1-17, vestments for priests; the New Testament does not show a temple but figure of a temple, as in both the local church and the entire "mystical church".30 1 Corinthians 3:16, 17, 6:19, *Unger's Survey of the Bible*, Hebrews 8:8-10 9:15, 12, 24, 13:16, 9:1.

The Tabernacle is to consist of a *Courtyard*, for the sacrificial of animals in forgiveness of sin; a *Holy Place,* the first place, temporary place for humans. And the Holy of Holies, the second place, the inner chamber, where the Ark of Covenant (the Ark) is to be kept, **shielded from view**. The inner chamber is the everlasting heavenly place of *conscience* in the heart and mind where God is. **On top of the Ark is a Mercy Seat, an atonement cover. 31 Spiritually, the Ark is the manifestation of God's presence on earth where, in the awesome aura of holiness, the Israelites meet with YAHWEH, their God.** [32] The two places are separated by a *Veil* symbolic to the body of the *Redeemer*, yet to be revealed, as the way:

"You shall make a Veil woven of blue, purple and scarlet thread
and fine woven linen...with an artistic design of Cherubim. [33a]

On the *Holy of the Holies*:

> *"Therefore...having boldness to enter the holiest by the blood*
> *of Jesus...by a new and living way which He consecrated for*
> *us, through the veil that is His flesh...having a High Priest over*
> *the house of God...of the good things to come, with the*
> *greater...perfect tabernacle, not made   with [human]*
> *hands...we were saved in this hope...*[33b]

Each item of materials used in the construction of the whole Tabernacle, bears a symbolic meaning and the focus is on sacrifice, judgment, cleansing and representing the *Ages of Dispensation.*

The Hebrew believed that by the blood of animal sacrifice they could pay the price for sin as the *chosen people* of God. They may have taken God for granted without a sense of right or wrong since the sacrifices defeated the object of the exercise, apparent in that they continued to use sacrificial animals. Therefore, the conscience of neither the people nor the priest was perfected by animal sacrifice, and the covenant was replaced by the *New Covenant* in Jesus, according to Christian theology.

Notes, references and comments:

31 Exodus 25:10-16, 25:22. 32 The *shekinah*, Hebrew word meaning "God's manifested glory" or "God's presence". This word does not appear in the Bible, but later Jewish scholars used it to refer to the dwelling place of God, especially the Temple in Jerusalem. The Bible contains conflicting information as to what was contained in the Ark. 1 Kings 8:9 says that inside the Ark there was only the two stone tablets of Moses. Hebrews 9:3-4 mentions three things, the gold jar of manna, Aaron's staff that had budded and the stone tablets. Numbers 4:5, 6, instructions to Aaron on how to cover the Ark; the scriptures record that no one can see God and live, therefore anyone who touches the Ark dies due to the Almighty's holiness and presence. Numbers 6:22-27, 18:19, shows how to bless people; Exodus 28:1-23 garments for high priests; Leviticus 1:1-7, rules for priests; 2:1-16, offerings. 33a Hebrews 5:3, 9:8, 9; Exodus 26:31-3. 33b Hebrews 10:19, 20: according to the New Testament by the blood of Jesus. The high priest in the sacrifices and offerings, in his person and duties Leviticus 1:1-17 and 7:1-38; Leviticus 16; and in the scapegoat, Leviticus 16:7-9, typifies Jesus respectively.

The *Holy of Holies* is to manifest its purpose for the coming of a redeemer whose blood, of infinite value,[34] would wash away man's sins; and in its Age of Dispensation represents a Messianic Kingdom in the reign of the Messianic-Redeemer in the end time. Under the Mosaic law descendants of Levi, of the Judah branch, one of the twelve tribes of Israel, became eternally sanctified priests. Dedicated to serve as mediators of people and God representing the whole nation Israel.[35] Moses anointed his brother Aaron and his sons as the first priests for daily worship. Once a year the one chosen from a body of Levite priests could enter and serve at the *Holy of Holies.* First, he had to be purified, sanctified, be hygienically clean in his person and abstain from relations with his wife for several days. He wore a breastplate with twelve precious stones representing all the tribes; and a string was tied to one of his ankles lest he erred and died so he could be pulled out, as none was sufficiently sanctified to enter the inner chamber.

Nomadic existence called for dismantling and re-assembling the Tabernacle, as with their dwelling tents. When dismantling, they place on the top of the Ark the Veil that separated the Holy of the Holies and the Holy Place; tachash skins (fine leather from sea animals); and a blue cloth on the top of all the layers. The Ark is concealed even from the Levites who carry it ahead of the people. After forty years wandering in the wilderness, the Israelites are almost in sight of the *Promised*. Moses dies and his generation almost diminished. Those left are born during the time in the wilderness.

Before Moses dies, he has completed writing the Torah and commanded the Levites to keep the scroll in the Ark, along with the Ten Commandments, <u>Aaron's rod</u>, and the jar of ***manna***.[36a] **Only Joshua and Caleb are left of the first generation since they left Egypt.Joshua leads them on as they carry the Tabernacle and Ark of Covenant. The Kohathites using the affixed poles carry on their shoulders the *Ark of Covenant* into the centre of the Jordan River**

Notes, references and comments:

34 Hebrews 8:8-13, 9:15, 12, 24,10:1-4, Luke 22:20, 1 Corinthians 11:25, 2 Corinthians 3:6, Galatians 3:16-18. *New Covenant & Administration of Fullness Times.* 35 with the exception of the last eight verses of Deuteronomy, which describe the death and burial of Moses. The Israelite literally but symbolically carried the message of redemption in the Tabernacle and each human body is a Tabernacle housing the spirit. The Veil is symbolic to the body of Jesus as the final Temple (Ephesians 1:19-22); for at the moment he dies, the *Veil* rents and opens the *way* for *all*, Jew and Gentile, to the final destination, the *Holy of Holies, the* place of the *skilled artist*: the *Promised Land.*

36a Exodus 28:1-43, Hebrews 5:1, Leviticus 9:22; Numbers 6:22-27, 18:19, Exodus 28:1-23; Leviticus 1:1-7, rules for priests; 2:1-16, offerings. David Zvi Hoffmann (1843-1921), Orthodox Rabbi, in his commentary to Leviticus, defended Mosaic authorship against the work of Julius Wellhausen, German Biblical scholar, and others. Today the majority of biblical scholarship accept the theory that the Torah has multiple authors and that its composition took place over centuries. Exodus 28:1-43, Hebrews 5:1, Leviticus 9:22; Numbers 6:22-27, 18:19, Exodus 28:1-23; Leviticus 1:1-7, rules for priests; 2:1-16, offerings. Deuteronomy 31:24-30, Moses also warns the people against their rebellion towards God.

And they cross to land; [36b] and they travel for twenty-eight days before they reach the *Promised Land.* The land is bounded by the Egyptian empire to the south and Mesopotamia to the north. Neither of them rules it but seven Canaanite tribes inhabit thirty-one fortified city-scattered areas each under its own king. The Egyptian Pharaoh has appointed regents in the area.

The Israelite engage in a number of battles, sometimes victorious but also facing defeat and casualties of their numbers. Things do not go smoothly as they meet with grave opposition. They resort to spying and other battle strategies. During these battles they do not set up the Tabernacle because of the prevailing circumstances, and the Ark remains separated from the Tabernacle. Sounding seven trumpets of rams' horns, circling the walls of Jericho, they take six days before they break the walls.[37] They settle amongst the tribes in areas [38] except the

Levites; for God is their inheritance and they name cities for the Levites within the conquered areas.[39]

During the time of Joshua the tribes are unified in faithfulness to YAHWEH and the land rested from war.[40] Joshua builds an altar of uncut stones at Mount Ebal in Schechem and they make burnt offerings to God;[41] and the Tabernacle and Ark of Covenant are revived. Joshua passes on at one hundred and ten.[42] Relatively chaotic years ensue, the Israelite enter into more battles.

In the war with the Philistines near Eben-ezer the Israelite take the Ark into battle in hope of securing victory, but they are defeated and the Philistines capture the Ark.[43] The tribes become a loose confederation without a central government then judges gain momentum and the era of Judges begins. The system of Judges as leaders was initiated by Moses before his death. Philistines experience a series of misfortunes and come to the conclusion that they were cursed by the Ark. They return it to the Israelite.[44] The judges were usually heads of families, tribal elders, or military leaders and divinely inspired. Their direct knowledge of YAHWEH enabled them to act as champions for the Israelite from oppression by foreign rulers. There were seven male judges in all, and one woman, Deborah.[45] The first judge, Othaniel, was son of Kenaz brother of Caleb who crossed the River Jordan into Canaan with Joshua, and 46 minor judges. [46]

Notes, references and comments:

36b Joshua 4:1-22; Joshua 4:5, they take memorial stones from Jordan River when waters had receded for them to cross. 37 Joshua 6:1-21, the march around Jericho. Numbers 35:5, cities for Levites. 38 Judges 4:5, 6:8 (era of Judges c1150-1025 BC). 39 Judges 4:5, 6:8; three minor judges; and Samson was the last judge: Judges 13-16. 40 Judges 3:7-11. 10:1-5,12:8-15. 41 Judges 1:25, "...and the people do as they please": Judges 17:18, 19-21. Era of Moses to Joshua. 42 1 Samuel 31:1-6. "...Saul was critically wounded; 2 Samuel 1:2-10, he was struck by one of David's men; Samuel 21:12, and 1 Chronicles 10:13, 14, "...the Lord took away favour from Saul and he committed suicide." 43 Hebrews 5:3, 9:8, 9, Ezekiel 40:45, instructions for two chambers, Joshua 18:1. 44 Hebrews 10:19-20, the blood of Yeshua. 45 Numbers 18:19. 46 Numbers 35:5, 4:5-6; 10:33-36, Joshua 4:5, Psalms 68:1, 32:8, 1 Kings 4:33

The Israelite continually alternate into unfaithfulness to God. In the era of Judges they become less unified and are at risk from neighbouring groups. A breakdown of religious sensitivity leads to deterioration and the *Tabernacle* and *Ark* do not feature in any way. Social breakdown and the civil war amongst the tribes follows.[48] The nomadic existence of Israel had ceased and for hundreds of years they had settled in Canaan, had won and lost an empire.[47]

God raised Samuel to lead the people but he was essentially a prophet and Israel prefers to have a king instead. As a headless society there is a vacuum for the rise of the monarchy, less religious but for a while, at least, they bring stability to a troubled people. Samuel is chosen to give them a king and Saul of the tribe of Benjamin receives the honour of becoming the first king of Israel. Despite his royal countenance, Saul does not trust in God. He fails to destroy pagan worship places, and plays no part in the *Ark*.[48] Oblivious to its meaning, Samuel and the people are seeped in idolatry. He rules forty years.[49] David is anointed as king when he is eight years old. He is the youngest child of Jesse, son of Obed, and his wife Nitzevet who is a Jewish woman.

The Davidic Covenant (the covenant) and *Administration of the Kingdom* may be read together with the *New Covenant and Administration of the Church, the* two covenants that relate to Jesus. Although the redeemer was to come through the people Israel as the chosen, they never appreciated or fully understood the significance of such privilege. As a result of this, several covenants had been made by God and a leader chosen for a particular period of time of the covenant. [1] The covenant was made with King David and spans from David's time to its special fulfilment in Christ in the *New Covenant* in the coming Kingdom. It secures paramount advantages to Israel through the house of David as an everlasting throne and an everlasting Kingdom.

An everlasting throne: Since the Babylonian exile, only one king of the Davidic family, Emmanuel Yeshua, has been crowned with thorns at His crucifixion. The covenant provides that this thorn-crowned King shall receive the Kingdom as David's Son and Lord when the time comes.[2]

The gospel of Matthew addressing Jews presents Christ as the Son of David, tracing his lineage back to Abraham ending with Joseph in Nazareth, and proclaims Him as King of Israel. [3]

Notes, references and comments:

47 1 Kings 4:33, Ezekiel 40:45. The Tabernacle references: 48 and 49 *Unger's Survey of the Bible.*

The Davidic Covenant: 1 *Unger's Survey of the Bible,* David's kingdom is in abeyance now, but will be restored some day. 2 2 Kings:241: The Babylonian captivity/exile refers to the time in Israel's history when Jews were taken captive by king Nebuchadnezzar II of Babylon. Captivity/exile and restoration of the Jewish nation were fulfilments of Old Testament prophecies. 3 He explains the Messianic significance in the number fourteen, the numerical equivalent of David's name in Hebrew, in the three stages in which he divides the ancestry of Jesus, and introduces Him as the rightful heir, Matthew 1:1-12; Psalm 110:1; Luke1:30-33, Acts 20:28. Samuel covers almost all the 40-year reign of king David; 1 Kings 2:11, succeeds Saul.

The everlasting kingdom: Luke addressing Gentiles presents Jesus as the son of man and traces His lineage to Adam, father of the human race.[4] Both the genealogies of David and Adam link Jesus to the Old Testament and its prophecies and promises of redemption.[5] Jesus, David's Son, shall rule over an everlasting kingdom, an earthly sphere with dominion extending over the entire millennial earth.[6]

The body of Jesus is the 'mystery' which in other ages was not made known. The Administration of the Church comes between Israel's rejection because of unbelief and the nation's restoration at the second coming of Jesus:

> *"If your sons will keep my covenant and my testimony which*
> *I shall teach them, their sons also shall sit upon your throne*
> *for evermore."* [7]

The Land Edict (the edict) was made while Israel was in the land of Moab and is distinct from but presumes the covenant given at Sinai. The edict is connected to the *Davidic Covenant* which directs that there are blessings for obedience and curses for disobedience. By misdemeanours from time to time Israelites were cut off from the land at Kadesh and from the covenant made at Sinai.[8] The Edict promises great mercies to the repentant and choice of life as opposed to death.[9] The Edict came to an end with the crucifixion of Jesus and was replaced by the *New Covenant and Administration of the* Church, according to Christian theology; that the *Davidic Covenant* is perpetual and continues to the coming Eucharist reign of Jesus Christ.[10]

Through the Ages of Dispensation the nomadic *Tabernacle* was transformed into a static temple, the Temple of Solomon at Jerusalem, where the Ark was subsequently placed as a place of safety.[11] A magnificent lavish edifice, Solomon's Temple endured for 376 years until it was destroyed by Nebuchadnezzar II in 486 BC, sent by God as punishment upon Israel.

Notes, references and comments:

4 The Du Bartas syndrome is apparent in the difference between Matthew and Luke in presenting the genealogy of Jesus: Matthews (Matt.1:1-17) begins with Abraham and moves down to Jesus, through David's son Solomon. Luke begins with Jesus and moves back through Abraham and Adam, through David's son Nathen. Matthew's arrangement is in 3 groups of 14 generations each (Matt.1:17), total 41 names, while Luke has 51 names. Psalm 72:1-20. 5 Luke 3:3-38. 6 *Unger's Survey of the Bible,* according to Christianity. Revelation 19:1. 7 Luke 22:20, 2 Samuel 7:4-17, Deuteronomy 30:1-10, though symbolically manifested in the Veil of the Tabernacle. 8 and 9 Deuteronomy 28:30. 10 *Unger's Survey of the Bible.* Menelik, offspring of Solomon and Sheba placed the Ark in the Church of Saint Mary of Zion in Axum, Ethiopia, guarded by a monk known as the `Keeper of the Ark'. 11 1 Kings 4:33, Ezekiel 40:45, Josephus, the Jewish historian who lived in the time of Yeshua says of the *Ark of Covenant*: "The innermost chamber measured 30 feet and was similarly separated by a curtain from the outer part. Nothing at all was kept in it, it was unapproachable, inviolable, and invisible to all, and was called the `Holy of Holies'. The post-exilic temple apparently contained no Ark." *The Wars of the Jews, Book Five* (Book V, Chap. V 5: Williamson, 30400.).

God established a covenant with King David,[12] a precedent in spiritual and temporal governance of the people under YAHWEH between the time of David (910-970BC) and the coming of Jesus Christ, who was and still is the fulfilment of his covenant. This covenant is a perpetual Covenant and it is to have fulfilment in the reign of Jesus in his second coming. [13]

3 Prophesy

Deuteronomy 18:18:

> *"I will raise them up a Prophet from among their brethren like unto thee, and I*
>
> *will put my words in his mouth; and he shall speak unto them all that I shall*
>
> *command him."*

Prophesy mentions no name of person or incident prophesied and interpretation involves deduction and reason but above all: `the gift of prophesy to interpret prophesy'. Prophesy is pre-announcement of God's divine revelation of the Almighty's intention, according to prophesy interpreters.

Ephesians 4:11 says:

> "And He Himself gave some to be apostles, some   prophets, some
>
> evangelists...some pastors and teachers."

Succession of Empires

Daniel 2:21 says:

> "And He changes the times and the seasons; wisdom unto the wise and
> knowledge to them that know understanding."

The Bible records God's displeasure by the Israelites' many sins, though God promised a nation and a company of nations.[1] The house of Judah repeated Israel's sins and was conquered and exiled by the Babylonians in 586 BC.[2]

Only a small politically weak group returned from Babylon to the province where the ministry of Yeshua took place.[3] Israel is contained in the prophesy of the succession of empires.

Notes, references and comments:

12 Psalms 89:2-38, 110:6. 13 Leviticus 23:1-44, feasts of the Lord; Hebrews 10:19, 20: according to the New Testament by the blood of Jesus.

3 Prophesy: 1 Genesis 12:1-3. 2 2 Kings 17:21-23, Israel carried to Syria, historically known as the ten lost tribes of Israel. In Deuteronomy 18:22, Moses established the test of a prophet: if he is speaking in the name of God the prophesy shall be fulfilled. If the word does not come to pass or come true, that is the word which God has not spoken. Failure to pass the test would doom the prophet, Deuteronomy 13:1-11. According to interpreters of prophesy, most Biblical prophesy has been precisely fulfilled which forms a basis for deducting the realisation of remaining prophesies.   3 Nehemiah 11:3-36, Israel's whole existence is preoccupied with the promise of land in which they live; they have engaged in many wars over the generations, and it is about their struggle over land, though bloodshed is YAHWEH's displeasure.Reference 3 continued below...

After 1600 BC the Assyrians were the super power over the Egyptians, Hittites, Mitannians, Babylonians and Elamites. The Israelites conquered and settled in Canaan, the peak of their power was from the death of Saul, the first king of Israel, to the reign of David and Solomon in the glory of Israel. The Assyrians were overthrown by Babylon as the first world empire - 625-539 BC.[4] Judah continued until the fall of Jerusalem in 586 BC and the ensuing exile to Babylon. Babylon was conquered by the Persians who became the Medo-Persia, second world empire - 538-330 BC.[5] The Persians were conquered by the Greco, third world empire - 332 BC.[6]

After Greco, Rome became the fourth world empire 31 BC-47 AD. [7]

Nebuchadnezzar's dream: Image with legs of iron; and Daniel's dream: Beast with seven heads and ten horns and Deadly wound is interpreted to mean the fall of the Roman Empire: 476 AD.[8]

Daniel's Dream: First Horn (plucked out) which foretold that the Roman Empire was to be resurrected **ten times**:

First under King Goiseric of the Vandals: 429-533 AD. [9]

Second resurrection under King Odoocer of Heruli, 476-498 AD.[10] Daniel's Dream third horn plucked out: Third resurrection under King Theodoric of the Ostrogoths: 493-554 AD.[11]

Daniel's Dream: Little Horn is symbolic of the Roman Church:

Three resurrections of Arian faith plucked out by the Little Horn.[12]John's Vision: Beast with horns of Lamb, speaks as Dragon, John's Vision: Purple and Scarlet Woman Riding on a Scarlet Beast with seven Heads. Roman Church influencing the last **seven resurrections** of the Roman Empire.[13]

Notes, references and comments:

Referene 3 continued: After a futile rebellion against Roman rule from AD 66-73 and 132-135, Jewish power shattered until re-established at the end of the Second World War in the Middle East as an independent state in 1948 supported by Great Britain and the United States of America by giving back to the Jews the Promised Land. Did this stop bloodshed to this day, between Jews and Arabs? Related biblical, religious and historical English terms include the Land of Canaan, the Promised Land, the Holy Land, and Palestine. All Jews are Israelite but not all Israelite are Jewish, Genesis 17:3-5, 21:12. Tudor Parfait recently found a genetic link between the Jewish priestly Kohanim and the Lemma tribe of southern Africa; and Chief Rabbinate of Israel in 2005 recognised an ethnic group living in East Asia as "descendants of Jews" from the Bi biblical half-tribe of Manasseh. Zvie Ben-Dor Benite, *The Ten Lost Tribes: A World History*. The division into two kingdoms was Israel's most serious blow, as later they became two competing kingdoms: ten tribes of the northern part of the land of Israel formed the house of Israel under Jeroboam. Benjamin and a few scattered of the priestly tribe of Levi formed the smaller house of Judah (from whence the term "Jew" came), southern kingdom under Rehoboam. After

931 BC, the Northern Kingdom of the tribe went its separate way until its fall to Assyria in 722 BC. 4 *The Times History of the World*, p.54. 5 Nebuchadnezzar foretold an Image with silver chest and arms; and Daniel's Dream said a Beast like a Bear and Ram with two horns. Nebuchadnezzar's dream described Babylon as an Image with head of gold; Daniel's Dream as Beast like Lion with Eagle's wings; 6 Daniel 2:32, 39; 7:6, 17; 8:5-9, 21. 7 Daniel 2:32, 40-43; 7:7, 8, 17; 13:1, 2. 8 Daniel 13:3. 9, 10 and 11 Daniel 7:8, and 9. 12 Daniel 7:8, 20-22, 24-27. 13 Revelation 13:11-17, 17:3-4. 14 8:3, 20:17.

Daniel's Dream: Fourth Horn, deadly healing:

Fourth resurrection under Justinian: 554 AD – developing imperial Restoration of two parts of the Empire.[14]

Fifth resurrection under Charlemagne, Crowned by Pope Leo 111 800 AD.[15]

Sixth resurrection under Otto the Great, 962 AD, crowned by Pope John X12, creating the Roman Empire of the German nation.[16]

Seventh resurrection under Charles V. Nebuchadnezzar's dream: Image with belly and bronze thighs; and Daniel's vision: Beast resembling Leopard with four heads, Daniel of Hapsburg: 1530 AD, crowned by Pope Clement V111.[17]

Eighth resurrection under Napoleon Bonaparte: 1804-1814, crowned by Pope Pius V11.[18]

Ninth resurrection under Hitler and Mussolini: 1933-1945, close collaboration with Pope Pius V11.[19]

The Tenth resurrection is prophesied as the European Confederacy of Ten Nations, controlled by a political dictator, the Beast, and a religious leader, the false Prophet;[20] that the European Union is heading towards replacing the United States as the global super power.

The national wealth of the United States reduced by 21.8 percent, while that of the European Union fell by 5.8 percent down to 22.2 trillion Euros but still a quarter of the world's entire wealth.[21] The Euro is one and a half times the US dollar.

The ten leaders, by political arrangements, are paving the way for a geopolitical area within Central Europe. This is the last of human governments as prophesied by Daniel, and complemented in the Revelation by John, as prior to the second coming of Christ.

Notes references and comments:

14 Daniel's dream and John's vision on first head. Daniel's dream fifth horn and

John's vision, second head, Revelation 13:15. 15 Daniel's dream and John's vision, sixth horn and third head; Daniel's dream seventh horn and John's vision fourth head; Daniel's Dream and John's vision fifth head; Daniel's Dream, eighth horn and John's vision fourth head; Daniel's Dream and John's vision fifth head; Daniel's Dream, eighth horn and John's vision, sixth head, Revelation 17. 16 Daniel's vision and dream, ten toes of iron and clay, and John's vision, tenth horn, seventh head with ten horns. 17 Weinland who claims to be one of two of God's Last Witnesses, and who advocates the 6,000 year notion of literal truth of humanity's existence on earth. Jeremiah, prophet of Israel, said Judah, the southern kingdom of Israel would be destroyed by Nebuchadnezzar, king of Babylon, that he would destroy the land to desolation: Jeremiah 25:9. He also said Jerusalem would be destroyed and the people would cease to laugh; that Jewish survivors would be carried off to Babylon, enslaved for 70 years: Jeremiah 25:11, punished by Pashur, one of the religious leaders: Jeremiah 20:2. Later archaeology and ancient history proved Jeremiah's prophesy: brilliant, eloquent and poetic prophesies, over a 60-year period (740-680 BC), during the reign of successive Judaean kings. Jeremiah proved himself by Moses' test many times over. 18 *Europe in Prophesy – The Unfolding of End Times*, Thomas Nelson Inc. Publishers. 19 *Europe in Prophesy – The Unfolding of End Times*, Thomas Nelson Inc. Publishers. 20 Revelation 13:1-18. Anti-Christ, along with "man of sin", lawlessness, and anarchy. *The Good News,* January- February 2010, pages 9-11, *Business Week*, September 16, 2009. 21 *The Economist* 24 October 2009, at the time of researching for this book 2009

Contemporary Europe is secular and multicultural but it will become strongly under-girded and supported by a pervasive religious element according to the interpreters of prophesy.[22] Due to changing world climate, views are mixed as to potential superpowers. Mentioned are countries such as Brazil, the Russian Federation and China - a return to Asia to what might seem to be its historical proportions of world population and economy.[23]

Ephraim and Manasseh.

God inspired Jacob to the prophesy that descendants of his two grandsons, Ephraim and Manasseh, would become a multitude of nations and become great powers on earth:

> *I will make your descendants as the dust of the Earth...if man could number the dust...then your descendants could also be numbered...and kings shall come from you... you shall spread abroad to the west and the east to the north and to the south....*[24]*And the land was not able to bear them that they might dwell together...their substance was great..."* [25]

Many writers and biblical researchers have explained Western races and their connections to the Israelites, particularly the Ten Lost Tribes. National greatness may not have been fulfilled by the Israelites in later years but possibly internationally. We should not assume that modern generations do not carry the genes of Israelites despite religious and cultural

Notes references and comments:

22 *The Good News* ditto and *Business Week* ditto. 23 *Brazil as an Emerging Superpower,* Mario Einaudi, International Studies, Cornell University; *China. The Next Super Power?* who has spread her tentacles into several countries in the field of structural development in recent years, what some consider as the prerequisite to superpower status - Geoffrey Murphy; *Russian Federation*, Steven Rosefields, University of North Carolina. Joseph S Nye, Jr. professor at Harvard author of The Future of Power. 24 Genesis 13:16; God to Abram, verse 14: *"... look northward, southward, eastward, and westward...*this would seem to mean entire world; for those who have not researched & recorded their genealogy does not mean they are excluded; every person on this earth has a long line of ancestry; 17:6: *"I will make you exceedingly fruitful..."* 21: *"..I will establish a covenant with Isaac",* miracle child of Sarah and Abraham, founder of the Jewish nation, courageous in defending his family, and a caring father who practised hospitality to others; and 12:1-3, 23: *"...leave your country...to a place I will show you..."* 25 Though one may add Africa particularly Ethiopia through Menelik, reputed to be son of Solomon and Sheba, though the evidence is scanty: Matthew 12:41, 42, 1 Kings 10, 2 Chronicles 9, and other sources would seem to support this. The descendants of Ephraim and Manasseh, sons of Jacob, father of 12 tribes and grandsons of Joseph, became Britain and United States as brother nations, *Business Week*, September 16, 2009; Genesis 49:1: Blessings: Jacob calls his sons, verses 22-26, Joseph exalted; 48:19, Joseph exalts his son Ephraim. Yair Davidy speaks on behalf of Brit/Am/Hebrew nations: the Ten Lost Tribes are amongst Western peoples...www.britain.org. Their sources include the Bible, Rabbinical Writings, History, Linguistics, Mythology, Archaeology, and numerous other disciplines.

differences. [26] The descendants of Ephraim became the British Empire, comprising four times a quarter of the earth's population and five times what was the territory of the Roman Empire.[27]

The British Empire dominated much of the earth, ruled over, and 'protected' many peoples of the world as no other empire in the known history of mankind, as the Royal Navy and Merchant Navy commanded the seas. The descendants of Manasseh lived among their cousins, the descendants of Ephraim in Great Britain, and moved westward to colonise North America. By the American Revolution in the early eighteenth century they broke away from the Empire to become the United States of America, a 'nation of nations', comprising immigrants from many parts of the world. By the nineteenth century Great Britain had become the dominant global superpower.[28] Out of the British Empire emerged leading countries of the Commonwealth: Britain, Canada, Australia and New Zealand, the Dominion of India, some Arab countries, other small territories and some African dependencies which became members of the British Commonwealth at the attainment of their independence from the mother country.

In the Second World War Great Britain fought solely against the Third Reich assisted only by her colonial forces (now Commonwealth) and joined by the Soviet Union in 1941. At the bombing of Pearl Harbour by Japan the brother nation, United States, was drawn into the war.[29] The cost of two world wars in less than three decades, policing the world and borrowing from the United States, brought Great Britain into financial and military stress. The United States replaced Great Britain as the world super power.[30]

Perhaps the End-Time Prophesy with predictions of the end of the world is one that has fascinated many people. In the late 1940s Jehovah Witnesses announced the exact date the world would end but the world is still here and more recent dateline predictions have also passed without event. The End-Time theory to the end-date of a 5,125-year-long cycle in the Mayan Long Count calendar on events of a transformation nature had been predicted to occur on 21 or 23 December 2012. A year the Mayans predicted as the year of unprecedented irreversible change in our world, related to a *New* age interpretation of

Notes, references and comments:

26 See reference 16 Edenic Covenant above: genes are carried through the succession of generations up to the present day in the inevitable factor of mixing genes (biology heredity). All people are one because their origin is one, divided by actions in the mode of the life we choose or chosen for us; distinction from others arises when a common group is formed and their characteristic traits and differences are determined by culture, circumstances, environment, language, and other factors; Genesis 17:4 Abraham: "...you shall be father of many nations;" and 21:12 "in Isaac", father of Jacob. 27 *Business Week* ditto; Britain: from the conquest of Ireland 1172 and much of France during the Hundred Years' War to the early 18th century. Emerged in later days, is the promise of global greatness to the descendants of Joseph, grandson of Abraham. 28 *The Good News, ditto* and *Business Week*, ditto 29 Imperial Japanese Navy

against the US naval base at Pearl Harbour, Hawaii, on the morning of 7/12/41 (Dec 8 in Japan). 30 Paul Kennedy *The Rise and Fall of the Great Powers*: "...debt and imperial over-reach are aspects to the rise and fall of empires."

transition: that Earth and inhabitants would undergo a *positive beginning of a new era.*Others said the date marked the end of the world, relating to Earth's collision with a passing planet referred to as Nibiru or black hole, physical or spiritual transformation; and some said 2012 would probably mark the end or the arrival of the next solar maximum. Islam believed in the return of the Madhi, Jesus, the Messiah, to defeat Masih-ad-Dajjal the false prophet and the golden age of peace before the final judgment. Buddhism believed in the coming of the next Buddha, Maitreya. The veils shall dissolve and the Physical and Spiritual realms shall merge, so said the Maori. The Zulu believed that the whole world would be turned upside down; and the current dark Kali Yuga age was heading for its end, according to Hinduism. None of these had been accepted by mainstream prophesy scholarship. [31]

Prophesy interpreters said the world was now at the eve of the beginning of the End Time and the *signs* as predicted were increased floods, tsunamis, wars in different places, diseases, human suicide bombings, population explosion, earthquakes, lawlessness, universal conflicts, increase of evil, natural catastrophes, all constituting the beginnings of sorrow.

It is true that the above have been experienced in many parts of the world and these signs had been a reality to the people experiencing them. In the devastating floods of Mozambique a woman gave birth to a baby up in the branches of a tree, moving someone in England to say:

"We cannot be affected by floods we are not a tropical country." [32]

Yeshua gives the analogy to these signs of the inter-advent Age as a woman in labour:

"Beware that no one leads you astray. For many will come in my name, saying

'I am the Messiah!' and they will lead many astray. And you will hear of wars

and rumours of wars; see that you are not alarmed; for this must take place,

but the end is not yet. For nation will rise against nation, and kingdom against

kingdom, and there will be famines and earthquakes in various places: all this

is but the beginning of the birth pangs." 33

According to prophesy interpreters, after the signs shall emerge the power of Satan manifest in the Anti-Christ, the world dictator and the breakdown of world traditional systems followed by false peace. 34 Prophesy of the End Time also predicted that the God of heaven shall set

Notes, references and comments:

31 Various media reports. These predictions did not meet the test of prophesy; life is an Infinite Journey, the earth is shaped like a globe, no beginning and no end. 32 Many floods have taken place in the United Kingdom in recent years and anarchism; which reduces the human condition as brutal cruelty ravages the infrastructure and is the product of poverty, disease and hunger; diseases are bred by war and kill more people than the wars themselves.33 Matthew 24:1-14; Luke 21:10,11. 34 The predicted dates came to pass without event: only the Almighty God knows what is and when it is going to happen.

up an eternal kingdom and existing kingdoms shall be disintegrated. Daniel also prophesied that after Babylon there would be a succession of empires the last of which would be rreplaced by the Kingdom of God. 35

Christian theology interpretation is that the Temple of God and the Jerusalem from Above, or the Heavenly Jerusalem in the Old Testament, are notions of outward sanctuary as having been replaced by the literal dwelling of God in the church; that the New Jerusalem is the city which is not heaven by itself since it descends from God out of heaven;36 and together with heaven it is the eternal abode and destiny of the redeemed of all the ages and all nations of the earth. Further that, these interpretations or eschatological beliefs are coincidental to the second coming of Jesus:

> *"I will make a new covenant with the people of Israel and Judah...I will put my law in their minds, and I will write them on their hearts."* 37

Millennia Rule has been prophesied as one thousand-year period of peace, love, fellowship, and harmony as intended in the Garden of

Eden.[38]

"Do not be conformed to this world but be transformed by the renewing of your minds, so that you may discern what is the will of God – what is good, acceptable and perfect". [39]

"The lofty looks of man shall be humbled... haughtiness of man shall be bowed down, and the Lord alone shall be exalted in that day." [40] *"Rome's door has at last opened to the Anglican's faithful to Christ's teaching. A Papal*
decree opens the way for Anglican priesthood to embrace Rome, while they
retain their traditional liturgy and their Marital status".[41]

The above refers to resignations of seven hundred Anglican clergy and three hundred laity to join the *Ordinariat,* a special section of the Roman Catholic clergy. [42]

Notes, references and comments:

35 Daniel 2:44.36 Isaiah 2:2-4. Some prophesied that the beginning of the *End Time* commenced from the year 2008; others said since Biblical prophesies have taken place and come to pass, why should the End Time prophesy not be realised and come to pass? 37 Jeremiah 31:31. 38 Revelation 20:1-6, 21:1-27; 1 Corinthians 15:35-58; Psalms 67:4. 39 Romans 12:2. 40 Isaiah 2:11. Zechariah 12:10; 13:1-2; Revelation 2:26-27, 5:10, 20:4 who keeps Jesus' works prevails; Isaiah 11:6-9: Wild and domestic animals shall live in peace; harmless serpents in peace with little children; military and wars discarded, money devoted to universal peace, people living on their own plots without fear of thieves, knowledge of God shall embrace the whole world: a kingdom of God. 41 *Europe in Prophesy – The Unfolding of End Times,* Thomas Nelson Inc. Publishers. Weinland, *God's Last Witness.* 42 *The Good News,* November-December 2009.

The counter Reformation in prophesy: What had been called the "Pope's power grab" was in tandem with the increased secular power of the European Union, made possible by the Czech Republic's approval of the Lisbon Treaty.[43] The Biblical prophesy of the End Time mentions a final revival of the ancient Roman Empire as foretold in the Books of Daniel and Revelation. The Advent of Jesus: First and Second:

"And He shall judge among the nations, and shall rebuke many peoples; and they shall beat their swords into ploughshares ...nation shall not lift up sword against nation, neither shall they learn war any more." [44]

The prophesy on the rejection and suffering of Yeshua:

"A tender plant - the infant Jesus carried our sorrows, wounded for our transgressions...for our iniquities and God laid all our iniquities upon Him...." [45]

Ancient and modern scholars have rigorously contested the above prophesy and it is universally acknowledged that these verses fit the person of Yeshua (Jesus).[46]

Daniel prophesied he saw in the night visions of one like the Son of Man who came with the clouds of heaven...he received eternal dominion, glory and Kingdom. Nations of all languages served him.[47]

Prophesy of a crucifixion is also described in the Old Testament by Isaiah, which though no particular person is named, fits the description and circumstances pertaining to that of Yeshua. [48]

Long before the coming of Yeshua David composed the verses of the Psalm:

"My God, my God, why hast thou forsaken me?" [49]

Notes, references and comments:

43 BBC Radio 4, 23/01/11, *The Economist* 24/10/09. 44 Isaiah 2:4. The Old Testament contains many prophesies about the coming of a redeemer to earth and that Yeshua was present in the world before His arrival at Pentecost, Ephesians 2:14: Pentecost: a) Jewish harvest festival, *Shavuoth,* on the fiftieth day after Passover, Leviticus 23:15, 16, anniversary of giving law on Mount Sinai. b) Christian festival held on Whit Sunday celebrating the descent of the Holy Spirit on Jesus' disciples after His death. Acts 1:4-6, 2. Roman Catholic church claims that Jesus took residence in the church at Pentecost; some theologians say the reference is to the growth of the Messianic Community Church, the *One in Messiah,* Jew and Gentile: *"For through Him we both have access by one Spirit unto the Father,* Ephesians 2:18, Daniel 7:13, 14. 45 Isaiah 53:1-12, 7:143, 11:1-10. 46 Ephesians 2:18-22. 47 Isaiah's prophesy is translated by Matthew, Mark Luke and John in the New Testament; Revelation 21:2, John's vision on holy Jerusalem, *Unger's Survey of the Bible, Major Themes of the Bible*, page 52. 48 2 Thessalonians 2:2-4, coming of Christ; Zechariah 4:6,

word of Lord to Zerubabel. 49 Psalm 22:1-21, 11:1, Matthew 27:26, Mark 15:15, Luke 1:1-35 and John 19, 20:25; refers to the humiliation and suffering of Jesus on the cross. Ezekiel: the practice of writing on wood dates back to the days of Moses, among the early Greeks, ancient Britons, and recently Sweden; KJV Concordance page 1144; 2 sticks represent Joseph and Ephraim and incorporation of Israel into Judah; that David shall be the people's prince forever; and Jesus is referred to as the son of David as king over their covenant of peace.

There are many Biblical accounts of the fate of the Ark, before, during and beyond the rule of kings of Israel with recurring degrees of idolatry. As such, they became increasingly oblivious to the existence of the *Ark*, its whereabouts or its meaning. In the eighteenth year of his reign about 20 BC, Herod decides to rebuild a Temple on the ruins of Solomon's *First Temple* at Jerusalem, on a rather magnificent scale but the meaning of the Ark of Covenant, as the message of the tabernacle is unknown to him. He is also seeped in idolatry. But the message of the Tabernacle and Ark of Covenant in its prophetic purpose of a redeemer is about to be realised during his time. 50

Notes, references and comments:

50 Isaiah 2:2-4; Daniel 7:13-14, on the advent of Jesus: well paraphrased poetically by Ian Wilson, page 175, *Jesus: The Evidence.* Isaiah prophesied the silence of Jesus before His judge (Pilate) when charged in the name of the living God; the prophesy was fulfilled as a perpetual testimony to the truth of the Gospel; Isaiah 43:7, Matthew 26:24. Symbolically, the prediction goes on to say that the house of the Lord shall be established on top of a mountain where many people shall go, shall be judged and many shall be rebuked; and the people shall lay down all their arms. The New Testament prophesy of Restoration: Acts 3:19-21, Peter's sermon on repentance, is all things prophesied will be fulfilled: The Biblical definition of Restoration is to bring back to the original state but Restoration in Scriptures means better than the original state: Hebrews 12:27, 28; According to the Law of Moses: "steal one, give back five": Joel 2:21, fear not: Mark 10:29; God restored Job's losses when he prayed for his friends twice as much as before. Exodus 22:1. Restoration to the Church means in the release of God's power all would know the disciples of Jesus. Job 42:10-12; Ephesians 2:20, Jesus chief cornerstone, 4:13 to the unity of faith and 2 Peter 2:20 look for day of the Lord.

THE VEIL

PART TWO

4 Who is Jesus?

"In the beginning was the Word ...And the Word was made flesh, and dwelt among us, and we beheld His glory, the glory as of only begotten of the Father, full of grace and truth." [1]

The Trinity

Son of God theory has been controversial, much debated by biblical scholars and not acceptable to some Christians.[1a] Arius (AD 250 or 256 –336) a Presbyter from Alexandria, Egypt, taught about the nature of the Godhead which implied God as the Father, Son (Jesus of Nazareth) and Holy Spirit. He emphasized that the Logos, Christ, second of the Trinity, was the first to be called into being by God as the agent or instrument through which God was to make all things. Christ was thus less than God, but more than man, He was divine, but He was not God. Much controversy surrounded Arius and threatened to split the Church. The newly-converted emperor Constantine convened (325 AD) the ecumenical First Council of Nicea, also known as the Nicene Creed.

In 379 AD antagonism arose between the disciples of the Nicene Creed which claimed that Christ was the same substance as God the Father; as did several other Christian sects within the Roman Empire. The opinion of the young presbyter Athanasius (later bishop of Alexandria) was that Christ was begotten, not made" and that He was of the same essence as the Father, God. The view of Athanasius was carried by the Council. Gregory, fourth century Church Father, defended the doctrine of the Trinity and at the time this made him one of the greatest champions of Christian orthodoxy.[2]

Notes, references and comments:

1 John 1:1 and 1:11; Jesus is portrayed as a magical figure, performing super acts, disappearing into the sky to some invisible world. There are many passages in the Bible which indicate that Jesus regarded himself as "humble", though he addressed God as "my Father". Interpretation of the Scriptures by Christian theology is that the children of God are the Israelite and that Gentiles are the adopted children. Can a loving God make a distinction that leads to the prejudice of favouring one from another? What then of the "equality of all people" taught by Yeshua? Yeshua is symbolic to the entire life of a human being, from conception to death but very few understand this, even those who think they are qualified to teach about Jesus. 1a such as Jehovah Witnesses, see

chapter 12 God of People.   2 J N D Kelly, *The Creed of Nicea in Early Christian Creeds*; Carol H Warren, *The Building of Christendom*, 1987, Rowan Williams, *Arius: Heresy and Tradition* - Revised Edition, 1987, 2001 – Synopsis; Readers Digest, *Facts at Your Fingertips*. Arianism was defeated in AD 787, Peter Brown, *The Rise of Christendom*, 2nd edition (Oxford, Blackwell Publishing, 2003). Some Christians do not consider Jehovah's Witnesses to be 'Christians' in any orthodox sense of the word, though they may have started as such, because they hold a 'non-Trinitarian' theology, believing that YAHWEH (Jehovah) is the only true God, the creator of all things, the "Universal Sovereign', that all worship should be directed to him alone, and that he is not part of a Trinity. They consider this marginalises to the point of elimination the very role of Christ, and say: *"This sets JW's outside the boundaries of mainstream Christianity."*

Reference 2 Continued below...

The new emperor Flavius Theodosius (347-395), known as Theodosius the Great, was also known for making Christianity the official state religion of the Roman Empire. His legacy is controversial: lauded as transforming the Roman Empire into a bastion of imperial Christianity, but he is also criticised for intolerance of other faiths and imposing draconian measures against those who did not follow Christianity. This went against the Christian teaching to *love one's neighbour.* Theodosius suppressed paganism and Arianism, taking the stand of Athanasius. He directed the convention of the second general council at Constantinople in 380 AD to clarify the norm. Theodosius was intellectually open-minded and he acquired a keen interest in history, though he did not apply or attribute Christianity to historical evidence.[2a]

Theodosius established the creed of the council of Nicaea, the Necene Creed, as a general principle for Christian orthodoxy. The newly recognized Christian Church sought to unify and clarify its theology and subjugated Arianism to describe those who disagreed with their doctrine of Trinity. The newly recognised Christian Church was *politically* under *the most powerful* authority of the time, the Roman Empire that later evolved into the Roman Catholic Church.[3]

John's gospel 3:16 and Genesis 1:12-31 says:

"For God so loved the world that He gave His only begotten Son, that

whosoever believeth in Him should not perish, but have eternal life."

Some Christians believe that the miraculous birth, as resurrection, although wonderful stories, are neither credible nor acceptable and are of no spiritual significance. Many who follow Jesus as Christians, in following the Church, believe that Jesus was born naturally,

Notes, references and comments:

Reference 2 continued: The persecution of Pagans in the late Roman Empire began during Constantine the Great's later reign, when he ordered the tearing down of some temples, through to Emperors Gracian, Valentinian II, and Theodosius I, Saint Ambrose's influence, Bishop of Milan. The first anti-Pagan laws by the Christian state started with Constantine's son, Constantius II, who was an unwavering opponent of Paganism on pain of death. Under his reign ordinary Christians started vandalising many of the ancient Pagan temples, tombs and monuments. 2a See reference 2 above. 3 All positive writings on Arianism had been destroyed but Arianism is an indication that there was a time before the *notion of Jesus as God*, when *only God* was thought to exist. Despite concerted opposition, Arian Christian churches persisted throughout Europe and North Africa, in various Goths and Germanic peoples' kingdoms, until suppressed by military conquest or voluntary royal conversion between the fifth and seventh centuries. The controversy over the Son's precise relationship to the Father had been debated long before Arius. Some say Jesus is theanthropic, Greek for `god-man' - both divine and human embodying deity in human form. The virgin birth theory holds that the conception of Jesus was asexual through a spirit, sadly, there was no scientific knowledge then to prove by means of DNA. Some say the Hebrew word for "young woman" was misconstrued to mean "virgin", language is the major communicating tool and any attempt to understand one's non-native language may give rise to assumptions leading to untruths.

some think perhaps illegitimate;[4] and other Christians worship Jesus like God. Jesus would most probably find this blasphemous.

Yeshua himself says:

> *"In vain do they worship me, teaching for doctrines the commandments of men...You reject the commandment of God, that you may keep your own traditions".* [5]
> *"I am the truth, the way and the life; No one comes to the Father but through me."* [5a]

God places Himself on the side of man, according to Pope John Paul II:

> *"He emptied himself, taking the form of a slave, coming*

in human likeness, and found human in appearance, he humbled himself, becoming obedient to death, even death on a cross (Philippians 2:7-8)... All individual and collective suffering caused by the forces of nature and unleashed by man's free will – the wars, the Gulags, and the holocausts: the holocaust of the Jews but also, for example, the holocaust of the black slaves from Africa".

The Definition or Creed of Chalcedon, also known as the Doctrine of the Hypostatic Union or the Two-Nature Doctrine defines Jesus as:

"In Jesus God and Man are in personal union; that which is divine is of personal union; that which is divine is of the same substance (the essential reality) as the Father God...; that which is human is of the same substance with us; and the two are united unconfusedly, unchangeably, indivisibly, and inseparably".

Jesus, born of woman, said:

"If you see one who was not born of woman, prostrate yourselves and worship him, that one is your Father." [6a]

Notes, references and comments:

4 Not necessarily the eldest of a large family, humble peasant family, in a small hamlet in the cosmopolitan and multicultural state of Galilee, under oppressive Roman occupation. By his story-telling Yeshua may have believed that it was the best way to reach the minds of his audience and was the most memorable way to put over his vision. 5 Mark 7:7, 9, about the popular customs and traditions of this world; Jesus calls such worship as the prophesy of hypocrites Mark 7:6 & 8; *Crossing the Threshold of Hope*, page 63. Jesus does not call himself 'God' 5a John 14:6. Clearly Jesus indicates he is the 'son'. Throughout the passages of the New Testament, Jesus asks us to revere God and not him. Some Christians call Jesus God. If we call Jesus God, what do we call God then? 6a *The Gospel of Thomas, the Sayings of Jesus,* No 15. Perhaps this was the reason for not including the Thomas gospel into the Bible. Under the dogma of the Godhead we may not look at God in isolation from the Son and Holy Spirit but as the *Trinity of the Godhead.* The history on the

Reference 6a continued below...

Ian Wilson asks:

"The real Jesus? Would Jesus endorse the Nicene Creed formulated in his name three hundred years later?" [6b]

National language is set and recognised by patriarchal authority. The use of "Father" and "Son" in relation to God and Jesus is either the masculine mind or poverty of language (though the first letter is capitalised). Nonetheless, the burning question is: Had the Nicene Creed, the contemporary authority, accepted the view of Arius over that of Athanasius would the notion that Jesus was of the same substance as God have gained momentum in Christendom and endured to this day?

The nature of a triune God is apparent in the New Testament in the following statement:

> *"Go therefore and make disciples of all the nations, baptising them in the*
>
> *name of the Father and of the Son and of the Holy Spirit."* [7]

Christ has been at the centre of faith and life in Christendom but there are many differing views on God and Jesus:

> *"The Enlightenment put to one side the true God – in   particular God the*
>
> *Redeemer; hence the existence of a Creator or of Providence was in no*
>
> *way helpful to science."* [8]

Notes, references and comments:

Interpretation of the dogma of the Trinity in Christianity is based upon the interpretation by the ancient councils of Nicaea and Constantinople, three hundred years after the death of Jesus in the fourth century.

Reference 6a continued: Deuteronomy 23:2: *"One of illegitimate birth shall not enter the assembly of the Lord; even to the tenth generation..."* The New Testament was written at a time when the notion of *illegitimacy* was still very much at its height; and the writers could not attribute greatness to one born illegitimate, so-called. Illegitimacy is a 'man-made barrier', an aspect of snobbery and a true loving God cannot place such a barrier on any person regardless of the circumstances of conception or birth. Over the centuries children have been born out of wedlock and they have become famous people performing great deeds which have lived through the centuries: Confucius (CA551-479 BC), one of his many quotes is *"What you do not want done to yourself, do not do to others".* Not unlike Jesus: *"Do unto others as you would wish them to do unto you;"* Leonardo da Vinci (1452-1519); Lawrence of Arabia (1888-1935), and others, including royalty. Words such as `bastard', 'illegitimate' are used by people who never bother to ask the most important question: *"Does the seed have any control over its conception as a human?"* Continued below... Perhaps the circumstances of the birth of Yeshua was God's gift for the abolition of the stigma man had attached to birth "out of wedlock". But man does not see the things of God. These offensive terms ought to be abolished and removed from dictionaries. There is no such a thing as an `illegitimate' child. 6b Ian Wilson, *Jesus: The Evidence,* page 175. Wilson asks the question historically rather than theologically, backed by evidence. 7 Matthew 28:19. Reference 8 continued below...

John's gospel explains that the divinity, humanity and office of Christ [9] was not a mere representative image of the Father's glory but the very brightness of that glory truly of the only begotten of the Father. [10]

Theologians say the major ancillary themes are internal and external evidence, including the witness of the Holy Spirit, which combine to authenticate the Bible as the fully inspired and authoritative Word of God. Many passages throughout the Bible corroborate the themes. Externally, the follow up ministry among Christian writers, who support this as truth.[11] Some say the tripartite Godhead is separate in functions but are in agreement in all the functions.

Hypothetically: Any person regardless of faith or creed who had never declared that s/he believed in Jesus or ever heard of him; and a Christian who attended church regularly, violated those tenets and harmed others - which one of these has followed Jesus? The answer is neither, according to Christian theology, unless one repents, confesses, accepts and believes in Jesus as a Redeemer. Some Christians say no amount of good deeds will get one into Heaven unless there is belief in Jesus. Is this not a misdirection and license to stray?

God is the Father of Christ by the declaration on the day Christ was begotten, according to Christian theology.[12] The Second Book of Psalms belongs to the time of David, after he had established the seat of his government at Jerusalem; and at the time when the nations which had been subdued by him were contemplating a revolt. The Second Book of Psalms prophesied the supremacy of the Messiah.[13] Another view is that those who believe in the Nicene Creed teaching do not understand that the Holy Spirit is simply the power of God, who is spirit and uses His spirit to do His will; the power is subject to God; and further that the Trinity does confound the truth about God.[14] Michael Servetus questioned the validity of

Notes, references and comments:

Referemce 8 continued: Pope John Paul II, *Crossing the Threshold of Hope*, pages 28-53. Enlightenment, the European intellectual movement of the late 17th and 18th centuries emphasising reason and individualism rather than tradition, also collectively known as "founding fathers" of that era in modern thought; also in Nirvarna Buddhist state of enlightenment. Does God, the Almighty, need helpers to control the universe? The notion of the Trinity may have been influenced by minds conditioned by the nature of human government. In most human governments, if not all, no head of state stands alone but is assisted by subordinates, in a hierarchical system of various descriptions, according to the culture of the government. The gospels are only other people's accounts of what they had heard. According to historical records, the original copy of the Bible was lost (see chapter 1 above). What we have today are copies of copies, no doubt to some extent affected by the *Du Bartas syndrome.* 9 John 1:15, 12, 34; Psalms 2:7; John 9:35; Matthew 11:27. 10 Timothy 3:15; Romans 10:17.11 *Unger's Survey of the Bible.* 12 Psalms 2:7. 13 Psalms 2:6. John 3:16 may indicate the affinity of the Father and the Son. 14 Ronald Weinland. 15 Richard Hooker, *World Civilizations,* on John Calvin (1509-1564), author of *Calvin's Institute of the Christian Religion.* Michael Servetus, Spanish scholar, Geneva 1553; ideals or any other situations become established by the contemporary power of men such as has been throughout in Christendom, Servetus was no match for Calvin.

the Trinity in the time of John Calvin, father of Calvinism.[15] From about 1514 Jesus came to be known as "Jesus the Christ".[16] Somewhere along the way, the word: `the' disappeared and it was thought that "Christ" was a surname. Yeshua in Greek Iesous; Jesu in Latin; Isa in Islam; Issa in Hindu; Jesus in English, and Joshua a variation. Jesus is known by many names: "the seed of woman";[17] "the seed of Abraham";[18] the "Prophet like unto Moses"; [19] "the priest after the order of Melchizedek"; [20] "the rod out of the stem of Jesse"; [21] "Immanuel, the virgin's son";[22] "the branch of Jehovah"; [23] and "the messenger of the covenant". [24]

With the universal rise of Christianity people around the world have called Yeshua by different versions of "Jesus", according to their culture. In most Bantu languages Yeshua is known as "Yesu". [25]

Some preachers describe the Trinity as a three-sided lamp in which God was both central and one of the sides; Jesus and the Holy Spirit were the other two. God's light it seemed could come from all three ways. Some Christians ask: If God was central why bother with the other two? Certain parts of this story are unacceptable to some Christians, as to non-Christians. To Mahatma Gandhi (a Hindu, 1869-1948) Jesus was the greatest teacher humanity has ever had and to his believers he was God's only begotten son.

Gandhi asks:

> *"If I do not accept this belief would it diminish its influence upon my life?*
>
> *I think not."*

He adorned the wall over his desk with a picture of Jesus and *The Sermon on the Mount* was a source of guidance and inspiration to him. He said to be a good Hindu meant that he would be a good Christian, no need for him to become a Christian to be a believer or try to follow the beauty of the teachings of Jesus:

> *"Jesus' own life is the key to His nearness to God. He expressed, as no other*
>
> *could, the spirit and will of God."*

Someone said:

> *"I believe in Jesus because if I am right, I stand to gain eternal bliss, and if I*
>
> *am wrong, I will have lost nothing."*

Another said:

> *"So long as I try to live by the Ten Commandments, I do not have to unravel*
>
> *or try to understand the complexities presented by Christian theologians."*

Notes, references and comments:

16 Flavius Josephus (1st century Romano-Jewish scholar, 37-100 AD); John 1:1-3 confirms Genesis 1:21; 3:14-10   17 Acts 17:3, 18:5, Daniel 9:326, Messiah."Christ", English term for the Greek *Kristos*, "the anointed one", standardised in the spirit of the Enlightenment in the seventeenth century as words to fit their Greek or Latin origins; Constantine was Greek, and `Christianity' was established during his contemporary political power. 18 Genesis 3:15. 19 God blesses the seed of Abraham to bless all nations on earth, Matthew 1:5, genealogy of Jesus from Abraham.   20 Psalms 110:4; Deuteronomy 18:15, the Lord will raise a prophet, Acts 13:23, God will raise a

saviour. 21 Isaiah 11:1, 10 and Zechariah 6:15. 22 Isaiah 7:14. 23 Isaiah 4:2. 24 Malachi 3:1, cross reference Matthew 11:10. 25 Author's oral testimony. There are many various scholars' interpretations of Jesus' existence in the Old and New Testaments.

Jesus the Christ has been well defined in *The Works of Josephus* in which are also several men named Jesus. Josephus distinguishes Emmanuel Jesus as the "Christ." Though allowances should be made for the oddities of translation by William Whiston in the *Works of Flavius Josephus*, contemporary of Yeshua. In the Jewish rebellion against Pilate, Josephus describes the man Jesus (Yeshua):

> *"There was about this time Jesus, a wise man, if it be lawful to call him a man, for he was a doer of wonderful works, a teacher of such men as receive the truth with pleasure. He drew over to him many Jews and Gentiles. He was [the] Christ. And when Pilate, at the suggestion of the principal men among us had condemned him to the Cross, those that loved him at first did not forsake him, for he appeared to them alive again the third day, as the divine prophets had foretold these and ten thousand other wonderful things concerning him. And the tribe Christians, so named from him, are not extinct at this day."* 26

John the Baptist preceded Jesus preaching in the wilderness, in Jerusalem, all Judea and around Jordan, saying:

"Repent Ye for The Kingdom of Heaven is at hand." 27

Josephus records History of the Jews and says of John the Baptist:

> *"Some of the Jews thought that the destruction of Herod's army came from God, and that Herod was punished very justly for what punishment he had inflicted upon John, that was called the Baptist ...who was a good man and commanded the Jews to exercise virtue...by righteousness towards one another and piety to God, and so to come to baptism"* .28

Christian theology teaches that Christ is the greatest of all men and is now in heaven as the glorified Son of Man, for He was born of the "seed of woman", Mary; as such He set the example or the way to glorification.[29] By virtue of His incarnation Christ not only possessed a temporary humanity but also a genuine permanent glorified human body for all eternity; and provides an eternal link between God and the redeemed. [30]

Christ is greater than Adam because He is Adam's creator; and that He is greater than Abraham because He existed in past eternity and was the object of Abraham's faith.[31]

Notes, references and comments:

26 *The Testimonies of Flavius Josephus concerning Jesus Christ, John the Baptist and James the Just,* page 52. 27 The *Works of Flavius Josephus*, page 34   28 *Unger's Survey of the Bible*, pp. 95, 102, John 1:42, 1-18, Philippians 2:5-11. 29 Matthew 3:1, Mark 1:2, Luke 1:76, 7:2729. 30 John 8:56-58. 31 Romans 5:17, 18: *"Christ is the source of life, greater than Adam the source of death".* If God delegated the function of Creation to Jesus, what then is God's function as the Almighty Creator? Are we to assume that God as the Supreme Spirit *has no limb to touch* and perform *material acts*? Is creation a mere material act? Or, are we to take these statements as poverty of

Reference 31 continued below...

Christ is greater than Solomon because He is the wisdom of God.[32] Christ is also the creator and owner of the universe and heir of all things.[33] Christ is greater than Jacob in the greatness of his gift: Jacob, their great ancestor, had given the people a well to drink from but Jesus spoke of giving His people rivers of living waters.[34]

The Apostle Paul in interpreting Christianity through the church at Colossi said:

> "God created all things through Jesus Christ ...by Him [Jesus] all things
> were created, that are in heaven,and that are on earth, visible and invisible,
> whether they be thrones, or dominions, or principalities or powers ..." [35]

The gospel of John says:

> "In the beginning there was the Word, and the Word was with God, and the
> Word was God. All things were made through Him... He was

before all

things and in Him all things consist." [36]

The Holy Spirit is viewed and presented by theologians differently. According to one view, the King James Version of the Bible contains an inaccuracy which is to be found in 1 John 5:7-8 (KJV – 1NKJV). Some words were deliberately added to the Scripture in order to encourage readers to believe that the Spirit of God is a person, a doctrine that the Bible does not teach.[37]

John's gospel presents the Holy Spirit as The Holy Spirit of God and not as a mere role model for good and not only one in counsel and purpose:

"Even the spirit of truth, whom the world cannot receive, because it seeth

Him not, neither knoweth Him, but ye know Him, for He dwelleth with you,

and shall be in you." [38]

"The Pharisees and the scribes have taken the keys of knowledge and have hidden them. They have not entered, nor have they allowed those who want
to enter to do so. As for you, be as shrewd as snakes and as innocent as doves." [39]

Notes, references and comments:

Reference 31 continued: language? The Bible says when Jesus resurrected and returned to heaven He re-delegated God's power to the Holy Spirit, the in-dweller of the Church. In the midst of all the delegating and re-delegating what is God's function? This indicates the typical characteristic of a mindset reflecting the hierarchical system of human government, where the `delegating device' reigns supreme. 32 Matthew 12:42; 1 Corinthians 1:30. 33 Colossians 1:15-17, Hebrews 1:2, 3, John 4:12. 34 John 14:7, 37-39. 35 Colossians 1:16, 17, Paul's statement indicates *enthusiasm over the top* and a *mindset* conditioned by a hierarchy, the Roman Empire legacy and role model to much of modern times. John 1:3, Hebrews 1:236 John 1:1-3, 36 Also indicates a mindset similar to that of Paul. 37 Wineland, *God's Final Witness,* page 203. 38 John 14:17, 16:7-15. 39 Sayings of Jesus No 39, the Gospel of Thomas

"It is not enough that another person has discovered the Truth. Each

individual must seek and strive to discern it and so engage in the Divine
labour of salvation of one's Soul, that is to say, the awakening and
liberation of one's Soul in conscious union with God." [40]

In the introduction to his book Ehrman says:

"As a historian, I am no longer obsessed with the theological question of how God became man, but with the historical question of how man became God." [41]

Ehrman is possibly the only one to have discussed frankly the extraordinary possibility, that Jesus had a twin brother; Thomas, also born of Mary: one child was divine, the other an ordinary human being. This bizarre situation is not without precedent, that is to say in classical mythology, in the supreme Greek hero Heracles (Hercules) and Iphicles, his twin. Alcmene had conceived a child with her husband, Amphitryon; the offspring was the mortal Iphicles; then she had been impregnated by Zeus, who appeared to her in human form in the guise of her husband Amphitryon. As a result, two foetuses (or feti, plural) grew in her womb, one the son of a mortal, the other the son of a god, Hercules, the immortal hero.That in the case of Mary, we would need to reverse the order. First she was impregnated by the Holy Spirit, while still a virgin (possibly based on the assumption of the virgin aspect). Not long thereafter, possibly Joseph (to whom she was engaged at the time) impregnated her with the child who was to become Didymus Judas Thomas, Jesus' twin brother. As the Trinity could not become a quaternity, Thomas was denied divine status.

The examples of Hercules and Jesus are dominated by the aspect of the "divinity" of one child. In other circumstances, we may look to the aid of science in explaining the mystery of twins, and the interplay of genetics. In 2006 a rare genetic chance produced twin boys, each with a different skin colour. [42]

Notes, references and comments:

40 Jesus' Sayings No 5, ditto. 41 The introduction to Bart Ehrman's book: *How Jesus Became God - The Exaltation of a Jewish Preacher From Galilee* (28 April 2014). Ehrman, ditto, though he does not explore the implications further. 42 *The Daily Telegraph* 25/10/06, accompanied by a picture of the twins, clearly one white and the other light brown skin with curly hair.

5 Is the existence of God a figment of the imagination of the human mind?

God has existed in historical stages according to the interpretation of human thought, apparent in various writings not only from the Bible writers to modern historians but also in the writings of other cultures of the world. The God of the philosophers of the Enlightenment was the offspring of human speculation. God is known by a *variety of assumptions,* all based on legacy, in a concept according to cultural conditioning. Not even the `Chosen People' the Israelite who wrote the Torah ever saw God. The great Biblical personages of the Old Testament who claimed to have spoken with God only tell of God in metaphorical terms as God of the Patriarchs from Abraham to Moses. The equation of God and Jesus in the New Testament was most probably in response to the cry for a *tangible God,* presented according to the view of the early theologians after Jesus. That is to say the different ways Christian leaders present or teach the message of Jesus.

If one chooses to follow Biblical evidence on the coming of Yeshua and his teachings plus the writings of earlier and modern historians, particularly the writings of Ian Wilson, supported by written archaeological evidence, and the *Works of Flavius Josephus* (albeit the translation of the latter was largely influenced by Christianity), oral testimony and general information, is the question whether God really exists necessary? [1]

Exodus 3:14 says that God said to Moses:

> "*I AM THAT I AM. Tell the children of Israel 'I AM has sent Me unto you'.*"

The belief that God is in some far away place from this earth where we shall go, *if we believe,* is influenced by the system of human government where the rulers are so far removed from the rest of the people in a hierarchical administration. There are those who realise or feel the presence of God in *everything*, in all daily deeds, in the very air we breathe in the here and now.

According to Christian theology, Jesus said:

"*...if you have seen me you have seen the Father".* [2]

Notes, references and comments:

1 The answer lies in the heart of each individual, for each dies a personal death as each gets a personal birth and faith lives in hope. The God of the believer is the only living God to the believer. All Christians, however devout, base their worship upon "faith" including church leaders; for no one is an eye-witness in this drama of faith. This also applies to all other faiths; faith is the light of eternal hope. The equality of all humans is apparent in birth and in death, therein is the one God. Bread is baked in many different forms and ingredients, but *bread* is *bread* to the eater and there is one God for all, even in non-Christian beliefs; the difference in methods of worship merely reflect cultural differences, all based on legacy. 2 John 8:19: Did Jesus utter these words or was that the language

Reference 2 continued below...

Some believe that God is the *Supreme Spirit* an abstract, *Omnipotent, Almighty* having infinite values, such as truth, love, grace, justice, healing, prophesies, peace, and is all-embracing: *without God there is nothing.* God's work and love for humans is expressed and praised by David's offering and prayer to God. 3

Quoting Matthew 23:9-10 Pope John Paul II says:

> *"Call no one on earth your father, you have but one father in heaven;* and:

> *"Do not be called master you have but one master, the Messiah. 'Be not*

> *afraid' of these words either."* 4

Independent Entities are found in the minute to the mighty where all things share the characteristic of being *unique* and *independent*, yet they are all *interdependent* and share a common *interrelation* in a grand orderly scheme. The Physical Laws of the Universe are immutable with no intervention. We are all subject to and abide subconsciously to a pre-ordained mechanism, what one may call a *magneto:* "supreme power" with mutant powers and mastery over all magnetic forces of the earth, bio-electrical patterns of all living beings; magnetosphere of the planets, which extends far into space. Magneto power is "for all practical purposes limitless". In other words "God's Divine Law", or Natural Law. God's major instruments for control are Time and the Sun which combines with Space in the orderly grand scheme.

In this grand scheme, humans are endowed with intellect, reason and free will. Regardless of their beliefs or anything else that may distinguish them from one another all are equal before the Divine Law of God. The forces that govern everything in the natural sense are *immutable* and apply to everything and to all, regardless of the importance of rank – the man-made barrier. Governmental or institutional systems, rules, things, groups, or ideals, routinely concentrate into *independent entities* with a *measure of time* allocation – each with

Notes, references and comments:

Reference 2 continued: of the recorder or translator of the event? Is it possible to see God? We `hear' God through Jesus and for most to how they have been taught and see with the mind, for some without Jesus. More fitting terminology is required for God in place of the earthly "father". Most fathers are great but some are monsters. "Reverend" is also applied to humans and men and women of the cloth take these titles. Regardless of their theological position, should man be revered? "Reverend" is mentioned once in the Bible and in relation to God: Psalm 111.9, King James Version only. The title "Lord" is applied to God or to Jesus as to humans. 3 Psalm 8:3-91, the Supreme Spirit makes everything *tick*. Dead things tick towards decay, to dust and beyond– in nature there is no cessation. What makes everything tick is not a long-bearded white man sitting on a throne above the clouds passing judgments, as presented by Christian institutions on posters in Africa, and around the world, whose priests, particularly the Roman Catholic, sported a long beard, Biblical white cassock and took the title of "Father", author's oral testimony. 4 Pope John Paul II, *Crossing the Threshold of Hope,* page 69. Magneto: electric generator using permanent magnets for ignition in internal combustion engines producing the required intermittent high-tension current independently of a battery.

different expectations. Death is a move into a different state for the body when the spirit moves away from it. Feet walk in terrestrial pathways of compound dust of billions of fossilised organisms that once lived in tangible, identifiable form. Archaeology proves that ancient cities are buried underground, what of the souls of the people who inhabited those cities? For all we know the roots of a tree may be feeding on human remains. Something has to die to bring forth new life: this is *interrelatedness in "true evolution".* All things interdependently revolve, self-regulating, and evolve as if detached from the forces that govern them. [5]

Living organisms and things have the infinite capacity to replicate or deplete - the mode of the growth of all things in the universe is seemingly out of nothingness. There are things that do not replicate such as minerals extracted for human consumption and existence; and/or the lavish usage of natural or other resources or materials, ideas, concepts, or anything else that phases out; or other things which dissipate, for example, wealth – such things are relegated to the *Realm of the Void,* the abstract dust bin.[5]

In the independence of entities, God is a *laissez-faire* engineer, ruling and controlling the entire universe by the Almighty's *pre-ordained magneto*, seemingly impotent and detached from us, moving one writer to say:

"God is the infinitely lazy creator". [6]

And another:

"And that inverted bowl we call the sky.

Underneath crawling, coopt, we live and die,

Lift not thy hands to it ...for

It rolls impotently on as thou or I." [7]

Pope John Paul II says:

"God created man rational and free, thereby placing Himself under

man's judgment...God's omnipotence was manifested in the

omnipotence of humiliation on the Cross." [8]

Notes, references and comments:

5 The second tenet of the *Edenic Covenant:* we may cut trees but without replenishment we do so at our own peril, trees retain water below and water is life. Most of us live in blissful ignorance of the invisible omnipotent power that governs our lives. Leaders at home and abroad, in every aspect of administration, dispensed the Roman model of *divide and rule,* despite that they carried the banner of Christendom in their supposed knowledge of what Jesus taught: *the equality of all humans,* but in Victorian prudish morality engaged in snobbery and slavery, for political, economic and other reasons. 6 Peter William Atkins, *Creation Revisited.* 6 Peter William Atkins, *Creation Revisited.* 7 Khayyam's view is not dissimilar, *The Rubaiyat of Omar Khayyam,* Persian astronomer/poet, translated by Edward Fitzgerald. 8 Pope John Paul II, *Crossing the Threshold of Hope.*

The ultimate finesse lies in the human being. The beauty and perfection of God's creation is the motivation to say in the human being *God unfolded into the ultimate finesse*: the perfection of the human body, for every part a use;[9] and the infinite capacity of the human brain, the mould of the master designer and myriads of them have emerged over the centuries, the good - and the evil directed by Satan?

It is said that Biblical writings were God inspired or God-breathed but we can also apply "God-breathed" to pre and post Biblical days: doctors; surgeons; humanists; philosophers; scientists, by empirical observation probed into the mysteries of nature itself showing in imaginable form the process of creation, applying hypothesis in the inexplicable areas and complementing the Biblical explanation of creation; as all those who invent or *do things for the good of humanity*.

Dr Chris Barnard's first heart transplant in South Africa was the dawn of the miracle of surgical human life saving, built upon researches of others before him; and over the centuries there have been many men and women whose ideals and vision in various fields lie in the legacy that permeates our entire existence over the centuries. They invented and established the comforts in facilities, too numerous to mention, that simplify our lives. Such was and is possible because of the "God within them". Winston Churchill, was the architect of peace in the era of the Second World War, and his colleagues, when the world was thrown into darkness by Hitler, a ruthless despot and his subordinates – *evil*, the other side of the coin. [10]

The distinction between others and Jews was anti-Semitism in the latter, aided by some in that interdependent aspect of all things. Despite his ideology of a pure Arian race, Hitler employed tens of thousands of Muslim volunteers to fight for him in his war campaign of human destruction.[11]

Notes, references and comments:

9 Save the breasts of the male body, perhaps as a finishing touch for decoration!
10 A *tenant in brief power,* like all power. Hitler engineered persecution of the Jews and others, thousands of Roma people were gassed in Auschwitz (see *Difference,* chapter 7 "Minorities, Travellers: Roma and Cypsy"). 11 BBC Radio4, 26/07/10, 20:00-20:30 pm; Hitler never fired a gun, and leaders hold the pen to a treaty that controls the lives of millions of people in the power of delegation. The war in Europe had concluded when Nazi Germany signed its instrument of surrender in 1945. As a result of Japan's refusal to accept the Allies' demands for unconditional surrender, the Pacific War dragged on.The USA dropped A-Bomb on the Japanese cities Hiroshima (06/08/1945) and Nagasaki (08//08/1945), may have brought the war to an end and the world's gratitude to the Alies for a safer world on the one hand, but what about the at least 129,000 deaths (the only use of nuclear weapons for warfare in history).. Those who survived suffered horrendous effects: at the initial stage was the greatest number of deaths with 90% due to thermal injury and/or blast effects, and 10%

due to super lethal radiation exposure, followed by deaths from ionising radiation; and delayed action resulting in numerous complications, mostly related to healing of thermal and mechanical injuries. Perhaps the people who died and those survivors were *sacrificial victims* for a safer world, in justification of the A-bomb, super lethal radiation exposure, followed by deaths from ionising radiation; and delayed action

Reference 11 continued below...

From 1930 through the Second World War millions of Jews in Germany, Poland and elsewhere in occupied Europe were persecuted and killed because they were Jews. They belonged to a self-defining religious group adhering to their faith, albeit biologically indistinguishable from the majority populations by intermarriage into Caucasian families over many generations. Some were as blond as the Scandinavians - but certain of their traits were highlighted by their persecutors (such as large nose, the beginning of cosmetic surgery, particularly for women). The acts of genocide which were committed against the Jewish 'race' in the name of the 'Aryan race' were directed against a name and a religion, a people whose mode of culture was similar to a family unit. The Second World War was an eye opener to colonised peoples that Europeans fought among themselves. The bombing of Pearl Harbour by Japan [12] indicated that the so-called backward races were capable of brutality as was the A-bomb on Hiroshima and Nagasaki – the interrelatedness of things in the good and bad found in all places.

> *"For we do not wrestle against flesh and blood but against principalities, against powers, against the rulers of the darkness of this age, against spiritual hosts of wickedness in the heavenly places..."* [13]

We exist in Three Realms (possibly more): Spiritual, Material and Void. What cannot be seen by the naked eye does not mean is non-existent. The Realms are all in the same place though in different mansions – God's house has many mansions and our passage through earth and beyond death is an *infinite journey*. **The Spiritual Realm** is timeless and invisible to the human eye but perceived by the human mind and death is the door to that realm. Grounded as we are in gravity in a split second our thoughts can spring to the other end of the world, *time-lessness* in harmony with *space*. Because the Spiritual Realm is intangible *faith in hope* endures. But Time is the instrument that operates only in the

Material Realm which is tangible, burdened by gravity a realm of death and decay. A fine line, as the split second of waking from sleep, the replica of death, or *invisible veil* divides this from the Spiritual Realm. Everything in the Material Realm changes by Time, the metaphor of the span of human life or any incident. In the Material Realm we see time differently.

Psalm 90:4, 5:

> *"For a thousand years in your sight are like yesterday when it is past and*
>
> *like a watch in the night you carry them away like a flood."*

2 Peter 3:8:

> *"But beloved, do not forget this one thing, that with the Lord that*
>
> *one day is a thousand years and a thousand years as one day."*

Notes, references and comments:

Reference 11 continued:resulting and delayed action resulting in numerous complications, mostly related to healing of thermal and mechanical injuries. Perhaps one could say the people who died and those survivors were the *sacrificial victims* for a safer world, if there was justification in the A-bomb. 12 Imperial Japanese Army (1871-1945). 13 Ephesians 6:12, though planet e*arth is crammed with heaven,* Elizabeth Barret.

Every seventh year was to be a Sabbath, a period of rest to the soil and the fiftieth year was to be a jubilee and the trumpet was blown to set all free of soil.

God was the only real proprietor and a house was considered as the fruits of human industry.

The Jubilee year was a season of rejoicing when the people were neither to sow nor reap but depended upon products without prior preparation of the land taken as common property. There were two grand distinctions: the liberation of servants or slaves and the return of property:

> *"...you shall count seven Sabbaths of years for yourself, seven times seven years and the time of the seven Sabbaths of years shall be to you forty-nine years... the fiftieth year claim liberty to all."* 15

The Realm of the Void is the dustbin of life which holds a magnetic force to takes things such as what we eat, drink, dissipation of wealth; phasing out of the stages of the span of human life from dot to infant, to child, to youth, and so on to old age - where did the baby go? Or material erased from a computer and other things that cease to be and pass away, both the solid and the abstract. At the end of all things, *decay* is master of the Material Realm.

Notes, references and comments:

15 Leviticus 25:8-17, 18-22. See Chapter 12, *God of People,* Other Faiths, on the similarity with African societies on crops, soil and fellowship on harvesting: Chinua Achebe, *Things Fall Apart.*

6 Genealogy of Yeshua

> *"And I will put enmity between thee and the woman, and between thy seed*
>
> *and her seed, it shall bruise thy head and thou shalt bruise his heel."*
> 1

From the above statement it is apparent that the context in historical time is the Garden of Eden, the "woman" is Eve and her seed is the first population of the earth. In the time of Joseph, the "woman" is Mary and her seed is Yeshua who would bruise the head of the serpent, agent of Satan. The "heel" is the lesser to the "head", the seed of woman triumphs over the seed of the serpent.

In the Old Testament the Messianic line is not with the first man Adam because of sin, according to Christian theology. He is bypassed in favour of Abel his son; for the genealogy of Yeshua is predominantly spiritual. God chose for meritorious reasons certain individuals to lead a particular generation from Abel to Yeshua. The genealogy progresses from Abel to Shem then Noah, a perfect man who perceived grace in God.[2]

The covenant idea progresses from Eden to Adam and Eve[3] through Noah on the emphasis for the obligation upon all humans to recognise the moral order.[4] God blessed Shem, as leader of his generation, and as father of all Semites.

Then the Almighty established as father of a multitude of nations,[5] Abraham, symbolic to a covenant with Abraham that came to the latter in a vision; and fulfilled through Yeshua incorporating the Gentiles into the Jewish nation. [6]

In Matthew's gospel Jesus is described as the son of Abraham.[7] The genealogy of Christ, head of the body of the church[8] consists of all who share Abraham's faith.[9] From Abraham to Jesus, according to Christian theology.[10] While Moses is the greatest figure in the Old Testament and is said to be the author of its first four books, he is not said to be part of the genealogy of Christ, save as part of Christ's Jewish connection; though he played an important role in freeing the Hebrew from Egyptian bondage during the Exodus and he was told to construct the Tabernacle, according to his vision on Mount Sinai.

Notes, references and comments:

1 Genesis 3:15. 2 Genesis 6:8-10, Seth was born after Abel who was murdered by Cain his brother. The line of descendants from Seth to Noah is often called righteous, in comparison to Cain's descendants who are called evil. Genesis 6:9 says Noah was the only blameless person alive. 3 Genesis 9:9. 4 Genesis 9:11, 12,13; 9:26, 27, the rainbow is the ensign in the *Noahic Covenant* as the sign of God's bond. 5 Galatians 3:8, 9. 6 Genesis 9:26, 27, Galatians 3:7, 14h nation, Genesis 15:5, *Unger's Survey of the Bible*. 7 Genesis 12:1-4, 17:23-27. 8 Genesis 15:6, before circumcision was instituted and circumcised Gentiles are included in the covenant. 9 Genesis 17:19-21., Matthew 1:1. 10 Ephesians 1:22-23, Galatians 3:7, Matthew 1:2-23. The genealogy of Yeshua as taken from the Gospel of Matthew in the New Testament: Abraham, Isaac, Jacob, Judas, Phares, Esrom, Aran, Aminadab, Naasson, Salmon, Booz (of Rachab), Obed (of Ruth), Jesse, David the King generations); Solomon, Rehoboam, Abia, Asa, Jehoshaphat, Jotam, Ozias, Joatham, Achaz, Ezekias, Manasses, Amon, Josias, Jachonias (14 generations, from the carrying away into Babylon); Salathiel, Zonibabel, Abiud, Ellakim, Azor, Sadoc, Achim, Elind, Eliazar, Mathan, Jacob, Joseph (husband of Mary), Jesus (13th generation? Perhaps printing error?).

Conception

"Your children are not your children,

They are the sons and daughters of

Life's leasing for itself.

They come through you but not from you.

And though they are with you

Yet they belong not to you."

Khalil Gibron [1]

Zechariah was performing his duties as priest at the alter of the Holy Place when the angel of the Lord stood on the right side of the alter. Zechariah was troubled when he saw the angel but the angel assured him; for his prayer for a child had been heard. His wife Elizabeth would bear a child whom they would call John. [2]

During the sixth month of Elizabeth's pregnancy, the angel Gabriel was sent from God into Nazareth to a virgin named Mary, who was engaged to Joseph of the House of David. [3] The angel Gabriel said to Mary that she was blessed among women:

> *"...therefore the Lord ...will give you a sign: Behold, the virgin shall conceive and bear a son, and shall call his name Emmanuel   ...the Lord shall give him the throne of David.* [4]

Mary was troubled by these words and asked:

> *"How shall this be seeing I know not a man?"* [5]

Gabriel replied:

> *"The Holy Ghost shall come upon thee and the power of the Highest shall*
>
> *overshadow thee; therefore the child born of thee shall be called the Son*
>
> *of God."* [6]

Mary went to a city in Judah into the house of Zechariah and greeted Elizabeth:

> *"When Elizabeth heard the greeting of Mary, the baby leaped in her womb and*
>
> *Elizabeth was filled with the Holy Spirit."* [7]

Jesus was to be born in Bethlehem and on God's direction the wise men should not return to Herod. Joseph fled from Herod, who gave an order to massacre all new born baby boys, and went into Egypt with Mary and the infant Emmanuel.[9]

Notes, references and comments:

1 Khalil Gibron, Author of *The Broken Wings*, a poetic novel first published in Arabic in 1912. 2 Luke 1:11-16, later this child became John, the Baptist of Galilee, City of Nazareth. 3 Matthew 1:17. 4 Luke 1:32, Emmanuel: God with us. 5 Luke 1:34.6 Luke 1:35. 7 Luke 1:40, 41; Joshua 21:9, cities of the Levites, descendants of Aaron, ancestor of Elizabeth. 8 Known as *"Massacre of the Innocents"*

The name was given to him by the angel Gabriel before he was conceived in his mother's womb.[9] Simeon, after he gave thanks, prophesied of Yeshua:

> *"As a light to lighten the Gentiles and the glory of the people Israel."* [10]

Prophetess Anna also gave thanks and prophesied that:

> *"They all look to him for redemption in Jerusalem."* [11]

In the Biblical law, the period between engagement and marriage, the woman is considered as the man's wife.

> *"...Joseph...did not know her [Mary] till she had brought forth her first born*
> *Son ..."* [12]

Science, complementing the Bible, enables us to understand that our journey begins before we are born. First the spermatozoon race has to be won. Along with fellow candidates, tails lashing, tips empowered by chromosome energy, agile void of limbs, all are accomplished swimmers, heading for the fertilisation point: the ovum. Concerted to the surface of the ovum they wreathe upon it, each one for itself in the competition to be conceived, break down the ovum cell's outer coating by releasing protein-dissolving enzymes. Two factors aid the winner: determination to out-race fellow candidates and head small enough to penetrate the ovum. Once through the gate, the ovum closes its barriers and the rest of her fellow contestants expire in infantile sperm but the winner does not escape mortality. Fusion of the nucleus of the sperm head and that of the ovum is the process of conception. [13] *God said: "I knit you together in your mother's womb:"* [14]

Notes, references and comments:

9 Luke 2:21, when Emmanuel was eight days old he was circumcised and was named Yeshua meaning "Yahweh is Salvation". 10 Luke 2:32. Since the New Testament was written after the death of Jesus, and his coming mentioned in the Old Testament in prophesy, one cannot help wondering where the details of his birth came from; though some say the writers were directed by the Holy Spirit. 11 Luke 2:36-38. 12 Matthew 1:25. If Joseph had brought Mary to open justice, though "he did not know her", he would have a ground to divorce her, as if she had committed adultery and would be seen as defiled but Joseph was a just man and he protected her, Deuteronomy 24:1-5, The angel of the Lord appeared to Joseph and assured him that the conception was by the Holy Spirit. This is a beautiful story, but the Almighty can breathe anything into existence or non-existence. 13 Dawkins' logic, *The Selfish Gene* - science sperm for short or seed Biblical; or Spencer's logic: "survival of the fittest", phrase coined by Herbert Spencer. Each spermatozoa carries a trio characteristic: *unique, independent* yet *interdependent;* Indibir Singh, *Introduction to Human Embryology for Medical Students:* a question of timing since the egg has a short period of time before it dissipates, and *The Great Sperm Race,* More 4 TV 11/07/09 22:35 pm. Reference 14 continued below...

Science And Currency of the Spiritual Realm

"Science without religion is lame,

Religion without science is blind."

Albert Einstein

Blood is the currency of the Spiritual Realm. The *Book of Genesis* explains the role of blood in several contexts: Blood cries from the ground. Without the shedding of blood there is no remission of sin.[1] Blood speaks. Blood is **Life**. The Biblical role of blood is complemented by God-breathed scientists in their intensive research, and empirical observation.

Blood cries from the ground: According to the Bible, each of the sons of Adam and Eve, Abel and Cain, brought an offering to God. Cain's gift was the fruits of his gardening labours and Abel's was the first born of his flock.[2] Because of God's preference to Abel's gift, Cain became jealous of his brother and murdered him. God confronted Cain that his brother's blood cried from the ground. Yet God forewarned that whosoever caused the death of Cain, vengeance would be imposed on him sevenfold.

It is also said in *Genesis* that the eating of meat was extended to humans by the grant of animal food, the only prohibition was:

"The flesh with the life thereof, shall ye not eat". [3]

This *Old Testament* imposition is religiously observed by Jews in *kosher* and Muslims in *halal*. Animals are slaughtered according to their teachings whereby blood must be drained from the animal before it is eaten.

Blood speaks through scientifically advanced medical methods and in carrying out tests of blood, will largely point to the ailment suffered by the patient or its absence.

Notes, references and comments:

Reference 14 Continued: Psalm 139.13, Jeremiah 1:4-5, "...*before I formed you in the womb, I knew you..*" In the knitting process: $1 + 1 = 2$; $2 + 2 = 4$; $4 + 4 = 8$, and so on, the microscopic dot of life, evolves by *time* and comes with everything making up the entire body – male or female, the *temple or tabernacle,* temporary abode of the spirit, replica of the universe. The baby enters the Material Realm with a vibrant cry, like the moment the universe was created. Pain from the sudden egress, anger and fright at separation from the protection of the womb, or charged with like velocity to the fertilising point at conception? God's overall embrace, *an overwhelming intake of air*, the God surrounding us in the very air we breathe. The universe has evolved over the centuries from its formation to the present day. The age of Earth is approximately one third of the age of the universe. An immense amount of biological and geological change has occurred in that time span, according to scientists. 1 According to the Bible: Hebrews 9:22. 2 Genesis 4:3-16. God's preference to Abel's sacrificial gift would reflect the characteristic of the ancient custom of sacrifice, before the shedding of the blood of Jesus, according to Christian theology; the meaning is twofold: God wanted to punish Cain and Cain took his punishment in the land of Nod, a place of penitence; and that vengeance belongs to God alone. 3 Genesis 9:3-5, 9:4; Leviticus 17:11. But to eat meat is to eat blood, according to some faiths, Hinduism for example.

God's covenants are made with blood, with chosen persons over the centuries, and in their particular circumstances.

Virgo intacta, Long lost in modern times is the breaking of the hymen of *virgo intacta,* of the wife, the flowing of the blood thereby mingled with the male semen, was the *covenant of marriage.*

A circumcision draws blood. In modern times circumcision is encouraged on non-Jewish male children for hygienic purposes, so it is said.

Passover: The blood of the lamb smeared on the sides of door frames saved the Israelites from God's angel of death. Yeshua symbolises wine as blood at the Last Supper as the end Passover in conjunction with the partaking of unleavened bread. The shedding of the blood of Yeshua in his horrendous death is a covenant between him and the believers in the *New Covenant.* According to Christianity.

Biological Motherhood is an important *primary* aspect of blood in the special position of women which patriarchal interpreters of covenant theology would not appear to have addressed. One could not imagine that God would have missed out this important aspect; and God may have done more in a **Maternal Covenant** with Eve for women of all succeeding generations because conception is the first step of human entry into this world. It is by the *Maternal Covenant* Yeshua was nurtured, as all humans. [4]

The *Maternal Covenant* is an aspect of blood connected with the ovum or seed of woman in the cleansing of the un-conceived ovum in the uterus to make way for new ovum, regardless of whether or not conception takes place for whatever reason. This is also as an aspect of a natural replication anddepletion before conception of life. Although science advanced considerably in some fields, the importance of blood for healthy child carrying and bearing was not pursued until the early nineteen sixties when the role of the Rhesus negative blood was discovered and babies were saved.

The Blood of Yeshua carries an important distinction and is of infinite value because of his special mission to earth and his sinless life. Before his advent animals were sacrificed for the atonement of sin. [5]

Blood is the prime source of Life: [6] the greatest medium through which the constituents of the body pass to become incorporated with its tissues. Pumped by the heart, blood circulates along trillions of cells with all their needs ensuring that they are kept in stable surroundings.

Notes, references and comments:

4 This is only author's belief and there is no Biblical evidence whatsoever; perhaps we can attribute this to the general masculine stance which paid less

regard to the position of women in almost all fields. 5 According to the writers of the New Testament: Ephesians 1:7; 2:13, Romans 5:9, redemption by blood of Yeshua; John 1:1-18; and Philippians 2:5-11. The blood of any human is valuable and the shedding of blood is a primary Biblical sin and a major crime in most human law. 6 Richard Walker et al.

Particularly in three ways: To **transport** oxygen from the lungs to all body cells, and glucose amino acids and other nutrients from the small intestine. Blood destroys metabolic waters, such as carbon dioxide from all body cells and urea from the liver by transporting them to the lungs and the kidneys respectively, the points of elimination of waste matter; and **regulates** the body's internal environment and maintains a constant body temperature by distributing heat around the body through liver and muscles. Blood **protects** the body by preventing loss of fluid from damaged blood vessels through blood clotting and by carrying white blood cells to sites of infection where they destroy invading pathogens. Where there is excessive loss of blood and the absence of medical help, such as blood transfusion, death would most likely follow. [6]

Blood types or groups: Everybody's blood looks the same, "red fluid", but there are very important distinctions. In the ABO system blood can be divided in four main groups: A, B, AB, and O.[6]

The surface of the cells in each group is different and will act as an antigen to plasma from another group, which carries the antibody. Group A cells will carry the antibody B in the plasma. Those in group AB do not carry either antibody, while those in group O have both antibodies but the cells do not have either antigen.[6]

Thousands of lives are saved by blood transfusions but they could be disastrous if the blood groups of donor and recipient were not compatible. The ABO and Rhesus factor antigens are very important in deciding which blood type someone should receive.

Within the ABO system people with blood group O are called **universal donors,** because their blood does not contain antigens. This means their blood can be given to anyone, irrespective of blood group. People with blood group AB are the **universal recipients** who can receive any blood group, because they do not make antibodies to antigens of A or B. [6]

How blood is made: Blood cells are made in bone marrow. [6] It is thought that stem cells in bone marrow give rise to all types of blood cells. Stem cells differentiate into other cells which give rise to red blood cells, white blood cells or platelets, approximately one per cent erythrocytes in circulating blood, are replaced daily, which means about three million enter circulation each second.

While the foetus is still developing it receives oxygen and dissolved food and gets rid of waste substances through the mother's blood supply.[6] During pregnancy the blood system of the mother and the foetus are in close contact within the **placenta,** but there is no mixing of blood, and are separated by a delicate physical barrier formed by the wall of the foetal blood supply.

The separation of the two blood systems is important for several reasons: The mother's blood is at a higher pressure than that of the foetus; the blood group of the mother and foetus may not be the same; the foetus has a **different genotype** to the mother since it has only inherited some of the genetic material from her; without the protection of special molecules in foetal cells, would trigger an immune response in the mother which might

Reference: 6 Richard Walker et al.

potentially kill the foetus; and the mixing of the two may result in **agglutination,** which is a clumping of blood cells. The foetal heart pumps blood to the placenta through the umbilical artery, and it returns through the umbilical vein.

At birth the placenta separates from the uterus wall and a limited amount of mixing may occur. An Rh negative mother may have an Rh positive child and at birth mother may receive some of the baby's blood and may hence become sensitised to it. To stop an immune response developing, she would be given an anti-D, a scientific development since nineteen sixties, injection promptly to destroy the red cells with the rhesus antigen. Prior to this foetuses died in the womb or soon after birth. If the mother develops anti-D antibodies and later had another Rh positive child, her immune response to it could cause damage to the child. [6]

The foetal blood develops uniquely and individually. For the foetus determination of sex is by the father's chromosome nucleus. Thus, there may be a difference with Yeshua; for it is said and claimed that Yeshua did not have a biological father. At the time of his birth there was no scientific contribution, otherwise DNA would have provided proof of this claim. Faith is the belief in something for which there is no proof, but the Almighty God knows all things, though some play God.

References: 6 Richard Walker et al. urea: crystalline component in urine.

Pathogens: agent that causes disease. Plasma: part of blood where corpuscles float. Erythrocytes: red blood corpuscles.

THE VEIL

PART THREE

7 Ministry of Yeshua

In the gospel of Mark Jesus is portrayed as an ordinary man and working as a carpenter in the workshop of his father Joseph. Like all Hebrew children from age three Jesus, along with his siblings, is taught the scriptures by their parents. [1] However, the Jesus of Thomas is free of the dogmatic cast that has held Jesus in ecclesiastical captivity since the New Testament. The Gospel is popular in America and the American Jesus is far closer to the Gospel of Thomas than to the crucified Jesus of the New Testament, according to Harold Bloom:

"What makes us free is the gnosis, and the hidden sayings set down by

Thomas form a part of gnosis available to every Christian, Jew, humanist,

sceptic, whatever you are."

In Jesus' sayings, as recorded by Thomas, Jesus may not have been an apocalyptic figure at all; Jesus does not use apocalyptic images to announce the coming of God's kingdom, but rather declares that the kingdom is already a present reality.

When properly understood, the Gospel presents salvation and life, according to Marvin Meyer:

"You encounter a Jesus who is unsponsored and free".

John the Baptist as a preacher was forerunner to Jesus. He preached in the wilderness, in Jerusalem, all Judaea and around Jordan, saying:

"Repent, the Kingdom of Heaven is at hand." [2]

When the Pharisees and Sadducees come to John to be baptised he refers to them as 'the generation of vipers', though he agrees to baptise them but tells them that:

"...there comes one after me who is mightier than I, whose sandal strap I am not worthy to stoop down and loose... who shall baptise you with the Holy Ghost for the repentance and remission of sin." [3]

Yeshua goes to the River Jordan to seek John in order to be baptised. It is the most remarkable moment of John's ministry. He recognises Yeshua as sinless. John performs a baptism on Jesus that takes place in adulthood. Thereafter, Yeshua proceeds into the

Notes, references, and comments:

1 It is said that there is a mysterious undercurrent in Mark's gospel that Jesus was much more than a prophet or an inspired healer: William Neil, *One Volume Bible Commentary* p.334. Matthew 18:11; 2 Matthew 3:1-2. 3 Mark 1:7, Matthew 4:1. As a boy Jesus pays a visit to the synagogue and they are awed by his remarkable knowledge of the Scriptures. On 'the missing years of Jesus, see Bibliography The Urantia Book.3 Mark 1:7, Matthew 4:1.

wilderness where he fasts for forty days and forty nights and he becomes hungry. Satan appears to him and tempts him to demonstrate his supernatural powers as proof of his divinity. He indicates three temptations: turn the stones into bread and eat; jump off a cliff and let the angels catch him; and surrender to Satan by receiving his kingdom as a reward.

Yeshua resisted the devil and the angels brought him nourishment.[4] Jesus actively begins to teach God's Word and invites *personal free will* to follow his teachings, inspired by the first disciples who are fishermen, Simon Peter and his brother Andrew, saying:

"Follow me and I will make you fishers of men". [5]

He embraces all those who were willing to follow him, regardless of their backgrounds or gender. He tells them that wherever they knocked at a door if they were not received they were to move on to the next house in the same street in whatever city they went:

"If anyone comes to me and does not hate his father and mother, wife and

children, brothers and sisters, yes, and his own life also, he cannot be my disciple." [6]

Notes, references, and comments:

4 Matthew 4:1-11; by his resistance Yeshua demonstrated the vital spiritual principle of 'Submit therefore to God. Resist the devil and he will flee from you. Muslims commemorate the 40-day fast of Jesus in the desert, an important aspect of the Islamic faith. 5 Disciples: Shim'on = Simon (Hebrew origin), also known as Simon bar Jonah, who is called Peter by Jesus, the Canaanite; Mattithyahu=Matthew (Hebrew origin), the tax collector, Mark 3:16; Ya'aqov = James (Hebrew origin meaning Jacob), son of Zebedee, his brother Y'hochanan = John, Mark 3:17-19; Lebbaeus Thaddeaus; Bar-Tôlmay = Bartholomew (Aramaic, which is related to Hebrew); Judah = Jude / Saint Jude (not to be confused with Judas Iscariot, Hebrew origin), John 1:45-51; Yehuda = Judas Iscariot (Hebrew origin, Betrayed Yeshua/Jesus); Cephas Kephas = Peter (Hebrew / Aramaic origin meaning "Rock"). Tau'ma = Thomas (Aramaic origin), Matthew 16:19, Mark 3:19; Andrew = Andrew (Greek origin, brother of Cephas / Kephas). Phillip = Philip (Greek origin); John 1:44, 12:2; Above are only 11 names, because there were 2 Apostles named Ya'aqov (James), who was son of Alphaeus, which brings the total to 12 apostles, including a tax collector and a revolutionist. Potentially 15 of them were Apostles but this is debatable. The progeny line of Abraham's obedience was in response to God and continued by the twelve Israelites whom Jesus chose to be His disciples, according to Christian theologians; though this view is not accepted by Judaism. Matthew 13:55: When Yeshua taught the Jews were astonished and said: "Where did this man get this wisdom...is this not the carpenter's son? Matthew 13:55, Is his mother not called Mary? And, his brothers James, Joseph, Simon and Judas [Thomas was also known as Judas]? Mark 6:3, Matthew 13:56: And, his sisters are they not all with us? Where...did he get all these things? John 11:16: "...then Thomas who is called the Twin, said to his fellow disciples 'Let us go, that we may die with Him.' " John 20:24-29. There are many passages in the Bile to indicate that Jesus treated women well, respectfully, sensitive to their needs, and included them in his ministry in several important ways, despite the male-dominated culture in which he lived. When it came to name the 12 apostles, only men were included. Is this what realy happened or was that a consequence of the masculine mindset of the recorders? 1 Corinthians 11:12: *"Neither is woman independent of man, nor is man independent of woman. For as*

Continued below...

The New Testament does not describe the unknown years of Jesus, also called his silent years, lost years, or missing years which generally refers to the period between Jesus' childhood and the beginning of his ministry. Two Russians recorded at different times the life of Jesus in India (where he was known as 'Issa'), [7] in 1884, by Nicolas Notovitch and in 1925 Nicholas Roerich. The latter recorded that:

> "At this time, an old woman approached the crowd, but was pushed back. Then Issa said,
> *"Reverence Woman, mother of the universe,' in her lies the truth of creation. She is the foundation of all that is good and beautiful. She is the source of life and death. Upon her depends the existence of man, because she is the sustenance of his labours. She gives birth to you in travail, she watches over your growth. Bless her. Honor her. Defend her. Love your wives and honor them, because tomorrow they shall be mothers, and later-progenitors of a whole race. Their love ennobles man, soothes the embittered heart and tames the beast. Wife and mother-they are the adornments of the universe."*

Disciples and Apostles carry different meanings in interpretation. A "disciple" is one who believes and tries to follow the tutor's moral values and teachings. Under such a definition women could not possibly be excluded from men to be considered disciples of Jesus because both men and women followed Jesus in His ministry, according to the New Testament. Some believe only a small number of apostles were chosen either by Jesus or by the original apostles. The Canonical gospels give varying names of the twelve disciples who chose to follow Jesus, some who were called by Jesus near the beginning of his ministry and those whom he also named apostles. [7] The Gospels record the constant failings, struggles, and doubts of the twelve men to whom Jesus said:

> *"But you shall receive power when it has come upon you and you shall be*
> *witnesses to me in Jerusalem and in all Judea and Samaria and to the end*
> *of the earth."* [8]

Notes, references and comments:
Continued from above: *the woman originates from the man, so also the man has his birth through the woman; and all things originate from God."* Matthew 4:19-25, 10:1-4. 6 Luke 3:13-19, 6:12-16, 14:26. See also the Gospel according to Hebrews. The primary disciples of Jesus who were his closest followers and who became primary teachers of the gospel message of Jesus; Christian scholars

disagree on the meaning of "apostle". The general scholarly meaning is: apostle spreads the teacher's words or *church planer.*. Greek *apostolos*, meaning `messenger' or `envoy', English equivalent `missionary' – mostly applied to one going out to spread religious faith. In 1894 Nicolas Notovitch published a book called *"The Unknown Life of Christ".* He was a Russian doctor who traveled extensively throughout Afghanistan, India and Tibet; and through the lovely passes of Bolan, over the Punjab, down into the arid rocky land of Ladak, and into the majestic Vale of Kashmir of the Himalayas. While visiting Leh, the capital of Ladak, close to the Buddhist convent Himis when he had an accident and broke his leg. This gave him the unplanned opportunity to stay awhile at the References 7 and 8 Continued below...

Sermon on the Mount contains the tenets for living and is a transition to the new era of love and mercy.; and surpasses all moral standards: they teach love, truth, charity, and peace which are eternal and indestructible.The Gospel of Matthew records the open air sermon as one incident though other scholars see it as having been delivered by Jesus during different times of his ministry.[9] Most Christian theologians believe that Jesus is the mediator of the *New Covenant* which portrays him as the true interpreter of the *Old Covenant* by Moses from the Old Testament and as a form of commentary on the Ten Commandments.

Surrounded by his disciples on a mountainside representing Mount Zion, Yeshua of Nazareth gave the *Sermon on the Mount* on moral teachings to a multitude of people.[10] The Sermon also contains the Lord's Prayer and other authoritative warnings. To many the Sermon on the Mount contains the central tenets of Christian discipleship and is considered as such by many outstanding religious and moral thinkers as one of the main sources of Christian pacifism.[11]

Matthew 7:12, the Law and the Prophets:
> *"Do unto others as you would wish them to do unto you."*

Then Yeshua says:

> *"Blessed are the poor in spirit for theirs is the Kingdom of Heaven; those*

> *that mourn; the meek; who hunger and thirst for righteous ness; the*

> *merciful; the pure in heart; the peacemakers; and the persecuted for*

> *righteousness sake.* [12]

As in all that Yeshua does it is clear that the *Sermon on the Mount* is not prescriptive but rather an appeal to the conscience of each in the audience. The laws of the Scribes and Pharisees are more exacting or demanding than the words of Jesus.[13] The ambience of the venue is like a *beam of light* from a hilltop radiating mercy and charity to the world [14]

Notes,references and comments:
Continued from above: Himis convent. Ancient scrolls reveal that Jesus spent 17 years in India and Tibet. From age 13 to age 29, he was both a student and teacher of Buddhist and Hindu holy men. The story of his journey from Jerusalem to Benares was recorded by Brahman historians. Up to the present they still know Jesus and love him as St Issa. Their 'Buddha'. In 1925 Nicholas Roerich (Russian) arrived at Himis. He was a philosopher and a distinguished scientist. He saw the same documents as Notovitch and Abhedananda and recorded his own travel diary the same legend of St Issa which have the estimated antiquity of many centuries. References 7 nd 8 continued: John 16:13, 14:17,14:26: the spirit of truth. 9 William Neil. 10 The Gospel of Matthew groups the teachings of Jesus into five discourses: *Sermon on the Mount*; *Instructions for Disciples*; *the Parables of the Kingdom*; *Instructions for the Church;* and a harsh *Denunciation of Scribes and Pharisees*. 11 Such as Tolstoy, Gandhi, Dietrich Bonhoeffer, Martin Luther King, Jr. among others; Carl Heinrich Bloch's paintings depict *The Sermon on the Mount* on Beautitudes and Blessedness. 12 Matthew 5:3-10. 13 Matthew 5:17-20; a Scribe is an ancient Jewish maker/keeper of records, or an ancient clerk; Pharisee, ancient Jewish sect noted for strict observation of traditional and written law, self-righteous person. 14 Matthew 5:14-16.

a standard or design for living. The mission and task of a disciple may extend to every willing believer to form a spiritual legitimacy; to be the salt of the Earth. [15]

"Intrinsic hate and anger are equivalent to murder." [16]

The real act of murder is not the killing of the physical body. This suggests the law written in the heart and conscience which places greater value upon the spirit than the physical body - if the mind is clean it cannot direct an evil act:

"The will to commit adultery is equivalent to the commission of adultery."[17]

Thoughts should be free from evil. In perjury oaths are not necessary but what is important is that speech should be truthful from where trustworthy and reliability will start.

> "Resist not evil but turn the other cheek.[18] Love enemies as friends." [19]

Under the Divine Law of God all are equal:

> "The sun rises upon the evil as the good and the rain falls upon the just as the
>
> unjust." [20]

On homosexuality, it is true that nothing specific is recorded in the four gospels of the Bible. However, to assume that Jesus was neutral on this issue might be to ignore a great deal of indirect evidence to the contrary.

There is nothing done in our modern world which was not done in the Biblical days and plus, but Yeshua chose to focus on *forgiveness of sin.* The gospels contain many examples of the forgiveness and mercy Jesus extended to men and women from all backgrounds and circumstances in life. [21]

> "Judge not lest ye be judged."
>
> "Therefore you are inexcusable. O man, whoever you are who judge, for in
> whatever you judge another you condemn yourself for you who judge practise
> the same things[22]...judge not that you be not judged." [23] There is no glory in
> wisdom, might, riches, rather exercise loving kindness, righteousness in the
> earth to delight God." [24]

Notes, references and comments:

15 Matthew 5:13. Basic fundamental goodness.16 Matthew 5:21-26.   17 Matthew 5:28; *Matthew 5:27-33, Jesus redefines adultery: thinking about any evil act which may lead to its commission.* 18 Matthew 5:39, not for the other cheek to be slapped too but to retaliate is no justice – walk way from a bad situation. 19 Matthew 5:44, this is similar to the Hindu principle: "Return good for evil", it

is harder to love someone who hates you but love is the Word of God. 20 Luke 6:4-17. References 21, 22, 23, & 24 coninued below...

> *"Do not look at the splinter in your brother's eye.*[25] *Love your brother like your soul, protect that person like the pupil of your eye..."*

When the priests rebuked Yeshua for sitting and sharing food and drink with publicans and sinners He replied:

> *"I came not to call the righteous but sinners to repent."* [26]

On marriage and divorce the Pharisees bring forth their self-righteousness. [27] The point was raised between Hillel and Schammi, on two conflicting Rabbinical views in confusing the political and judicial on the moral aspect of divorce. Hillel favoured the man's right to divorce his wife from mere opinion without proper proceedings. Schammi rejected any such right. The Pharisees tempted Jesus on this question and Jesus said a man should not set aside his wife for any cause, as man and woman were originally combined in Adam. Then they asked why Moses commanded a writing of divorce. Jesus replied that man's heart had become hardened, originally that was not the position, that the married couple should adhere to the original intention.

The idea of marriage as a divine institution is to be realised in this life and that sacred union was that the man and his wife are joined into one man within the limits of their united earthly life. Jesus said:

> *"...who divorces his wife, except for immorality, and marries another, has committed adultery and whosoever marries her who is divorced commits adultery.* [28] *If a woman divorces her husband and marries another, she commits adultery."* [29]

Notes, references and comments:

References from above: 21 John 8:1-11. Continued from above: The incident of the woman caught in adultery is a case in point which raises a number of issues. In extending forgiveness to this woman, Jesus certainly did release her from all past and future condemnation at the same time silenced the vociferous crowd. Some traditional Christian leaders, including Born Again Christians and other modern denominations, harp about the sins of others, particularly on homosexuality, as they take the high moral stand. 22, 23 & 24 Romans 2:1, 1:20, Matthew 7:1-25, Luke 6:37, 38, Jeremiah 9:23. Adultery takes two people to perform but the man or men she committed adultery with are not mentioned in the Bible. They went `Scot free' as the expression goes; a typical example of the patriarchal characteristic of the Bible, reflecting the mindset of the writers who chose to deride women and ignore the faults of men. 25 Luke 6:41, Matthew 7:3; the meaning of "brother" is not literal but rather enjoins love for one's *fellow being.* 26 Mark 2:15-17. clear example of the forgiveness and mercy extended by Jesus is given in John 8:1-59, stoning of the woman in adultery. In Uganda a gay man was stoned to death by Christian men and women in August 2013, BBC World Service August 2013. *27 Matthew 19:3-12, Pharisee: Aramaic, p'risayyd; Hebrew, parus; Greek, Pharisaisos; Latin phariaeus. Jesus reflects a liberal mind on both the parties to a marriage and recognises only the fault of adultery. 28 Matthew 19:9. 29 Mark 10:12.*

One of Jesus' disciples said it would be better not to marry at all.[30] Jesus replied that those who are inclined and are able to marry may do so; there were three types of eunuchs: those born as such; made eunuchs by men and have no choice; and those who have made themselves eunuchs for the Kingdom of Heaven. Those who marry should remain committed and stay faithful to each other in matrimony. Jesus said children of the world marry and are given in marriage but those who shall be resurrected from the dead and enter Heaven neither marry nor are they given in marriage: [31] The body on earth is a vessel in sex gratification. In Heaven there is no need for marriage or to gratify the flesh. Those who make it to Heaven do not die; they are equal to the angels as children of the resurrection are the children of God. [32] In a different scenario, contrast the words of Jesus with those in Deuteronomy:

> *"He who is emasculated [castrated] shall not enter the assembly of the Lord[33]*
>
> *one of illegitimate birth shall not enter the assembly of the Lord; even to the*
>
> *tenth generation none of his descendants shall enter the assembly of the*
>
> *Lord."* [34]
>
> *"You shall destroy all the places ...where they served their gods...[35]*

The mind of a child is all innocence. When children were brought to Jesus the disciples rebuked them, but Jesus laid his hands on them, blessed them, and said those who humble themselves as little children are great in the Kingdom of Heaven; and those who receive one child in the name of Jesus receives Jesus. [36]

"V*erily I say unto you, except ye be converted and become as little children,*

ye shall not enter into the Kingdom of Heaven... [37]*I have said that whoever*

among you becomes a child will recognize the (Father's) kingdom and will

become greater than John."

"Suffer little children, and forbid them not to come unto me, for such is the

Kingdom of Heaven.[38]

"...From Adam to John the Baptist, among those born of women, no one is

so much greater than John the Baptist that his eyes should not be averted." [39]

Prayer is a Petition, praise or thanksgiving, the tool, the key to God, particularly praying for others for forgiveness. God did not manifest in Yeshua to condemn the world but that the world might be saved through him. When others pray for us it is a sign of goodwill.[40]

Note, references and comments:
30 Matthew 19:10. 31 Luke 20:34-38. 32 Luke 20:34-37. 33 & 34 Deuteronomy 23:1, and 23:2: The Old Testament condones the perpetrator's sin of judging and exclusion, child and eunuch are not responsible for being such. A eunuch is a castrated man and rendered so to serve in a harem, in Pharaoh's or Roman bed chamber, or Indian mogul households. 35 Deuteronomy 12:2, draconian intolerance of other faiths. 36 Matthew 18:4, Luke 18:16. 37 Mark 10:6, Genesis 1:27, 5:2. 38 Matthew 18:3-5. 39 The Thomas Gospel which appeared in part between 30 and 60 CE, only mentions John the Baptist once Thomas 46. Matthew 19:14. References 39 and 40 Continued below....

When you pray for something, remember to pray for God's will, not your own:

"O My Father, if it be possible, let this cup pass from me...

nevertheless not as I will...but as you will." [41]

"But God must be fully present when we are praying...pray for the dead in the hope of eternal life. [42]

"Suffering is a test of both physical and spiritual strength... standard of the Cross remains the key to the interpretation of the great mystery of suffering which is so much a part of the history of mankind." [43]

Religious duties of church, alms giving, fasting and prayer and ostentatious practice of religious obligations, or the thought of getting credit for being pious should be shunned. Prayer should take place in a closet. [44]

In *The Sermon on the Mount* Jesus indicated the *Lord's Prayer* [45] as a guide to prayer in seeking help to withstand evil and is amplified in other passages.

The prayer covers everything for a good and wholesome existence. Accoding to the Christian interpretation:

1. God: "Our Father who art in heaven, hallowed be thy name."

2. God's reign: "Thy Kingdom come" indicates Reverence [46] to and acceptance of the omnipotence of God. "Thy will be done on Earth as it is in Heaven." Acceptance, of whatever the will of God may be.

3. God's provision: "Give us this day our daily bread." not only food for sustenance of the body but more so spiritually. By faith in God through Yeshua prayer changes things as you want it but according to the will of God, for God knows your need before you ask it. [47]

Note, references and comments:

References 39 and 40 Continued: Mark 10:16, humility is greatest virtue: Matthew 18:1, unless you are converted-4, who receives child; pride is greatest sin: Matthew 11:8, clothed in soft garment are kings. Matthew 2-12, Psalm 59:12, sin of mouth and words. Proverbs 8:13, pride and arrogance does not fear of God. 16:18, pride before destruction. 29:23, pride will bring one low but humility retains honour. *40 "No man is an island", John Donne. A good sermon is a prayer and a lamp unto our feet. How powerful is prayer? When Hitler was persecuting the Jews, they must have prayed to YAHWEH; and all those persecuted by leaders and others around the world throughout the centuries no doubt pray to their particular God; but pain only disappears when its measure of time has passed – hence we bow to* "Thy will be done.": *41 Matthew 26:39, Psalm 88:2, Revelation 5:8, Matthew 6:5-7; 6:9-15. C S Lewis says:* "Pain is God's megaphone" *42 Job 22:27. 43 Pope John Paul II, ditto. 44 Matthew 6:5-7; Prayer is a matter between the individual and God. When people gather together in prayer it is an expression of fellowship in a common faith but some dismiss prayer as insignificant. 45 Matthew 6:9-15. 46 Psalms 111:9, the word `reverence' appears in the Bible once & is applied to God: Psalms 111:9, KJV only. 47 Matthew 6:8, 19:24; No insincere verbal assertions of loyalties to God but sincere acts intended for the good of others. Christ's Golden Rule is the norm, complete self-giving, doing God's will alone.*

4.God's pardon: "Forgive us our trespasses as we forgive those who trespass against us." Forgive so that God may forgive you.

5. God's purity: "Lead us not into temptation"...Temptation is the path to adverse deeds. Materialism takes second place for the purpose of identifying with God.6. God's deliverance: "...but deliver us from evil."

4.God's pardon: "Forgive us our trespasses as we forgive those who trespass against us." Forgive so that God may forgive you.

5. God's purity: "Lead us not into temptation"...Temptation is the path to adverse deeds. Materialism takes second place for the purpose of identifying with God.6. God's deliverance: "...but deliver us from evil."

6.God's power: "For thine is the Kingdom, the power and the glory, forever and ever"; acknowledgement of God's eternal kingdom, omnipotence and glory. One cannot worship two masters, God and Mammon.[48] Anxiety about the future is unnecessary for birds do not sow seed but they are fed. [49]

7. Amen = So be it.

Commercial exchange is the essential inter-relation for human existence. We live in a system that preys upon the gullible consumer and encouragement of borrowing by those who benefit by charging interest.

The expenses scandal concerning members of the Westminster Parliament and the bankers in receipt of exorbitant bonuses [50] is a manifestation of self-interest and is among the causes of the financial crisis of the twenty-first century.

> *"It is good neither to eat nor to drink anything whereby others*
> *are offended*
> or made weak." [51]

Notes, references and comments:

48 Matthew 6:19, 21, 24: money, 6:25 clothing, 6:31 food, 6:34 bread, 14:31 Mammon and greed, Psalms 16:8, doubt. 49 Matthew 6:26, 6:25-34, future; Philippians 4:3, be registered in the book of life; 4:4, rejoice in the Lord always, 4:7 be redeemed through Jesus, 4:9, 1-5, and 6-8, be received in the peace of God, Hebrews 5:7. 6:8,19-24; pray for a miracle but ask what is the will of God and base your prayer upon it for God's authority over it. According to Baha'u'llah: Prayer in its purest state serves to bring us nearer to God and helps us to attain the divine presense, a means to converse with God, and burns away the veils that shut us from God. *50* BBC World Service, 12 July 2009 and other channels of the media: a major spiritual crisis and moral bankrupt; Isaiah 14:12-14, "Lucifer how you have fallen, you who weakened the nation"; If members of the government & institutions place themselves above the law, they provoke public anger, not only from those who put them in the position of government in the first place, but also the general public: References 51 & 52 continued: *51* Romans 14:21; "All animals are equal but some are more equal than others", *George Orwell, Animal Farm.* The words of Martin Luther King Jr: "*As long as there is poverty in the world I can never be rich, even if I have a billion dollars... "*

Judas did not know what to do with the twenty pieces of silver he received from the Jewish priests for informing against Jesus. He tried to return them to the priests but they refused it. Upon counsel the silver paid for a potter's field as a burial ground for strangers.[52] Paul in his first letter to Timothy says the love of money is the root of all kinds of evil:

> "We brought nothing into the world and it is certain we can carry nothing out of it; that as for those in the present who are rich, they should not be arrogant or to set their hopes on the uncertainty of riches; and that in their wealth they would do good by being generous and ready to share" [53]

Though the borrower should take personal responsibility for repayment of debt:

"*He shall lend to you, but you shall not lend to him; he* [the lender] *shall*

be the head and you shall be the tail." [54]

A rich man asks Jesus how he could aspire to the Kingdom of Heaven: "Good Master", he commences.. Jesus asks him why he was calling him good master; for "good" can be applied only to God, then Jesus said:

"Follow the commandments: do not commit adultery, do not steal, do not bear
false witness, honour your parents, and love your neighbour. Sell all you have
and give to the poor." [55]

Yeshua and his followers enter Herod's Temple where the courtyard is filled with livestock. It is the *Festival of the Passover.* It is noisy, brisk with trading, selling and buying oxen, sheep and doves for sacrifice and money-changes set upon tables. The gentle Yeshua loses his cool becomes extremely angry and he takes some cords weaves them in a small whip. He pours out the commodities, the changes of money, spilling coins on the ground, overthrows the tables and chairs of the sellers and money changers. The non-Gentile priests' are showing no respect for a place of prayer, he stops them from using the Temple as a `market place' and drives them out. As he cleanses the Temple of greed and profit Yeshua says:

"Is it not written, my Father's house shall be called an house of prayer

for all nations? But you have made it a 'den of thieves.' " [56]

Notes, references and comments:
52 *Jeremiah 7:8-11, Mark 11:15-17, the* expenses scandal *concerning members of the Westminster Parliament and the bankers in receipt of exorbitant bonuses, the latter to their clients' losses; and the high salaries paid to those at the top of organisations is a manifestation of self-interest, and one of the main causes of the gap between the rich and the poor. In any organisation the cleaner is just as important to the organisation because the chief executive cannot do the cleaning. 53 Timothy 6:7, cross reference Ecclesiastes 5:5, James 1:17, Genesis 31:16 and Ephesians 5:20. 54 Deuteronomy 28:44, Proverbs 22:7 cross reference 2 Corinthians 9:6, Psalms 10:2 on persecution of the poor by the wicked.55 Matthew 19:10-12, the greater the congregation at Passover, the more profits from interest charged by them. 56 Matthew 21:1 2, Mark 11:15-17.*

Jersalem is a central exchange mart and the Temple vaults serve as safe deposits in which every type of coin is represented, carried out by the *shulhani*, exchange banker. Distant traders bring their money in large denominations since small coins are cumbersome, for the transactions they charge a fee ranging from 4% to 8%. The *shulhani* also receive money to deposit for investment for which they charge an interest, contrary to Jewish law regarded as the sin of `usury'. They misconstrue `usury' to mean that interest can be charged to those who are external to their own sect but not amongst themselves.

In Judaea the connecting medium of money is not unlike the difference of languages and cultures. The coins are Roman, Greek, Syrian and Jewish. The Jews are allowed to issue coins only in bronze, Roman assarion (one cent). Large sums are expressed in talents and minas. The Syrian stater, about 50 cents; Roman denarius, 20 cents, the Greek drachma, is equivalent to denarius; and the stater is accepted as equal to the Jewish shekel 1/50 of a mina; and about 65 cents for two persons as tax to use the Temple. The denarius is the usual day's wage for a labourer in the field and it is also the coin of tax to the Emperor. Quadrants: 1/4 of a cent is the Jewish perutah or lepton, which is worth 1/8 of a cent. [57]

We may dig deeper to find the origin of money in the Galilean society of the time of Jesus. It all came down to the lack of stability in the monetary system, unlike the time of Roman emperor Julius Caesar (100-44 BC), before the ministry of Yeshua.Caesar took back from the money changers the power to coin money and then minted coins for the benefit of 'all'.[58]

When the Jews come to the Temple at Jerusalem they can only pay their entrance with a special coin, the `half shekel', the equivalent of half an ounce of silver and of assured weight – "the special coin" without the image of a pagan emperor, but according to the Jews, it is the only coin acceptable to YAHWEH.

The special coin is scarce, the bankers had cornered the market on them and so they raise the price to whatever the market could bear. They use their monopoly on the coins for exorbitant profits, forcing the Jews to pay whatever they demanded. It is in the last year of Yeshua's ministry, and the only time, that Yeshua uses physical force against anyone by throwing the bankers out of the Temple. They were in violation of the sanctity of the Temple, and defiling a place of prayer with their greed to make profits. Yeshua told the bankers that *they thought they could steal, murder, commit adultery, lie, and burn incense to Baal and all those other gods; and by entering the Temple they were fooled into thinking they would never suffer for their deeds.*

Notes, references and comments:

57 the famous widow's mite. The High Priest had ordered that only Tyrian shekels would be accepted for the annual half-shekel Temple tax because they contain a higher percentage of silver. The value of coins depends upon the content of silver within. Pilgrims carry coins from their home towns, most bearing the images of Roman emperors or Greek gods which the Temple priests consider as idolatrous. Vast numbers of Jews come to Jerusalem taking with them considerable sums of money in foreign currencies. Foreign coins have to be changed and often handed over to the Temple authorities for safe deposit in the Temple Treasury. 58 The great soldier, conqueror, classical writer of Roman prose, lawyer, politician, statesman and dictator of the Roman Republic; Caesar means a supreme ruler, emperor, dictator or autocrat. Referemce 58 continued below...

Then Yeshua says:

> *"It is easier for a camel to go through the eye of a needle, than for a rich man*
> *to enter into the Kingdom of Heaven.* [59] *But the harlots and the publicans*
> *shall enter the Kingdom of heaven."*
> *"Enter through the narrow gate. For wide is the gate and*
> *broad is the road*
> *that leads to destruction and many enter through it. But small*
> *is the gate*
> *and narrow is the road that leads to life and only a few find it."*

Jesus does not mean that a camel is a creature holier than the bankers or the rich. The "Eye of a Needle" is a narrow secure gate within a gate in Jerusalem; and because of its size and shape, as the eye of a needle, it is impossible for a camel, a humble useful beast of burden, to go through the gate without first unloading its burden. [60] It was said that to charge interest to members of your own sect was the sin of usury but not to those who are not of your own sect. **The sin of usury found its expression by John Calvin in its revival under the Protestant doctrine which created the model that would dominate Western European culture and thought in the mid sixteenth century in Geneva.** [61]

All are in awe, disciples and others, of Yeshua's authority in God's sacred place; while the common people are impressed by the extent of his rather unexpected authority, the chief priests and scribes become alarmed. He had not come to their attention until the Temple incident and they begin to fear his popularity. Demitrius a man from the Temple runs from the Temple all excited and reports to Annas that the new preacher was threatening to destroy the Temple and he was seducing the people to follow his new faith.Annas is the first high priest appointed at the time of the newly formed Roman province of Judaea in 6 AD and at this time he is still one of the nation's most influential political and social figures. While there

Notes, references and comments:
Reference 58 continued: A member of the 'Julian' dynasty, Gaius Julius Caesar was his actual name and his surname "Caesar" remained as a title of successive emperors. History biographers have presented a number of reasons why Caesar was assassinated. Author buys the account by Andrew Hitchcock 2006, The French Connection-History of the Money Changers: *With this new vision, there was a large supply of money. Caesar established many massive construction projects and public works and won the love of the common people but the bankers hated him. His colleagues, including his beloved Brutus, ended his life by sticking daggers into his body. Roman money supply became reduced by 90 percent, the consequences were the common people lost lands and their homes. After his death plentiful money ended in Rome, taxes increased, as did corruption. 59 Matthew 19:23, 24;* **one of the attendants at the Temple, Dimitrius, runs from the Temple to tell Annas that the upstart preacher was creating a commotion at the Temple.** *The way to God is narrow and the gate cannot take riches; they may not realise it but riches can be a burden; a harlot is a Biblical prostitute or promiscuous woman; and publicans were considered as the worst kind, they were tax collectors of Roman revenue and were regarded as traitors by fellow Jews. 61 BBC World Service, 12 July 2009. Calvin was prominent under the Protestant church, following* The Acts of the Apostles, *divided church organization into four levels: Pastors, Teachers, Elders and Deacons, Richard Hooker,* World Civilizations Home Page **for Information."The sin of usury should be brought back now", comment by Ann Pettitor, political economist, The Guardian. Usury: lending money on interest payments, Biblical sin but practised in Christendom, under Islamic Sharia Law usury is not permitted. The Mosaic law scriptures protect the poor from exploitation by the wealthy.**

is always friction between the Sadducee and Pharisees, two groups who make up the Sanhedrin, they now share a `common' problem: they are threatened by the popularity of what they think is an `upstart preacher', preaching a faith alien to them. Although Yeshua is a Rabbi he has been preaching a `radical new doctrine'.

No one is allowed to deny the truth of the established faith in Judaea, Judaism; and its denial leads to the supposed tendency to shake and corrupt the fabric of society; although the Romans are not part of Judaism, they give freedom of expression of faith to the Jews.

On the evening before the feast of the Passover Yeshua had sent one of the disciples to book a room with an inn-holder where they could have the Passover meal. While they were eating he told his disciples that he had earnestly desired to eat the Passover with them before he suffered. [62]

He predicts He will suffer soon after the meal before he accomplishes his mission and symbolises his body to unleavened [62] bread, which he breaks, gives thanks, and gives it to his disciples:

> "This is my body which is given to you in remembrance of me." [63]

Then Yeshua symbolises wine as his blood in a cup, gives thanks and says:

> *"This is the token of God's new covenant to save you sealed with the blood I have poured out for you.*
> *"Drink, ye all of it; for this is my blood of the New Testament, which is shed for many for he remission of sin."* [64]

Then Yeshua tells his disciples that he would not eat the Passover again until all barriers of human fears were defeated; and life restored in the bodily resurrection following his death. Jesus provides hope to His followers:

> *"And, I confer on you a kingdom, just as my father conferred one on me, so that you may eat and drink at my table in my Father's kingdom ..."* [65]

Notes, references and comments:
62 Luke 22:15-22. 63 1 Corinthians 5:7, 8. 26:2-5, assemblage at Caiaphas to take Jesus by trickery but decides not to during the feast to avoid popular uproar.

64 Luke 22:19, 20, Mark 6:50. The act of sharing, KJV translation, Greek: kuinonia, partnership/fellowship; painting known as the Last Supper by Leonardo da Vinci; Matthew 1 Corinthians 10:16, 2 Corinthians 5:1; Unger's Survey of the Bible, Hebrews 8:8-10, New covenant in Jesus 9:15-24, Jesus mediator of the covenant; "...purge out the old leaven..." means that upon ressurrection the believer receives a new body of eternal life. 65 Luke 22:29, 30; Do people eat in Heaven? Can anyone visualise what Heaven is? Our knowledge is based on legacy. Yeshua, wilfully and obediently, allowed himself brutally to sacrifice his body on the

Reference 65 continued below...

Jesus transformed the meaning of the elements of the Passover meal into a New Covenant thought. The bread now represents the body of Jesus which would be given and the cup his blood for the forgiveness of sin; and that a new way was being prepared through Jesus, after the old order of the Old Testament satisfying it forever, according to Christian theology. Christian denominations observe the Passover differently. Jehovah Witnesses do not take Holy Communion of bread and wine in the belief that there are only one hundred and forty-four thousand righteous persons who are qualified to do so:

> *"Twelve thousand seated from each tribe: Judah, Aser, Nephthalim, Manasseh, Simeon, Levi, Issashar, Zebulon, Joseph, Benjamin,* Reuben and Gad." [66]

The Roman Catholics believe that through the Holy Communion they take Jesus into their heart. However, in Roman Catholicism, the congregation had not taken wine, but only the priest consumes a large goblet of wine.[67] *This has now changed and the congregassion does partake of the holy wine, Blood of Christ which they believe is also transsubstantial.*

Body refers to the Unleavened Bread and Jesus' words are simple in symbolising as a remembrance of his life on earth. He was the Living Word in flesh and blood. Yeshua was born with a human body and lived as a human being but a sinless life. He was entombed and his body never came into contact with earth, according to the Bible, and this in itself is a mystery. [68]

Notes, references and comments:
*Refeence 65 continued: cross (or stake) to reconcile each of us to God by paying the debt of our sins, according to Christian theology. He makes a simple request that we remember this act of love he performed on our behalf, because h*e values every life on earth *and wants to see and eat with each of us at his table someday in Heaven. According to Christian theology, the Lord's Supper commonly referred to as the communion is one of two special ordinances Jesus instituted while He was on earth. The ordinance of communion commemorates and typifies the suffering and death of Jesus. The other is baptism symbolising Christ's resurrection. 66 Revelation 7:5, 7:1-18, 9:1-15, which goes back to the original 12 tribes of Israel. Ronald Weinland: "Neither traditional Christianity nor modern Judaism observes the Passover as God and Christ command and as such they fail to know the "eternal" God and Christ,* God's Last Witness, *p 41.   68 People generally feel strongly about the disposition of their bodies after death; some choose internment rather than cremation; what of those who were devoured by lions or crocodiles or in a plane crash and disappeared above the clouds? God holds a blue print for each one of us and does it matter how the body is disposed? Provided it is done in reverence to God and respect to the departed one. See Part 1, Chapter 1, Mosaic Covenant, The Tabernacle.*

The body is a temple, a tabernacle, temporary house of the soul during its earthly sojourn:

> *"Do you not know that your body is the temple of the Holy Spirit who is with*
> *you, whom you have from God and you are not your own?*[84]
> *For we know*
> *that if our earthly house, this tent, is destroyed, we have a building from God...*
> *eternal in the heavens."* [69]

The human earthly body performs the wishes of the mind: touchable, fragile, and vulnerable to death and decay. Body and spirit (soul, as "mind") are always at odds; body carries the five senses: touch, sound, sight, taste and smell; craves for more, has a memory of "pleasurable" experiences and mind argues for abstention, but the body, the solidity; and the abstract boundless spirit, are inseparable partners in earthly transit, until death:

"This I say then, walk in the spirit and you shall not fulfil the lust of the flesh...

flesh lusts against the spirit...contrary the one to the other; so that you cannot

do the things that you would.

"Watch and pray, that ye enter not into temptation; the spirit indeed is willing, but

the flesh is weak. [70]

"For we wrestle not against flesh and blood but against principalities... powers
of the rulers of the darkness of this world, against spiritual wickedness in
high places." [71]

The human is a triune being: spirit, body and soul, woven into the mystery and essence of our being, as the image of the supreme designer, manifested in the bodily gift from parents - generations upon generations pass through body.

The soul has its origin in the spiritual worlds of God. It is exalted above matter and the physical world. The individual has his beginning when the soul associates itself with the embryo at the time of conception. But this association is not material; the soul does not enter or leave the body and does not occupy physical space. The soul does not belong to the material world, and its association with the body is similar to that of a light with a mirror which reflects it. The light which appears in the mirror is not inside it; it comes from an external source. Similarly, the soul is not inside the body; there is a special relationship between it and the body, and together they form a human being. [72]

Notes, references and comments:
69 1 Corinthians 6:19, Proverbs 20:22. 70 2 Corinthians 5:1. 71 Galatians 5:16, 17, Matthew 26:41, Ephesians 6:12; the struggle between humans and spiritual forces of the Devil, powers of the rulers of the darkness of this world. 72 The Teachings of Baha'u'llah, Reflections on the Life of the Spirit, Life and Death *page 35, Ruhi Institute, Book 1. Baha'i Books UK,*

Abuse of body is thought of the mind, where mind fails to abstain - overindulgence in: food, the most delectable, comforting and essential item; fluid; drugs; lack of sleep/rest, sex; over-eating batters the body and leads to obesity, whereas bulimia finds consolation by reaching out for food.

Body language: bodies talk, at peace, in anger, no need for words. The human touch, literally in touch with people is rooted in the body, stands up to be in touch with other bodies.

Body moves to numerous acts: dance in harmony to the tune of music or sport among others. Thou hast given me a body to communicate pleasures of the flesh. Removal of the body is the internet, the telephone, mechanical and impersonal, in touch by technology. Fall in love and surrender body and soul – love of the beloved, reaching out for the love of a person, to express the desires of the mind.

The body as an object is the taker of life's blows in the full toll of the years; a form of abuse over the centuries in the market place for slavery, forced labour, the body of a little child exploited in child labour at factories, production for gain, or abused by a warden.

By the passage of time the body evolves from dot to mass, in lifespan stages, suffering appropriate pain, as baby's pain at teething, yet death and decay heeds no age or rank. We daily heed mundane things for hygiene to maintain physical cleanliness in the endless battle for the sacredness of the body, a battle against *decay,* servant or agent of the *realm of the void.* Body is estranged, and when wounded, oozes out evil smelling substances, a burden, a broken body by accident, illness, stroke, or whatever, fails to serve or follow wishes of the mind. In advanced age mind is willing but the body is weak, save in dentia where mind precedes body in weakness, a kind of stroke in the mind.

8 Arrest, Trial And Condemnation

The incident at the Temple was the culmination of the animosity towards Yeshua, the basis of accusation that triggered decisive action leading to his betrayal and arrest. The charges commenced with blasphemy, the preaching of a novel radical faith, with the tendency to shake and corrupt the fabric of society. [1]

Notes, references and comments:
1 Jesus was regarded as rebellious against the accepted norms yet he was teaching about one true God not unlike the God of the Pharisees and Sadducees. Deuteronomy 6:4: Hear, O Israel: The LORD our God [is] one LORD; Isaiah 44:6: Thus saith the LORD the King of Israel, and his redeemer the LORD of hosts; I [am] the first, and I [am] the last; and beside me [there is] no God." That he not only broke the Sabbath but also called God his father, making himself equal with God; he was healing the sick without licence, he has not followed the procedures to become a registered healer within the community; he is preaching falsities against Judaism; and he had called the Sadducee and Pharisees a `generation of vipers'. Yeshua had also exposed the illegal taxes imposed and collected by the Sanhedrin from the people by the commotion he created in the Temple.The Romans gave  freedom to the Jews to worship YAHWEH, following their forefathers. Pilate is not concerned about `God', a concept unknown to the Roman leaders who themselves were `gods'; and regarded the concept of some intangible deity as `cranky'.

The Sanhedrin call up a meeting and the members are unanimous in their view that Yeshua's intention is to publish the probable effect of his words. The upstart preacher is presenting a threat to the Romans and Jewish Temple officials in their mutual status quo. Caiaphas cannot afford to tolerate someone who is challenging his comfortable position. They decide that Yeshua be arrested but they are presented with the difficulty that the authorities did not hear his preaching, as they are above the peasants who were drawn to his meetings. The officials do not know him in order to arrest him within all the crowds at Passover - it would be impossible to identify him. The Sanhedrin members decide to arrest him at night after the crowds have dispersed, they are in league with Judas Iscariot, they pay him 30 pieces of silver and he undertakes to identify Yeshua by a kiss.

The Sanhedrin gather and pay for information on the things Yeshua said in his sermons and teaching including that: he has been working on Sabbath, a day of rest and prayer which is contrary to Rabbinical rules, he healed a sick man on Sabbath and when confronted he replied:

> "My Father has been working until now and I have been working...the Sabbath

was made for man and not man for the Sabbath. Therefore, the son of man
is also Lord of the Sabbath." [2]

Thus they incorporate the information and make up a case of 'blasphemy' against the upstart preacher. The book of Exodus on the Sabbath and draconian measures for failure to keep the Sabbath

...

God said to Moses:

"You shall keep the Sabbath...for it is holy to you. Everyone who profanes
it shall surely be put to death; for whoever does work on it, that person shall
be cut off from among his people... [3] *He not only broke the Sabbath but*
*also said God was his Father making himself **equal with God."*** [4]

Notes, references and comments:
2 John 5:17, 5:7-9; Mark 2:27, 28,3 Exodus 31:14, 31:16, 20:8-11: compare the Old Testament to Yeshua's healing on Sabbath.The Mosaic code is the fundamental and basic written law; there is also the Talmud containing ancient, traditional and Rabbinical interpretations; and also contents of the Talmud traditions and commentary orally transmitted through centuries; and it shall transpire that Israel will mediate this redemption to all the nations of the earth during the kingdom age: Unger's Survey of the Bible, Hebrews 8:8-10, 9:15-24, Encyclopaedia Britannica, Eleventh edition, Vol. 14, page 273. 3 According to Christian theology, when man fell God's Sabbath in creation was broken then God began working in redemption; and when Yeshua defied the Sabbath in his healing, it means that when Christ redeems Israel, in the seconds. 4 John 5:18, perhaps Jesus should have obtained a licence to heal on Sabbath according to the rules; Genesis 2:3. Sunday worship was
Reference 4 continued below...

They are again faced with another difficulty. Tiberius is the current Caesar who rules with an iron fist and he is anti-Semitic. Rome is in power and in full control of Judaea which means any arrest, trial and verdict must be conducted by the state through its prefect or governor in Judaea, as a colony of Rome. Therefore, the Sanhedrin have no authority to `arrest' and an arrest by them would be illegal. Not only were the Sanhedrin officials usurping the role of the Roman state but had ignored their own justice system. In fact, the arrest of

Yeshua was conducted under no legal system of any kind, supposedly tried under the Mosaic Code and Caiaphas sat as sole judge. Yeshua is accused of the offence of *blasphemy* and of challenging the validity of Jewish authority. At this stage there is no mention of treason. After questioning him Caiaphas realised that he had no power to put him to death and that the proper forum to try him was before Pilate, the governor, under the Roman code of criminal procedure.

When the case for blasphemy collapsed they looked to the charges likely to appeal to the Roman state, "treason and sedition".5 It was impossible to identify Yeshua within the crowds at Passover, the officials do not know him, to arrest him. They decide to arrest Jesus at night after the crowds have dispersed. They conspire with Judas Iscariot, they pay him 30 pieces of silver and he undertakes to identify Yeshua by a kiss. 6 The Sanhedrin plotand succeed in convincing the Roman soldiers that Yeshua was guilty of treason and sedition because he had been building up a powerful following.

There were number of irregularities in these proceedings: On a capital charge such as the one Yeshua is charged with no proceedings ought to have been conducted on the day preceding the Sabbath or on any holy day; or of any festival, or commenced on a Friday where the proceedings would be adjourned, or continue to the Sabbath, or on any of the Biblical holidays; Yeshua had been subjected to a secret examination; and on the occasion before Caiaphas as the sole judge, the Mosaic Code states:

> *"Be not sole judge, for there is no sole judge but me".*

Notes, references and comments:

Reference 4 continued: established by Roman emperor Constantine when in 323 AD he issued a Sunday-keeping edict to venerate the Sun-god in 323 AD, its origins are Pagan, see Part 4, Chapter 9. According to Christian theology, the *Mosaic Covenant* was replaced by the *New Covenant* in Christ and it fulfils predictions made by Jeremiah: 31:31-34, Psalm 66:4, 67:4, Hebrews 8-12. The Jewish Sabbath and the Sunday worship in Christianity are two totally different things. Sabbath keeping is legalistic and is the logo of the *Mosaic Covenant*. The commandment of Sabbath keeping represents the moral law of God only adapted as a requirement of the *Mosaic Covenant* and elect nation Israel. In practice it has no relevance to Church or Christianity. 5 The upstart preacher was presenting a threat to the Romans and Jewish Temple officials, according to them, in their mutual peace and prosperity in the *status quo*. Caiaphas, chief of the Sanhedrin, could not afford to tolerate someone who, he felt was challenging his comfortable position. 6 **Then they treat Yeshua like a yo-yo. He** is first brought to Annas, influential first high priest of the Roman province of Judaea. He subjects Yeshua to a brief private secret examination, then he sends him to the home of <u>Caiaphas</u> where the latter is holding a Sanhedrin meeting.

The Sanhedrin verdict is a unanimous verdict of guilt rendered on the same day which would have the effect of an `acquittal', according to the Hebrew natural law. This makes the verdict of `guilty' invalid and therefore a sentence ought not to have followed on an invalid verdict. Yeshua had been arrested, tried and found guilty in a `single day'. Caiaphas' reply to Pilate was that if Yeshua were not a criminal they would not have brought him before Pilate; and the latter tells them to take him and judge him themselves according to their own laws.

There was no consensus among the false witnesses and their testimonies were contradictory. His followers acclaim Yeshua as prophet, miracle performer, healer, defender of the poor and the oppressed. Then members of the Sanhedrin trump up the *charges of treason* against the government of Rome based on Yeshua's sayings on "the coming Kingdom of God", plus sedition. By now it is very early in the morning, they are eager to dispose of him, they are pushing for quick action to prevent the followers of the accused to organise a support protest.Then the accused is brought before Pilate to answer the charge of treason and sedition against the Roman state.

The charges of Treason and Sedition were based on seduction against the Roman State and included: A threat to destroy the Temple; seduce people from their ancient allegiance; and interference with money changes. Pilate came out to them and asked what the man was accused of but he was unconvinced that there was a case to answer. If found guilty, the charges would carry the death sentence upon which the Sanhedrin were intent. Pilate regards Yeshua's belief not unlike that of the rest of the Jews, the belief in some unseen being. According to them, Yeshua was a novel crank because he was preaching a God different from the Jewish God, albeit there was a similarity in a *one true God*. Nontheless, The Sadducee and Pharisees have organised an `officer' and men with lanterns and weapons.Judas, as pre-connived, approaches Yeshua
and says:

"Hail, Master!" and gives him the `kiss of death' on the cheek. Yeshua looked at the officers and asked them who were they looking for and they replied: *"Yeshua of Nazareth."*
Jesus says to them:

"I am he...have you come out as against a robber, with swords and clubs to take
me...I sat daily with you, teaching... and you did not seize me? [7]

Notes, references and comments:

[7] The officer followed the mode of arrest as taught to the soldiers involving physical pain to the accused: his right wrist was grabbed in a twist of his arm behind him, knuckles touching between his shoulder blades and tied with the other arm. At which point he became prisoner of the state. Matthew 26:47-68, Mark 14:49, Luke 22:53. The account by these three gospels are similar but they differ from John's account (the *Du Bartas syndrome*) John 1 John 17:21, 1 Corinthians 12:13, cross reference Romans 12:4-6.8 Matthew 27:19. [9] The Bible does not mention the name of Pilate's wife. The Apocryphal book, the *Gospel of Nicodemus*, identifies her as Claudia Procula, granddaughter of Emperor Augustus, and that she was a convert to Judaism.

Herod is also in Jerusalem from Tiberius to pay respect to the Jewish leaders for their *Festival of Passover*. Pilate is also in Jerusalem from his residence in Caesarea to keep order during the Passover. Pilate discovers that Yeshua is a citizen of Herod's province and decides that he will divide the grave responsibility by sending Yeshua to Herod to be judged. Herod is glad to see Yeshua since he has been wanting to meet the man he had heard so much about. He questions Yeshua on many points but he receives only `silence'. Then he asks Yeshua to do some `juggling' for his amusement but he is still met with silence – the golden stance which speaks volumes. While the priests and scribes vehemently accuse him. The incident of Yeshua brings Pilate and Herod together but finding nothing to condemn Yeshua he sends him back to Pilate. The case of Yeshua is still unsolved and still in Pilate's hands, as the Sadduces had replied that they could not put him to death, for that was for the state, and Pilate summons Yeshua into the governor's residence.

When questioned by Pilate, Yeshua answers:

"*My kingdom is not of this world.*" [8] .

Before Pilate sat on the judgment seat, Claudia Procula, his wife had said to him:

"*What are you going to do with that just man? ...have nothing to do with that*

just man , for I have suffered many things today because of my dreams of

him." [9]

When Pilate says:
"Do you not know that I have power to crucify you, and power to *release you?*"
Yeshua replies:
"*You could have no power at all against me unless it had been given you*
from above. Therefore the one who delivered me to you has the greater sin". [10]

The priests and scribes mock Jesus as "the Messiah" [11] and say:
"*Shall you sit on the right hand of the power of God?*
"*Are you the son of God?*
But Pilate continues:
"*Are you the King of the Jews?*"
Ye say that I am." [11]

Notes, references and comments:

8 Matthew 27:19. 9 The Bible does not mention the name of Pilate's wife. The Apocryphal book, the *Gospel of Nicodemus*, identifies her as Claudia Procula, granddaughter of Emperor Augustus, and that she was a convert to Judaism. Jesus was abandoned by the public crowds and by his followers in his darkest hour, is the way of the world: The end of the life and political career of Julius Caesar, or Margaret Thatcher and the hostility of her all-male cabinet members,

are prime examples. 10 Matthew 27:11-26, Mark 15:1-16, Luke 22:63-71, John 18:28-40 The Gospels of Matthew, Mark, Luke and John give differing accounts on the trial of Yeshua, reflecting the individual mindset. 11 John 19:11, Hebrews 10:11.

Yeshua explains that the Kingdom he speaks of is not of this time; and when questioned about the accusations by the Jewish hierarchy, Yeshua answers nothing. Pilate finds Yeshua *not guilty* of the charges against him. To these assertions Yeshua replied that whatever he may say they would not believe him.

When the priests asked Pilate to change the mocking title: *King of the Jews* to: *"...He said he is King of the Jews"* (emphasis added).
Pilate replies:
> *"Leave it as I have written ".*

Pilate sees that he is accomplishing nothing and he has a riot before him. The crowd yell:

> *"His blood be on us and on our children!"*

Pilate regards Yeshua as a `harmless enthusiast' but fears the crowds and for his own security stifles his conscience, resisting Claudia's counsel and he wants peace. He gives up a man he believes to be `innocent' to the will of the people – after all, what is the death of one Jew? At the Feast of the Passover it was customary to release to the multitude one Jewish prisoner whom they choose. Then Pilate tries to use this custom as an excuse to release Yeshua and he asks the crowd whom he should release: Barabbas the notorious prisoner or Yeshua?" Passing the buck" as he publicly washed his hands in a bowl of water symbolising before the multitude that he was innocent of the blood of the just accused. The paid and planted individuals in the crowd call for and initiate the mob's chant for the death of Yeshua as they shouted:

"Crucify him!"

Procula's plea is a little voice in the wilderness as Pilate is influenced by the crowd despite his own better judgment. The barbaric punishment that followed against Yeshua was the norm upon the guilty.

FROM THE SIXTH to the ninth hour - three o'clock in the afternoon -there was darkness all over the land just before Yeshua dies. [12]   At that moment Jesus was carrying all the sins of the world. God had turned away, the Almighty could not look upon sin. [13] God had turned away because the Almighty could not look upon sin. Then Yeshua cried in a loud voice:

Notes, references and comments:
12 Luke 22:67-69. Yeshua was crucified outside of the city wall at Golgotha, Calvary Hill or Place of the Skull. That he was crucified on a cross is debatable. The Christian patriarchs inherited the adoption of the words `cross' and `crucify', which are nowhere to be found in the Greek version of the New Testament. They are mistranslations of the Greek words *stauros*, an upright pole or stake,
References 13 & 14 continued below...

"Eli, Eli, lama sabachthani"

"My God! My God! Why hast Thou forsaken me?"

Then Yeshua cried again loudly:

"Eloi, Eloi, lama sabachthani?"

"My God My God For what have you forsaken me?[14]

The above was addressed to God but misunderstood by those who stood there. The words indicated not only an appeal but also disbelief that God had alienated him, the son; at the same time showing the agony of his sacrifice; forsaken, abandoned in his darkest hour, a sin bearer who had committed no sin.

Yeshua then said:

"Father into Thy hands I commit my spirit." [15]

He gave up the spirit and breathed his last.

"... behold the veil of the tabernacle was rent in two from top to bottom; and the earth quaked, and the rocks split..." [16]

Women at the crucifixion were Mary mother of Yeshua and his mother's sister; Mary, wife of Clopas; and Mary Magdalene, all looking on.[17] The women who followed Jesus from Galilee ministering with Him, were also there looking on from afar: Mary, Mother of James and Lese; Joseph's mother; mother of Zebedee's sons; Salome; and certain women who had been healed of demons by Jesus. A rich man named Joseph of Arimathea, disciple of Jesus, asked Pilate to release the body of Jesus and Pilate gave the order. The body of Jesus was placed in a sealed tomb. Mary Magdalene and mother of Joseph observed where Jesus was laid after he died.[18] Mary Magdalene and one referred to in the Bible as "the other Mary" sat opposite the tomb. On the first day of the week Jesus rose and appeared to Mary Magdalene;[19] then she went to the tomb early, while it was still dark. She saw the stone had been removed from the tomb, she went to Simon Peter and another disciple and told them. The New Testament of the Bible says God is love and truth through Jesus who said:

Notes, references and comments:
Refeences 13 & 14 continued:*Dictionary of the New Testament Words.* Noun and verb *stauros:* to fasten to a stake or pole, are to be distinguished from ecclesiastical form of a two-beamed cross, the latter's origin is ancient Chaldea (Babylon). Crosses were used as in the symbols of Babylonian Sun-god: Dr Bullinger's *The Companion Bible*, appx. 162. Rev. Alexander Hislop, *The Two Babylons*, pp. 197-205 calls the cross "this Pagan symbol...the Tau, the sign of the cross... of Tammuz, the fake Messiah...Tau of the Chaldenians...and Egyptians...form of the letter "T". *Encyclopaedia Britannica*, 11th Ed. Vol. 14, p.273: "...in Egyptian churches the cross was a Pagan symbol of life borrowed by Christians and interpreted in the Pagan manner..." There is a long list of more evidence. However, the cross is more convincing than a beam: when a priest places the Bible and the Cross, rather than a beam, upon the coffin of a departed loved one, it somehow brings comfort: author's anectdotal testimony.   13 Romans 3:20. 14 Matthew 27:46-47. 15 Luke 23:46. 16 Matthew 27:51-54. 17 Matthew 27:55-57, Mark 15:40, Luke 8:2. 18 Mark 15:47. 19 Matthew 27:61, Romans 16:3, Mark 16:9.

"Greater love hath no man than that a man lay down his life for his friends." [20]

Jesus removed all barriers between people and came to fulfil the prophesies and promises of the Old Testament as confirmed in the New Testament with its own prophesies and promises for the End Time; and that this is Jesus' teaching on the Spirit who will guide the church into all truth in self-preservation as He turns to face His cross, according to Christian theology:

> "*I have overcome the world…I pray that they all may be one…by one spirit we were all baptised into one body, whether Jews or Greeks, whether slaves or free and all have been made to drink into one spirit.*" [21]

The Pit of Hell and Death is about Jesus' ultimate victory over death. The conclusion to the Old Testament in the companions of the group of twelve short recollections of prophesy of the typology in the Book of Jonah [22] and the sign seen by John in the Book of Revelation, New Testament, [23] are said to be metaphoric and prophesy to the presence of Jesus in the Pit of Hell and Death. Jonah was commanded by God to go to Nineveh to preach against the wickedness of that city. Jonah disobeyed and boarded a ship in the opposite direction to Tarshsh and God sent a tempest which rocked the ship. The skipper and the crew feared a shipwreck, attributed the tempest to Jonah's presence, and they cast him overboard. He was swallowed by a whale in whose belly Jonah remained for three days and three nights. He was conveyed out on to the shore by the whale and Jonah resumed his mission to Nineveh. John in the Book of Revelation gives prophesy of the fifth angel:

> "*I saw a star fall from heaven into the earth and to Him was given the key*
>
> *to the bottomless pit.*" [24]

Jesus' own interpretation of the typology of Jonah is that after His death on the cross (or beam) he would play in the imagery of Sheol, found in Jonah's prayer:

Notes, references and comments:
20 John 15:13, 17:21. According to Christian theology, Jesus took a new body by resurrection after His death symbolising that by faith in Jesus the human body would again become purified to its original state as before the fall of Adam and Eve. Only and until then could the human body be justified in the presence of God. 21 Hebrews 5:10. The question is: how well has man adhered to this "oneness" theme, in the world of Christendom, leaders as followers? The word

"Tabernacle" in Roman Catholicism refers to the altar where the priest performs his priestly function, while the meaning of the "Ark of Covenant" is altogether bypassed. The view of Lee Warren is that each of us is Melchizedeck: *king and priest* in our hearts and minds, representing the temple where Yeshua ministers; David's Psalm 110:4 prophesied Yeshua as a priest forever after the order of Melchizedeck. 22 Genesis 10:11-12, Matthew 12:38-42. 23 Revelation 7:1-8 and 14, typology, Biblical type, *tupos* Greek. 24 Revelation 9:1-15.

"I am he that liveth, eternity of the eternities, and was dead and behold Iam

alive for evermore, Amen. I have the keys of hell and of death." [25]

When Jesus dies he fulfils the prophesy of the parable of Jonah and stays three days and three nights in Sheol in the bowel of the earth and takes from Satan the keys of hell and death. According to the Bible New Testament, at the bottomless pit, Jesus resurrected dead saints who had been imprisoned by Satan and they went into the Holy City where many saw them. When Jesus opened the pit there came forth smoke as from a furnace darkening the sun and the air as horses in battle came out of the smoke not to prey on vegetation but to torment only those who lacked the seal of God on their foreheads - even death fled them. [26]

Notes, references and comments:

25 Revelation 1:18, Sign is son of man, Jesus as Jonah's sign to the Ninevites, Luke 11:30, Jonah became sign to Ninevites, so also the son of man. 26 Matthew 12:38-4. Locusts likened to "horses in battle."

THE VEIL

PART FOUR

9 Assumed Divine Mandate

> *"If one purges the Judaism of the prophets and Christianity as Jesus Christ taught it of all subsequent additions, especially those of the priests, one is left with a teaching which is capable of curing all the social ills of humanity."*
>
> > - Albert Einstein

The Apostolic Age is the cradle of Christianity and the first phase of papal supremacy in the Roman Catholic Church. The Bishops of Rome claimed that 'church' was instituted by Christ and that papal succession is traced back to Peter the Apostle in the first century [1] but this is a matter of dispute and much debate.

The conversion to Christianity of Paul or Saul indicates two factors: the merits and demerits of faith and its consequences and the blessing of forgiveness. Saul was an ardent promoter in the persecution of Christians.[2]

Paul hated Christians and he made it his goal to capture, then bring them to public trial and execution after the crucifixion of Jesus. He swore to wipe out the new Jewish sect of the Christian church known as *The Way:*

> *"I persecuted the followers of The Way to their death, arresting both men and women* [and children] *and throwing them into prison, as also the high priest and all the Council can testify. I even obtained letters from them to their brothers in Damascus, and went there to bring these people as prisoners to Jerusalem to be punished..."* [3]

Saul was present when Stephen, the first Christian martyr was killed by an angry mob:

> *"...they all rushed at Stephen, dragged him out of the city and began to stone*
> *him and Saul was there, giving approval to his death."* [4]

Notes, references and comments:
1 Matthew 16:17-19, it is difficult to visualise how Jesus could have instituted something that was conceived and established a good while after his death. 2 Galatians 1:13-15; to find knowledge of God see Proverbs 2:3-5, Philippians 3:4-6. Saul was a Hellenic Jew, a tent-maker, and after the crucifixion of Yeshuaa he

became a Pharisee. This powerful sect demanded strict observance of law and tradition. Christianity was held to be contrary to those tenets, teaching a new way to salvation through Jesus. Saul was highly educated for his era in Jewish beliefs about God, Philipplians 3:4-6. He was born early in the first century A.D or late in the last century BC. He was known by different names and titles: Paul of Tarsus, Paul the Apostle, and the Apostle Paul, the latter may have been attributed to his Roman citizenship. In Cilicia he was known by the Jewish name of Saul. No one can claim to Love God while hating others: 1 John 4:20; Acts 22:6-11. 3 Acts 22:4-5. 4 Acts 7:57 to 8:1, 8:3. After Stephen was martyred Saul was foremost in promoting Christianity after his conversion, and he went from door to door in Jerusalem to find people who believed that Jesus was the Messiah.

The Law in Paul's day stated that a man hung upon a stake was "accursed of God." [5] From Saul's viewpoint, these words were clearly applicable to Jesus; and those who followed Jesus as the Messiah were blasphemous, they deserved to suffer as blasphemers; and Saul believed that he was doing God's will.

First-century Jews expected the Messiah to be a glorious King who would free them from the hated yoke of Roman domination. That the one who was condemned by the Great Sanhedrin on a charge of blasphemy and thereafter impaled on a torture cross (or stake?) like an accursed criminal could be the Messiah was completely unacceptable, and repellent to their way of thinking.[5] But Paul seems to have been especially zealous in his campaign when he persecuted both men and women as he began to destroy the church. [6]

But something happened to Saul as he travelled to Damascus in search of Christians to destroy, according to his own account:

"About noon as I came near Damascus, suddenly a bright light from heaven flashed around me. I fell to the ground and heard a voice say to me:

`Saul! Saul! Why do you persecute me?'

"Who are you?" I asked.

`I am Jesus of Nazareth, whom you are persecuting.'

"My companions saw the light, but they did not understand the voice of him who was speaking to me."

"What shall I do, Lord?" I asked..

"`Get up,' the Lord said, `and go into Damascus. There you will be told all that you have been assigned to do.' My companions led me by the hand into Damascus, because the brilliance of the light had blinded me." [7]

Also, Roman emperor Nero fabricated Christian scapegoats and the followers of Jesus were vigorously persecuted by the Romans as Jesus himself had predicted:

"...they shall persecute you ...for my name's sake...some of you shall they cause
    to be put to death". [8]

The irony of Christianity is that the same Roman Empire that crucified Yeshua at the behest of Jewish elders, led by Caiaphas the Jewish high priest, took the persona of Yeshua transformed him into *Christ* and made Christianity the religion of the Empire. [9a]

Notes, references and comments:
5 Deuteronomy 21:22, 23. 6 Acts 8:3, yet, Paul surpasses in his *analysis of Love* Galatians 3:13, see Chapter 10 below. 7 Acts 22:6-11, 9:4, 9:1-9. 8 Matthew 24:9, Luke 21:12; despite the many Christian lives Saul had destroyed, he repented, confessed, was forgiven (we hope). 9a `Christ' is the Greek `Christos' for the Hebrew Messiah, meaning *the annointed one*. Costantine was born in Moesia, modern Serbia in 272 AD, Moesian father and Greek mother, any person living within the boundaries of the Roman Empire was considered a citizen of Rome during late third/early fourth century irrespective of ethnicity. The hybrid religion interpreted as "a combination of two Sun-symbols, known as the Ax or Hammer-symbol of the Sun or Sky-deity", ancient symbol of the Sun, also connoting sensuality or fertility. *"It has served us well this myth of Christ"*, so said Pope Leo X, according to John Bale (1495-1563), *The Pagent of the Popes*.

In 312 AD Roman Emperor Constantine defeated Maxentius at Milvian Bridge in Rome and was convinced that his victory was attributable to the power of the new deity, Jesus. Constantine was a Sun-god worshipper. He had a vision of the cross superimposed on the sun symbol of the Sun-deity, Chi-Rho, also the centre of cosmic religion, the astrological religion of Babylon; emblem of the Chaldean or Babylonian sky-god - as the imperial ensign and thereby succeeded in uniting both divisions of his troops, Pagans and Christians in a common worship.
Subsequently "Chi" had been explained as representing the first letters of *Christos*, "Chi" was Pagan origin, dating from the year c. 2500 BC.[9b]
The unrest between the increasing numbers of Pagans and Christians led Constantine to favour the rising popularity of Christianity, and he combined Sun worship and the Messianic belief in Jesus. In 325 AD he was politically motivated to unify Rome under the single religion of Christianity. Paganism existed in Europe before the birth of Jesus. By continuing with Pagan symbols, dates and rituals into the expanding

Christian faith, Constantine created a hybrid religion that served both the Christians and the Pagans. Though he mistook Jesus for Apollo, the son of the Greek god Zeus..

The Roman Catholic Church claims succession of the Pope from Peter by the confession of Peter in response to his acknowledgement of Jesus' divinity when Jesus said:

> *"Blessed are you, Simon Bar-Jonah... you are Peter, and on this rock*
> *I will*
> *build my church, and the powers of death [gates of hell] shall not*
> *prevail*
> *against it. I will give you the keys of the Kingdom of Heaven."* [10a]

Notes, references and comments:
9b Constantine only requested to be baptised at his death bed in the year 337, many years after he took Christianity as the religion of the Empire. This could be a pointer that Christianity was used as a rallying political instrument in governing the people. Another Pagan proof of this is found on a coin of Ptolemeus III from the year 247-222 BC. n the Egyptian churches the cross was a Pagan symbol of life borrowed by the Christians and interpreted in the Pagan manner. Post 314 AD coins of Constantine sho w an even-armed cross as a symbol of the Sun-god. Prior to this a Roman religion for Rome existed, adopted by Zoroastricism, an ancient semi-dualisticmonotheist religion of Greater Iran, adopted in differing forms as the generally inclusive overarching state religion of the Achaemenid Empire and subsequent Parthian and Sasanin (or Sassanid empires. 10a Matthew 16:17-19; Ephesians 1:22-23, 3:19, 4:13; Galatians 1:15–16; There is an African proverb that says: "*The first man in the field is chief.*"

According to non-Catholic Christians, the key to the Kingdom of Heaven is held by every believer who accepts Jesus as the Redeemer by the rent of the *Veil,* symbolic to his body which separated the *Holy Place* from the *Holy of the Holies* at the moment of his death.[10b]

The apostles were esteemed as evidence of authority and orthodoxy in the second century AD. Paul's epistles were accepted as scripture and two of the four gospels: Matthew, Mark, Luke and John, were associated with apostles as were other New Testament works. The New Testament says *nothing directly about Peter's connection to Rome*, an early Catholic tradition supports such a connection but such claim is external to the New Testament. That Peter was bishop of Rome is disputed by positive evidence and negative evidence corroborates that Peter was bishop of Rome. A 2009 critical study by Otto Zwierlein concludes that: "*...there is not a single piece of reliable literary or archaeological evidence*" that Peter ever was in Rome. [11]

From Roman Empire to *Roman Catholic Church* is the development of Christianity. It is said that after the crucifixion of Yeshua His message was spread beyond the Jews; and that Paul, and later Peter, the apostles, were foremost in spreading the message of Yeshua as Jesus. The Priory of Sion believes that Constantine and his male successors through the Christian Church successfully converted the world from Matriarchal Paganism to Patriarchal Christianity by waging a campaign against sacred matriarchal Pagan beliefs.[12]

Notes, references and comments:
10b Non-Catholic Christians argue that the bishop of Rome held greater esteem and not greater authority than the other bishops. The Catholic Church claims an unbroken Papal succession which runs back to Peter who was invested with the "keys of the Kingdom of heaven". One gets the impression that Jesus delegated his power to the Pope through Peter, but this is a monopolistic usurpation as first in line to the true God, though this statement may be only symbolic. Easter and Passover overlap. The Passover is Christian Holy week with the Jewish eight-day celebration of passover, both of equal gravity. First, their absolute mould is spring; in both the calendar is adjusted to ensure that the holiday is celebrated at the beginning of spring. In the belief that the resurrection took place on a Sunday, the church, the First Council of Nicaea in 325 determined that Easter should always fall on the first Sunday after the first full moon following the vernal equinox. Hence Easter remains without a fixed date, which coincided with the start of Passover on the 15th of Nissan. **The rabbis understood the verse "You go free on this day, in the month of Aviv" (in fact, means fresh ears of barley), Exodus 13:4 to restrict passover to early spring. Easter is Pagan in its origin. Secular culture celebrates the spring equinox, whilst religious culture celebrates the resurrection. 11 Otto Zwierlein, *Peter in Rome.* 12 Dan Brown, *The da Vinci Code.* Some historians have challenged this traditional view of Peter's role in the early Roman Church. Most Catholic, Protestant and other scholars in general say Peter was indeed martyred in Rome under Nero. The See of Rome is traditionally said to be founded by Peter and Paul, who had invested it with apostolic authority. Nonetheless, they *substituted humanity for divinity.* Dan Brown (page 125) states: "Their brutal crusade to re-educate the pagan and feminine worshipping religions spanned three centuries,
Reference 12 continued below...

They were called `Pagan' during the rise of Christianity because they were not enlisted in the 'army' of the Roman Christ. The Code of Justinian [13] enacted Orthodox Christianity into law by Theodosius, who also confirmed ecclesiastical leadership of the Roman Church and ordered all Christian congregations to submit to the authority of the Church. Dissenters were labelled heretics for *not believing* in Christianity and subject to the death sentence and exclusion from the protection of the establishment.[14] **By the ninth century the power of the Roman Catholic Church was enhanced by its association with the Holy Roman Empire of Charlemagne and his successors. Relations between the popes and the Holy Roman Empire deteriorated in the Middle Ages and the existence of an alternative Roman tradition in the Byzantine east led to the separation of the Catholic and Orthodox Churches, worsened by the intervention of the Crusaders against Byzantine Muslim enemies. European history from the Renaissance onwards shows a link with the splitting of the Western Church into Catholic and Protestant.Not only Europe sought to travel the Roman road, however. Arabia after the death of Mohammed (632 AD) became a religious empire in the Islamic world, spread by Arab armies outside the Arabian Peninsula through much of the Middle East, North Africa and the eastern coast of Africa, before the arrival of Europeans in that area. 15**

Notes, references and comments:
Referemce 12 continued: employing methods as inspired as they were horrific. The Catholic Inquisition published the book that arguably could be called the most blood-soaked publication in human history. *Malleus Maleficarum* – or *The Witches Hammer* – indoctrinated the world to 'the dangers of freethinking women' and instructed the clergy how to locate, torture and destroy them. Those deemed 'witches' by the Church included all female scholars, priestesses, gypsies, mystics, nature lovers, herb gatherers and any women 'suspiciously attuned to the natural world.' Midwives were also killed for their heretical practice of using medical knowledge to ease the pain of childbirth – and suffering, the Church claimed, that was God's rightful punishment for Eve's partaking of the Apple of Knowledge, thus giving birth to the idea of Original sin. During three hundred years of witch hunts, the Church burned at the stake an astounding five *million* women." **Gilbert Grindle (1892) *The Destruction of paganism in the Roman Empire,* pp 29-30. Most of the destruction was perpetrated by Christian monks and bishops. Michael Routery (1997), *The Serapeum of Alexandria, The First Missionay War. The Church take over of the Roman Empire.* 13 Known in English as Justinian 1 (482 or 483 AD), Codex, codification of Roman law that served as a basis for law in Europe;**

no English translations were made of the Codex until the 20th century. 14 Will Durant, *History of the King James Version of the Bible.* Much of Europe became Christian by 600 AD. The irony is that the same Roman Empire persecuted *believers in Christ* before establishing Christianity as the religion of the Roman Empire. But the ideals of any institution evolve when current leaders pass on.Reference 16 continued: ordinary people, as heads of institutions in the private sector. Biblical passages reflect the masculine mindset of the contemporary Biblical society as in `God the Father'. Was it inescapable that a patriarchal *mindset* would have perceived and translated God as masculine? One Christian view is that by calling God Father, formality is removed, personalises the Almighty, and brings God closer to humans, but why should God be Father and not Mother? "It's interesting to speculate how it developed that in two of the most anti-feminist institutions, the church and the law court, the men are wearing dresses," **Flo Kennedy,** *Florynce R. Kennedy Quotes.* **The Tenth Commandment** says: *"Thou shalt not covet thy neighbour's wife"* - not 'husband'. 15 Author's oral testimony passed down from previous generations and various sources.

Church and Government is apparent in early Christianity. Since the beginning of time there have been politicians behind every aspect of human existence; and behind them there have been philosophers in the religions of the world: Hinduism, Judaism, Christianity, Islam and other such branches of major faiths including myths, cults and the so-called primitive forms of worship.When the Roman Empire collapsed the Western Church preserved much of the learning and traditions of Rome and became the dominant force in the medieval world. As a religious empire and by an assumed "divine mandate" the Roman Catholic Church took a political, cultural and spiritual role. It was the only major governing institution to preserve the authority of the Roman times and almost the only unifying influence in Western Europe. 16

It is said that God is the Father of Jesus by the declaration on the day Jesus was begotten.17 The Father begot the Son and this was acknowledged by the Son and this affinity, if one can use this term, is just as profound a mystery as the essence or being of the *Father.* The pronoun "Him" as applied to God gives the impression that God is man (male); and terms such as "King" or "Lord" applied to God and to Jesus are also applied to mortals. This style of address may be attributed to male dominance, to class or hierarchical distinctions, or to possible linguistic poverty, though the latter is less likely. "Reverend" is a term which appears only once in the Bible but *only in reference to God.* 18 Prophets and ministers are to be shown respect for the position they hold without the show of pre-eminence, grandiose, glittering ceremonies or the carrying of religious titles.[19] The Bible describes Jesus as of humble birth and in mode of life. In humility of spirit he said:

"Don't you be called Rabbi as a religious title, whoever shall exalt himself
shall be abased and he that shall humble himself shall be exalted. [20] *...*
in vain they worship me, teaching as commandments the doctrines of men". [21]

Notes, references and comments:
16 Christendom shares the patriarchal characteristic of the Western hierarchical system where the head of state as the pope is far removed from the ordinary people, as heads of institutions in the private sector. Biblical passages reflect the masculine mindset of the contemporary Biblical society as in `God the Father'. Was it inescapable that a patriarchal *mindset* **would have perceived and translated God as masculine? One Christian view is that by calling God Father, formality is removed, personalises the Almighty, and brings God closer to humans, but why should God be Father and not Mother?** "It's interesting to speculate how it developed that in two of the most anti-feminist institutions, the church and the law court, the men are wearing dresses," **Flo Kennedy,** *Florynce R. Kennedy Quotes.* **The Tenth Commandment says:** *"Thou shalt not covet thy neighbour's wife"* **- not 'husband'. 17 Psalm 2:7. 18 See Part 1, Chapter 2,** *The Holy Bible,* **some facts from the Holy Scriptures, Psalm 111:9 KJ Version only; Chapter 7, Ministry of Yeshua, Prayer, God's purpose. 19 Acts: 12-23: "...immediately the angel of the Lord smote him, because he gave not to God the glory..." The majority receive accolades according to the concept of those who recommend them, but to use the same titles for God and Jesus as for mortals is rather presumptuous 20** Matthew 23:12. 21 Mark 7:7. "Pope" means *Papa,* Father of all Fathers. Pharaohs, Roman emperors, absolute monarchs and kings were revered as divine and some painted by artists in "divine image". Zeus, Jupiter and Heracles were worshipped as gods by Roman armies; and the Pope has been regarded as *divine* by worshippers (author's oral testimony): can a human being be *revered as divine?*

Pope John Paul II quotes the words of Jesus:

> *"Call no one on earth your father, you have but one father in*
> *heaven...words such as 'Holy Father' or 'Your holiness'...seem*
> *inimical to the Gospel.* [22] *Do not be called Master you have but*
> *one master, the Messiah...be not afraid of these words either."* [23]
> *In such a climate all abstractions vanish. Dogma becomes*

flesh,blood, life. The theologian becomes witness and shepherd." [24]

Mary and the Virgin Birth of Jesus is the tenet of Roman Christianity as is the perpetual virginity of Mary. According to the Nicene creed, as revised by the First Council of Constantinople, Jesus was the incarnate of the Holy Spirit and Virgin Mary. The Apostles Creed states that Jesus was born of the Virgin Mary, not of sexual union between man and woman.

According to Pope John Paul II:

> *"Mary is the new Eve, placed by God in close relation to Christ, the new Adam, beginning with the Annunciation through the night of his birth in Bethlehem, through the wedding feast at Canaan of Galilee, through the Cross at Calvary, and up to the gift of the Holy Spirit at Pentecost. The Mother of Christ the Redeemer is the Mother of the Church."* [25]

Mary, mother of Jesus is surrounded by mythology in the Catholic Church, idolised and revered as saints whose statues adorn the churches. Some Catholics say she is not revered but respected as a `mother' who gave birth to a redeemer. Other Catholics discard God and Jesus altogether and pray to Mary as their saviour. The appreciation of art is an appreciation

Notes, references and comments:
22 In the first chapter of *Crossing the Threshold of Hope*, entitled *The Pope: A Scandal and A Mystery:* why does the Church use *hostile* words? 23 and 24 Pope John Paul II, *Crossing the Threshold of Hope*, page 6. mother though few follow a role model. Most significantly God chose to manifest through Yeshua by the *Maternal Covenant* with Mary. God chooses, for the benefit of humanity as a whole, certain individuals as outstanding personages to fulfil a certain role. Mary is a mother who witnessed and endured her son's horrendous death through the worst punishment that could be imposed upon a human being. She is a mother deserving respect among mothers and women. See Part 2, Chapter 6, Currency of the Spiritual Realm. 25 Pope John Paul II, *Crossing the Threshold of Hope*, page 212. Like the conversion of Yeshua to Jesus, the Hebraic Miriam was also converted to Mary. The Roman Catholic dogma of the virgin birth in the *perpetual virginity of Mary* is somewhat mystifying. Once a woman has given birth the natural way can she remain a virgin? With God everything is possible, of course, but the purpose of eternal virginity of Mary is unclear. Some Christians believe that the conception of Jesus is more significant than His birth, while others do not. Does it matter whether Jesus was born out of wedlock or

of the Holy Spirit?

of aesthetic beauty but idolatry is prohibited in the first of the Ten Commandments:

> *"Thou shalt have no other gods before me".* [26]

Christmas is a Pagan Festival as is Easter. In the hustle and bustle of Christmas commerce and festivities as we know them and Christ is replaced by Santa Claus. When people celebrate Christmas in tandem with its commercial aspect how many relate the event to the birth of Jesus? [27]

Jesus did not approve or direct the observance of Christmas and he spoke on the traditions of men and that Scriptures cannot be broken.[28] He warned against Pagan worship customs to honour the true God.[29] Daniel's prophesy was that religious men would attempt to change times and law including God's festival seasons. [30] On the coming of Christ, Zachariah says keep the *Feast of the Tabernacle*.[31]

10 The New Covenant and Administration of the Church (*New Covenant*) was necessary because of Israel's disbelief and rejection of Yeshua the Saviour whose birth among them was the privilege bestowed upon the nation Israel, according to Christian theology.
The *New Covenant* was secured by the blood of Jesus which bought the Church of God.[1] It replaces the Land Edict and the body of Christ is the Church: the mystery which in other ages was not made known.[2]

In the meantime God is visiting the Gentiles to take out of them "a people for God's name"; and is said to be the mystery which holds together believing Jews and Gentiles in a completely new entity. The Church, through the blood of the *New Covenant* shed at Calvary is called the *Dispensation of the Holy Spirit* because the spirit has been especially

Notes, references and comments:
26 Mary is an inspirational role model for wife and mother though few follow a role model. Most significantly God chose to manifest through Yeshua by the *Maternal Covenant* with Mary. God chooses, for the benefit of humanity as a whole, certain individuals as outstanding personages to fulfil a certain role. Mary is a mother who witnessed and endured her son's horrendous death through the worst punishment that could be imposed upon a human being. She

is a mother deserving respect among mothers and women. See Part 2, Chapter 6, Currency of the Spiritual Realm.. 27 Over spending, over indulgence and the "birthday boy" is left in the cold. Alexander Hislop, *The Two Babylons,* the Pagan festival of Christmas began at least two thousand years before the birth of Jesus. 28 John 10:35 and note 21 above. 29 Deuteronomy 12:29-32. 30 Zachariah 14:16.The good thing about Christmas is the fellowship and goodwill that people share, but why not spread the "spirit of goodwill" throughout the year? 31 Leviticus 23:1-44; Matthew 5:17-19. God's annual holidays are the: *Passover Feast of Unleavened Bread; Pentecost Feast of the Tabernacles; and Trumpets,* which disclose God's plan, according to interpreters of Christian theology. References 1 & 2 continued below...

manifested by Christ's formation and indwelling of the Church. The age will be consummated by Christ's completion and glorification of the Church.[3] The church is a mission representing Jesus beseeching humans to be reconciled to God:

> *"...by one Spirit we are all baptised into one body."* [4]

According to Christian theologians, Church was coined by Jesus but How could he, when `church' was established three hundred years well after his death? Church is a creation of the Apostolic Age:

> *"God who made the world and everything in it...Lord of heaven and earth, does*
> *not dwell in temples made with hands.*
> *"Nor is He worshipped with men's hands, as though He needed anything, since*
> *He gives to all life, breath, and all things."*   Acts 17:24, 25.

Church is not a building or a technical designation of any kind. The *role model* for living lies in the *Sermon on the Mount* delivered by Yeshua in the *"open"* space. A building sheltered from the natural elements is *where believers may gather in common fellowship* or *collective worship* but worship can take place anywhere, even in one's closet. The interpretation of the New Testament by theoloians, the church is broken down into three categories: the church throughout the world,[5] the church throughout a region [6] and the church in a city.[7] A local church comprises all believers and denominations based upon understanding of the universal church. Members are followers of Christ the head and belong to the same body of the church.[8] Paul speaks of all Christians as members of Christ, of one Mystical Body.[9] The mystical church is any assemblage of people called out of the creation into the *New Covenant* representing all the saved of the age; distinguished from the local assemblage whose understanding of the mystical church is based upon an understanding of the universal church which refers to all God's people. Christian mysticism is the development of

Notes, references and comments:
1 1 John 16:17, 8, 13, Unger's *Survey of the Bible;* Jeremiah 31:31-34; Matthew 5:17. *2* Luke 22:20; Acts 20:28, 15:14; 1 Corinthians 12:12, 13; Ephesians 3:9. 3 John 16:17, 8, 13, Ephesians 2:74, 5:25; 2 Corinthians 11:2. 4 Romans 6:3, 4; Ephesians 1:20-23, 1 Corinthians l2:l3, Over the centuries much emphasis has been placed on structures called "church", some of which are of considerable opulence, managed as a business while those who worship in them are clothed in poverty. *Church* is a Christian invention and is a *label or identification* of Christianity. 5 Acts 9:31. 6 1 Corinthians l2:l4. 7 1 Corinthians 1:2. 8 Colossians 1:18, 2:18-20, Ephesians 2:7, Acts 15:14, 2 Corinthians 5:20: not unlike governmental regional administration. 9 Corinthians12:12-31, Colossians 1:18, 2:18-20, Christian mysticism refers to the development of mystical practices and theory within the tradition of Christian teaching. It has often been connected to mystical theology, especially in the Roman Catholic and Eastern Orthodox traditions. St Paul did not use the word "Mystical" but there is a re-emergence of mysticism both outside and inside the Church. It was developed more recently to bring out the claim that this union is unique and there is no parallel to it.

mystical practises and theories within the Roman Catholic Church. [10] The Temple of God [11] and the Jerusalem from above or the Heavenly Jerusalem are copied by Christianity from the Old Testament outward sanctuary, replaced by the claim of the literal dwelling of God in the church. [12]

Love Analysed by Paul shows that God works through people and things as we can reach God through love and kindness to others. In his letter to the Romans Paul explains that love should be without hypocrisy.[13] Bless those who persecute you and do not curse them. Live in harmony with one another. Do not be arrogant but associate with those who are humble.

Bless those who persecute you, bless and do not curse.[14] The following phrase embraces all the commandments:

"You shall love your neighbour as yourself." [15]

The love of God is explained in the beautiful love story of Ruth and the love for her mother-in-law, Naomi, the great grandmother of King David: a story that reflects a peaceful picture of domestic life in a time of anarchy and trouble.[16] Paul analyses love amongst other values:

"If I speak in the tongues of mortals and of angels but do not have love, I am a noisy gong or a clanging cymbal; and if I have prophetic powers and understand all mysteries and all knowledge, and if I have all faith, enough to remove mountains, but do not have love, I am nothing. If I give away all my possessions and hand over my body to be burnt but do not have love, I gain nothing.

"Love is patient and kind. Love is not envious, boastful, arrogant or rude. Love does not insist on its own way. Love is not irritable or resentful. Love does not rejoice in wrongdoing, but rejoices in the truth. Love bears all things, believes all things, hopes all things, endures all things. Love never ends. Now faith, hope and love abide, these three; and the greatest of these is love." [17]

Notes, references and comments:
10 *Newsweek,* 5 Sept 2005, many people seek a mystical experience in America. 11 Galatians 4:26, Hebrews l2:22. 12 1 Corinthians 12:12-31, Colossians 1:18, 2:18-20, Ephesians 1:22-23, 3:19; 4:13; Dennis McCallum and Gary De Lashmutt, *The New Testament Definition of the Church,* from the Introductory Study Guide: *Understanding Ministry;* Bride of Christ or Christ's Betrothed refer to the love and loyalty existing between Christ and believers, such titles or phrases indicate enthusiasm over the top and they add nothing to the knowledge of what Yeshua is about, and are frivolous and vexatious. 13 Romans 12:9,11:13, Romans 1:18.14 Romans 12:14. 15 Proverbs 10:12; Lord Atkin, a judge in the House of Lords defined the neighbour principle in the case of *Donoghue v Stevenson:* "Your neighbour is not the one who literally lives next door to you but the *effect of your act* upon any person – even one who is at the other end of the world from you" because we owe a duty of care to others. The facts of the case: In Paisley, Scotland, a snail was contained in a bottle of ginger beer and the purchaser sued the manufacturer of the ginger beer and she won. 16 The *Book of Ruth* is one of those of two books in the Bible named after women, the other book is *Esther.Notes, references and comments.* 17 1 Corinthians 13:13, 13:8, Matthew 22:36-40, John 4:9, 10.

Generosity:
   "Love envies not, Envy is a feeling of ill-will to those who are in the same line as ourselves". [18]
Humility:
   "To put a seal on your lips and forget what you have done. Love counts not itself. Is not puffed up does not behave itself unseemly, seeks not her own, is not easily provoked, thinks no evil." [19]
A Pharisee put the question to Yeshua:
   "Which is the greatest commandment of the law?"
Yeshua replied:
   "Love the Lord thy God with all thy heart and with thy soul, and
with
      thy entire mind." [20]

Spreading Roman Christianity

   "They came with the Bible and told us to close our eyes and pray.
When we
      opened our eyes, we had the Bible and they had the land."
                                             Bishop Desmond Tutu.

From late eighteenth century to early nineteenth century missionaries carried the Christian banner to Africa and other places under imperial flags, based on the Berlin Conference of 1884-1885 (to divide Africa among

European powers) involving Britain and other Western European powers. Its characteristic carried the Roman legacy: *divide and rule* in which people were placed in categories of *colour* (operated on "class" strata in the mother countries). Our entire existence to the present day had been conditioned by *skin colour* and *class* though in recent years the term "class" is, for *political correctness,* avoided in speech but not in practice.
The Roman Catholic Church, as the universal mission covered more territory globally than other Christian denominations. In their schools, the boys were taught horticulture and the girls were taught needlework but both sadly lacking academically. No member of the congregation was permitted to read the Bible but directed to constant prayer as set by the church administration following the Roman Catholic Church Bible, distinct from the regular BiblEducation for the lower classes (so-called) in the late 1800s was a much controversial issue and regarded with

suspicion. The Catholic Church wherever it spread its wings stood apart with more senior authority than the governmental administration, other Christiane.

Notes, references and comments:

18 Romans 12:9, 11:13; a spirit of courteousness. It is said that God has revealed love to humans through Yeshua for whose sake mercy has been extended to the fallen. Do only what Yeshua did with the Father, whatever the Father asked Him to do: love others, help the needy, share our resources, keep our lives clean, offer forgiveness and bring others to God. "Love" motivates us to obey God. 19 Romans 12:9. 20 Deuteronomy 6:5.

denominations to a lesser degree in the governments' policy of "non interference". In *blind faith* people conformed to the demands of institutionalised imperialism. Despite that church administrators represented God they were riddled with racial and class discrimination as the regimes they operated under. [21]
The characteristic traits of Jesus were presented, on posters and drawings, as those of a Caucasian: white skin, long golden hair, blue eyes, though garbed in Biblical dress, the image impressed upon the Christian dominated world. It

is highly unlikely, that Jesus, a Jew, would have had the characteristic traits of a Caucasian, unless he had been born among the exiled Jews in Europe. The colonisers saw it best to introduce and establish a God with their own characteristic traits; for they could not pay tribute to one with a dark skin, regardless of noble deeds. Does it matter whether Jesus was sky-eyed, or otherwise, with golden or black hair, white or otherwise? This mattered to the rulers of that era.

Nature's persistence to replicate is blind to social constraints of colour or any other distinctions. Children born to local indigenous women in the colonies and white men of the ruling class were relegated to a miscegenation category. In prudish Christendom, children born out of wedlock were treated as the scum of society. The process of the conception is one, and the seed has no control over its conception. Some nuns and priests in the convents told such children that they could never enter heaven because their parents were not married as they were conceived in sin:

"...the weight of shame from illegitimacy was dumped squarely on the child". [22]

Fundamentalists hold that baptism is for adults and older children and criticise the Catholic Church's practice of baptising infants; that baptism should take place only after one has become "born again" and fully understands the meaning of baptism and "accepted Jesus Christ as personal Lord and Saviour;" that at the instant of acceptance, the adult becomes a Christian, and salvation is assured forever when baptism should follow. The Roman Catholic baptism of infants is based on "man's original sin", an important doctrine within the Roman Catholic Church, as explained in depth by St Augustine and formalised as part of Roman Catholic doctrine by the Councils of Trent in the 16th Century.

Notes, references and comments:

21 Author's oral testimony. 22 Kate Edie's classic description of the foundling or adopted child in her book, *Nobody's Child*, page 6. There is no such a thing as an illegitimate child even one conceived by rape; at that time there may have been only illegitimate parents. This was by no means confined to the colonies. Charles Dickens well illustrates in *Oliver Twist* child born out of wedlock and the plight of orphans; similarly, the novels of Catherine Cookson, on which movies have been based, well illustrates the point.

The Catholic Church has regarded unmarried mothers as adulterers and their babies were buried outside of the confines of sanctified ground of burial within the Church, never saw heaven or hell but left in limbo, and causing torment and panic to the   mothers. Between 1925 and 1961 nearly 800 babies died at St Mary's, one of many unwed mothers homes run by the Catholic Church, where the babies were buried in bulk. This placed a dark period of the country's history onto American consciousness. The homes of unwed mothers were designed to punish the mothers and house their children. The young mothers were forced to work in indentured servitude, and if their children survived childbirth and infancy, they were often given up for adoption.

Ferris Cochran (formerly Andrew Michael Gallagher Irish born in 1957 who was adopted by an American couple), North Carolina man once owner of a successful business was born in the now infamous Tuam centre, where 800 babies may have been discarded in a massive septic tank. Now the subject of investigation, with authorities using ground sensor equipment to explore the tank. [23]

Cochran says:

> *"...of every bit I knew was that this was a very evil orphanage. "It was evil for the orphans and it was evil for the unwed mothers. My mother was persecuted for out-of-wedlock sex... I could not walk, I could not talk, I had never been held by anybody when they received me at 18-months-old. These are the things that gave me the driving force to... go to Ireland and see where I came from. "I wanted nothing but to look at her and say, 'Look, you went through Hell...the bottom line is the decision that you made was the right decision...I'm safe, and I've had a good life in the United States. It's time for you to just close your eyes, rest, and know that what happened 50 years ago turned out to be a good story." [24]*

There is nothing in the Bible to indicate that anyone would suffer for the sins of another and Jesus said:

> *"Judge not, lest ye be judged."*

Notes, references and comments:

The Archbishop of Dublin acknowledged that what happened in Tuam and St. Mary's could have happened elsewhere across the country; that there is a need for a full investigation into convent-run mother and baby homes; update 6/23/2014: The Associated Press clarified new details of this story; Produced by Editors: Megan Quellhorst, T J Raphael; Contributor Henry Molofsky. How can a loving God banish little innocents into limbo? 24 Cochran never met his birth mother, but through his visits to the location where the home once stood and his tireless research into his past, he learned that his birth mother was among those whom the Tuam Center shamed. It was not an orphanage, it was a place where unwed mothers had to repent their sins: The Catholic Church usurpation of the powers of God.

But Jesus does not specify:

> *"Whosoever receives a child in my name, receives me".* [25]

> *"...the condemnation of God by man is not based on the truth, but on*

> *arrogance ...underhanded conspiracy...in our time the same condemnation*

> *has been repeated in many courts of totalitarian regimes. And isn't it also*

> *being repeated in the parliaments of democracies where, for example, laws*

> *are regularly passed condemning to death a person not yet born?"* [26]

Regardless of colour, creed or rank over the centuries men have spread their seed wherever they went with or without the consent of women: estate owners on slave women; European colonists in the areas they colonised; Second World War Hitler's German soldiers in the countries he invaded; the American soldiers in the unpopular war of Viet Nam; invading Bantu from the Congo down to southern Africa; and others around the world without exception. [27]

Western-culture orientated Christianity mainly derived from Greco-Roman roots was exported by missionaries universally. The most popular was the Roman Catholic Church – *Catholic* means universal. Those representing the Vatican, most affluent religious institution, lived in relative comfort, and preached to the poor of the poorest clutching a penny to buy eternal life:

> *"Blessed are the poor, for they shall inherit the Kingdom of Heaven".* [28]

Notes, references and comments:

25 Matthew 18:5. 26 Pope John Paul II, *Crossing the Threshold of Hope,* page 65. Not all parents welcome the gift of a child who may end up reared by others. Snobbery is the architect of illegitimacy. Abortion kills an innocent life for choice and the law allows it, some are killed without the law, illegal abortions. In either the foetus is without protection. The situation has somewhat evolved from adoption to abortion. Life begins at conception, Psalm 139:13: Prophet Jeremiah and Apostle Paul were called by God before they were born, Jeremiah

1:5; Galatians 1:15. 27 Germane Greer, *The Female Eunuch.* Within this male dominant sex, children were born and are being born today. There are also a good number of women who have and still do consent to male overtures and conception takes place. But as said above, there is nothing in the Bible to indicate that anyone would suffer for the sins of another. 28 Author's oral testimony. 16th century religious Reformation, major reformers Martin Luther and John Calvin, had far-reaching political, economic and social effects, after Reformation the basis of main religious institutions: Roman Catholicism, Eastern Orthodoxy and Protestantism; this also removed pictured church windows, liturgy and allowed ordinary people to read the Bible; the depth of the divine Scriptures could only be understood by those qualified to do so, to impose their will on the ignorant. Agents or employees in institutional administration deal with the public and take the brunt of the system of shortcomings but the top is far removed from day to day administration, its inconveniences and consequences. The Vatican, a huge business enterprise, was no different. Some agents violate human rights in serving the public, while others with compassion. Pontius Pilate did not tell the Roman soldiers to scourge Yeshua to the extent they did but that is the characteristic of "carrying out orders."

The Vatican influence and its reaction against Protestantism was to send out the message that:

> *"Outside the Roman Catholic Church there is no salvation".* [29]

The general attitude of Christian denominations, the Roman Catholic Church and all, was that to be saved people should renounce their values and culture. Though the Church of Scotland Mission abroad was different by emphasising the perpetuation of local culture and tradition, and deviation from the preservation of ancient family names was not permitted. Christian names for newborn babies or for new Christian converts as the first or Christian name was the norm. [30]

The Vatican stance promoted a view of Church and missionary work and the Christian banner was to invite African peoples – and people in other areas of the world - into the mystery of life and death as understood through the Gospel message intrinsically. Disciples of Christ were disciples of all nations.

Jesus said:

> *"All power is given unto me in heaven and in earth".* [31]

On the question of a Catholic minority compared to other religions by the year 2000 the answer given by Pope John Paul II:

> *"Pilate, who, pointing to the Nazarene crowned with thorns after His*
> *scourging, said: 'Behold the man!' (John 19:5) did not realise that he*
> *was proclaiming an essential truth, expressing that which always and*
> *every where remains the heart of evangelisation."* [32]

At The Hands of Wardens children have been abused as headlined in the media by men of the cloth and other men. The child's mother turns a blind eye to the abuse; while some mothers severely punish the child for having evil thoughts about a "holy priest". [33] Because of the stigma attached to the family and the power of the Catholic Institution, the child was sacrificed as *fear led to silence*.

Abuse is predominantly by some male relatives in the home of the child. Priests (some in "sheep skin") were welcomed into a child's home as they took a secretive attitude towards

Notes, references and comments:

29 This sounds like an example of trading competition. Genevan reformer Calvin: *"beyond the pale of the church...no forgiveness of sins, no salvation.."* Martin Luther Protestant leader: *"...belonging to the church is necessary for salvation..."* 30 Author's oral testimony. 31 Matthew 28:18; the fundamental problem with Christianity lies not with the message of Yeshua but the post-Jesus Christian messenger which has its roots in the Apostolic Age. 32 Pope John Paul II, *Crossing the Threshold of Hope*, page 104. 33 Author's oral testimony.

sex, publicly push it aside while they were titillated by it. There is nothing in the Bible to indicate that Yeshua taught celibacy. Before the fourth century Catholic priests married and on death inheritance went to the eldest son, the factor being the problematical relationship the Catholic Church had with real estate and inheritance of land. After the fourth century celibacy was imposed and inheritance went to the bishop or to the church. [34]

O'Gorman classic quote on the stance of the priest:

Colm O'Gorman well illustrates the sexual abuse of boys by Catholic priests. He was abused by his priest over a period of years and betrayed by his Church. He took legal proceedings against the Pope and won. But child abuse is not confined to the Catholic Church.

In countries where there is limited "access" to women (who are fully veiled), for example in Afghanistan. Dance teachers take the boys as young as four-five years old under the pretext of "protection" and teach them to dance and sing for the gratification of men. In the high incidence of poverty, families agree to give the child away as a means of livelihood. 36

However, it should be noted that sexual abuse is not confined to the Catholic priests, perhaps one could say rather to the "male species". From the excerpts of an article written by Sam Miller, 12% of the 300 Protestant clergy survey admitted to sexual intercourse with a parishioner; 38% acknowledged other inappropriate sexual contact. In a study by the United Methodist Church, 41.8% of clergy women reported unwanted sexual behaviour; 17% of laywomen have been sexually harassed. 1.7% of the Catholic clergy has been found guilty of paedophilia. 10% of the Protestant ministers have been found guilty of paedophilia.37

Notes, references and comments:

34 Austin Cline, *History of Celibacy in Roman Catholicism.* They ought to marry and move from hypocritical celibacy but abuses are not confined to unmarried men. 35 Above all, *truth,* one of the greatest values of human existence, was hidden and gave way to anonymity, Colm O'Gorman, *Beyond Belief.* Not only those children who come under Roman Catholic protection suffer, because of the size and "universal" characteristic of the Catholic Church, the numbers are greater; but children suffer in most parts of the world under different circumstances. Head of the Church of England, criticised the Roman Catholic Church for child abuse (media reports 04/04/10), but a thief is a thief only when caught. Trevor Bailey was abused from age five by a curator of the Church of England, interviewed by BBC Radio4 28/03/10, 9:00 am. A guest speaker revealed that as a boy he had been abused by a Rabbi, BBC 1, *The Big Questions,* presented by Nicky Campbell, 11/04/10 and various media reports. Some white Catholic priests with local women parishioners in foreign missions added to the miscegenation population, Author's oral testimony. 36 Marcia G Yerman, *Daily Cos* member; known as *Bachi Bazi,* literally meaning "playing with boys",

young boys, known as "dancing boys", targets of sexual abuse in male environments, BBC World Service, 05/04/08, 24/05/11.37 Sam Miller, Non-Catholic prominent Cleveland Jewish businessman.

The scale of cover up is explained by O'Gorman who states that an independent research commissioned by American bishops was carried out by John Jay College of Criminal Justice. They found that sexual abuse by clerical personnel in active ministry in the Catholic Church was widespread across the United States: affecting 95% diocesan priests; in 1952 and 2002 4% of all priests had been accused of sexually abusing a child; 10,667 allegations involved rape and abuse; and in the United States alone the Catholic Church was aware of more than 7,100 cases. [38] The children of a place in Nigeria were branded witches, beaten, tortured, and killed in the name of Christianity. When approached the leader of the country promised to protect the children but no action was taken against the perpetrators.[39]

Jesus said:
> "...those who offend a child it would be better for them that a   millstone were hanged about the neck and drowned in the depth of the sea". [40] "For nothing is hidden that will not be made manifest, nor is anything secret that will not be known... [41] For God will bring every deed into judgment, with every secret thing, whether good or evil." [42]

The Commendable Aspect on the Roman Catholic Church is explained by the excerpts of an article written by Sam Miller. The Church educates 2.6 million elementary pupils and high school students everyday in the USA at the cost to that hand to the American taxpayer of 18 billion dollars a year. The graduates go on to university studies at the rate of 92%. The Church has 230 colleges and universities in the U.S. at the cost of 10 billion dollars a year

Notes, references and comments:
40 Matthew 18:1-7. 41 Luke 8:17.23. 42 Ecclesiastes 12:14. A conquered people deserve less, some got worse under the Christian banner since: The Portuguese in Brazil no method of exterminating Indians had been spared by those from the so-called civilised cultures; the Aborigines in Australia and the Sioux Indians in America were confined to reservations. Various Media reports: On the point of return of Aboriginal land rights to indigenous Australians by the Commonwealth or territory governments of Australia is based on recognition of dispossession. The worst stigma in Christendom is the *slave trade* plus racial discrimination. But compare with Eastern Europe, ethnic cleansing is on par

with the holocaust as the Tutsi of Africa. In imperial history, whether crucial or insignificant, when interests of the indigenous conflicted with those of white people the indigenous lost. Throughout the centuries no empire ever educated the local indigenous people. European colonies were no different and the education of locals was left to faith denominations in their missions abroad. Schools may have been subject to government control policy to harmonise and avoid disparities in the education system. 38 Miller ditto. 39 Channel 4 News, 12/11/08: Gary Foxcroft, an Englishman, "Saving Africa's Witch Children"; BBC World Service 24/05/11. In the United States, Warren Jeff of the Fundamentalist Church of Christ Latter Day Saints in Texas was jailed for abducting and holding 42 children from ages of sixteen to seventeen. A Christian Texas ranch girl of fourteen was forced to marry a much older man against her will; and there were incidents of children sexually abused in Fort Concho.

to the Church, and a savings on the other enrolment of 700,000 students. The Catholic Church has a non- profit hospital system of 637 hospitals, which account for hospital treatment of one out of every five people - not just Catholics - in the United States today. [43] Many a Catholic priest has assisted parents of children (and the children) caught in the drug culture of the 1960s and in numerous other circumstances in a variety of ways. [44]

As William Neil puts it:

> "We are all caught up in the paradox of progress and civilisation so that things good in themselves like national pride, scientific development, and improvement of living standards bring us many curses as blessings in their train, if they do not end in total disaster for all whom they seek to benefit".

Children over the centuries:
I am the child who was killed at birth – I was born female in China.
I am the child who was abandoned – I was born female.
I am the child who was glorified - I was born male.
I am the child who became a king.
I am the child who became a slave.
I am the child who was nipped in the bud [abortion] – because I would shame the good name of the family.
I am the child who became homosexual – I was killed by a group of Christians in Africa.

I am the child of the twenty-first century who never made it to the future:
  I was bombed in Gaza.   I was bombed in Israel.
Kings, lawyers, doctors, politicians, scientists, economists, professionals, the magnates, priests, and every adult, regardless of rank...all were children once.

11 The Palestinian Covenant on Messianic Administration (the covenant) was made while Israel was in the land of Moab as separate and distinctive from the one made with them in Horeb besides the one made at Mount Sinai, according to Christian theology.[1]

Notes, references and comments:
43 Sam Miller ditto. Author's oral testimony. An institution is an *entity* that may, and does, survive longer than the succession of administrators, for the span of human life mostly turns out to be shorter than that of an institution. 44   An institution is not a barrel of apples where one or two bad ones would contaminate the lot. Many did and do carry out their duties humanely. Oral testimony is overwhelming in the humanitarian activities of the Roman Catholic Church, as other Christian and non-Christian denominations, particularly in death: the placing of the cross and the Bible on a coffin by a priest, brings comfort to the bereaved; and it does not matter whether Jesus died on a cross or on a beam, the cross is more expressive than a beam. The commendable aspect of Roman Christianity (as other Christian denominations) is also the general fellowship it provided, and still provides. to its members and services such as schools, medical facilities. Especially where a death occurs to the destitute the compassionate funeral services were and are tremendous. In this respect the Islamic communities are similar as are other faith denominations in bringing comfort to their communities.
Reference 1 continued below...

The covenant contains a promise that after God dispersed[2] the Israelites among the nations as punishment for disobedience and the rejection of a redeemer, Yeshua will re-gather them after the Tribulation[3] and return them to their land after they repent of their sins and look to YAHWEH. The covenant is closely linked with the Mosaic Covenant, and some scholars say the two are joined together at the beginning of the Millennium and is part of the Abrahamic Covenant.[4] The covenant shall be completely fulfilled in the millennial reign of Yeshua. Many writers advocate a variety of prophetic theories, some think the rebellion was largely a fulfilment of a large part of Daniel's prophesy:[5]

And Jesus went out, and departed from the temple: and His disciples came

to Him to show Him the buildings of the temple. And Jesus said unto them:

"See ye not all these things? Verily I say unto you, There shall not be left here

one stone upon another that shall not be thrown down." [6]

The covenant ushers in the millennial age and like the Davidic Covenant finds fulfilment in kingdom blessing; and comes into effect at the end of the Tribulation period when the remaining Jews see Yeshua and receive Him as their Messiah. They will nationally repent and mourn for their sin of rejecting Yeshua and admit before all their acceptance of Him as King. YAHWEH will then, in Yeshua, forgive them andthe entire land grant promised to Abraham, all will be restored to them and all Israel will be saved nationally in a day.[7]

Notes, references and comments:
Reference 1 continued: *Unger's Survey of the Bible*, Deuteronomy 29:1-29, 30:1-10; It is unclear why Christian theologians have interpeted this Covenant as `Palestinian', when Canaan, the promised land, only came to be called `Palestine' after the Philistines had conquered Israel in Canaan, long after the death of Joshua; Moab is located across the River Jordan from Israel, where the Israelites encamped before they entered the Promised land led by Joshua, and where the Covenant was made, Numbers 22:1, 26:63 and 13:32.The covenant was made in 1400 BC at the end of Israel's forty-year wandering in the wilderness prior to their entry into the land of Canaan. The covenant replaces the Mosaic Covenant which ended with the crucifixion of Yeshua. The destruction of Jerusalem and dispersal of the Jewish nation in the Roman conquest of Jerusalem in AD 70 was ignited by the Jewish rebellion against Roman rule. 2 Deuteronomy 30:1. 3 Deuteronomy 10:3. 4 Ezekiel 16:60, Deuteronomy 29:1, Luke 22:20; Acts 20:28; 1 Corinthians 12:12, 13; Ephesians 3:9. Acts 15:14. 2 Deuteronomy 30:1. 3 Deuteronomy 10:3. 4 Ezekiel 16:60, Deuteronomy 29:1, Luke 22:20; Acts 20:28; 1 Corinthians 12:12, 13; Ephesians 3:9. Acts 15:14. 5 Daniel 11:1-45, others say as explained in portions of the book of Matthew 24:1-51, John 16:8, Ephesians 1:19-22, Luke 21:20. 6 Luke 19:41-44, 21:20 records Yeshua weeping openly when he foresaw the tribulations to come. Ezra 5:2 records building of the temple. The Temple was destroyed by the Romans during the Jewish uprising against Roman rule in AD 70, only a few years after its completion. From this point Judaism was spread around the world by exiles. It is prophesied that in the End Times the Jews shall build a temple ultimately to become occupied by the man of sin, the Anti-Christ, 2 Thessalonians 2:47. 7 Matthew 24:1, 2. Despite that Israel was the chosen nation, they did not choose God, hence they did not possess all the promised

land. The divine intent of the Palestinian Covenant refers to Abraham's salvation, lines of Ishmail and Isaac, according to Christian theology.

The covenant arose from the point that the whole generation of Israel, which had taken part in the covenant at Sinai, had not observed its tenets and because the *Old Covenant* included succeeding generations, its replacement was essential to maintain its duties and privileges, according to Christian theology.[8] The Order of Melchizedek is attributed to Yeshua:

> *"Yahweh hath sworn... Thou art a priest forever after the order of Melchizedek."* [9]

The millennial Temple shall be established by Yeshua for the duration of the kingdom age in the New Jerusalem; for the redeemed of all ages; the city, as the "Temple of God" in the New Jerusalem, shall be part of the new heaven and new earth in the sin-cleansed universe. [10]

The commission of sin with lawlessness[11] and sin relate to unrighteousness; and that to *confess sins* earns God's forgiveness from all unrighteousness;[12] and if we deny commission of sin by not repenting the word of God is not in us, according to Christianity. On the confession of sin some do not support the notion of confessing to a priest because he too is not without sin.[13]

According to Paul, no human is inherently righteous. All have sinned and have come short of the glory of God.[14]

> *"He who is without sin let him cast the first stone."* .[15]

The New Covenant and Administration of Fullness Times (the *New Covenant*) is based on the redemption work of Jesus and has application not only to the Church of Christ in this age but also to the restored nation of Israel in the age to come, according to Christian theologians. And, God provided a way of salvation for all believers in Christ, necessary as a means by which the true humanity of the Messiah could enter into human history. Christianity concludes that the permanent possession of a coming Messiah will flow from

Notes, references and comments:
8 *Unger' Survey of the Bible.* 9 Psalms 110:4.`Melchizedeck' is a combination of two Hebrew words: *melek*=king, and *tsedeq*=righteousness, denoting king of righteousness and is a 'typology' rather than a person. Melchizedek was the King and High Priest of Salem (Jerusalem) in the days of Abraham, Genesis 14:9-18, 14:18-20.Revelation 21:9-22:5, 21:1, 2. 11 Page 143 Concordance,

Holy Bible KJV; Isaiah 2:1-22; 1 John 3:4, NKJV. 12 1 John 5:17. 13 Since the moment of Yeshua's death when the *Veil of the Tabernacle* rent, believers gained direct access to God. It may be best to confess directly to God through Yeshua. See Part 3, Chapter 8, the *Crucifixion and Veil of the Tabernacle.* 14 Romans 3:9, 10, Perhaps one of the greater sins is to dwell upon the sins of others. Some Biblical sins have been relaxed by society, particularly divorce and remarriage. Jesus erased the old draconian order of the Old Testament, the beginning of the era of love, forgiveness, and peace. 15 Romans 3:23, 8:3:-7, Galatians 3:21, 22, Isaiah 64:6. Yet, some have the tendency to pontificate upon homosexuality, prostitution and other sins (so-called) on their high moral ground in the condemnation of the actions of others, a deviation from the teachings of Yeshua, whom they called Jesus Christ.

the lineage of Abraham through Isaac, not from Abraham through Ishmael. The timing of Isaac's birth is c.2061 BC. The birth of the Messiah's true humanity is over 20 generations into the future. It is also known as the Covenant of Grace, which Paul refers to as "fullness of time." [1]

The *New Covenant* requires obedience to the Old Testament Mosaic law, because the wages of sin is death. Jeremiah predicted that a redeemer would come to fulfil the Law of Moses and to create a new covenant between God and people. The old covenant was written in stone while the *New Covenant* is written in the human heart:

> *"I will make a new covenant with the people of Israel and Judah...and on that day I will put my law in their minds, and I will write them on their hearts.* [2]

After the last supper, Yeshua took another cup of wine symbolising his blood, said:

> *"This wine is the token of God's new covenant to save you – an agreement sealed*
> *with the blood I will pour out for you."* [3]

Believers can share in the inheritance from Yeshua who is the mediator of the promised eternal relationship with God.[4] In Israel's case the *New Covenant* is new in that it is the basis for the out calling of the new people of God, the Church, according to theologians, and it supersedes the *Mosaic Covenant* which Israel broke.

The *New Covenant* does not alter or conflict with the *Palestinian, Abrahamic* or *Davidic Covenants.* Although its blessing is in the future and assured by God's faithfulness, it includes spiritual regeneration and fellowship with God as a result of forgiveness and the complete removal of sin. [5] The *New Covenant* will cover kingdom age and the perfect age of New Heaven and New Earth that follows, guarantees eternal salvation, wherein is dispensation of the fullness of times. This perfect age is the prelude to eternity, when Jesus will surrender His perfect Kingdom to the Father, that God may be "all in all".[6]

"Behold the days have come ...that I will send a famine in the land, not a famine
of bread, not a thirst for water but of hearing the words of the Lord." [7]

Notes, references and comments:
1 Galatians 4:4, Romans 6:23, Unger's Survey of the Bible. Genesis 6, 9 (Noah); Genesis 12m 15m 17 (Abraham); Exodus 19-24 (Moses); 2 Samuel 7 (David); and finally in the New Covenant founded and fulfilled in Christ: In the *New Covenant*, we see the place of the Ark, in the heart, as emphasis is placed upon the spirit, the Ark of Covenant in the *Holy of the Holies;* Psalm 2 and 110, Isaiah 53, Philippians 2:5-11 and Revelation 5:9-10. 2 Jeremiah 31:31-34. 3 Luke 22:20. 4 Hebrews 9:15. 5 Jeremiah 31:33, 34. 6   Revelation 21:1 Corinthians 15:28. See also: Isaiah 46:9 on the power of God; Daniel 12:4 on the tribulations of the End Time and the increase of human knowledge by the command of God. 7 Amos 8:11.

Redemption means Salvation representing the entire work of God where by faith humans are rescued from the ruin of sin and receive eternal life now and eternal glory by the grace of God, [8] according to Christian theology. Sanctification is part of salvation, the setting apart of a saved person for God's worship and salvation embraces the past, present and future: Past tense: Humans were saved when they believed in Jesus.[9]

Present tense: the believer is being delivered from the power of sin by continuing in union with Jesus as seen by God in Jesus, progressive persistence to God's work and following God's will. [10]
Future tense: the believer will yet be saved into full conformity, the final phase of sanctification when the believer sees Jesus as made like Him and eternal destiny in glory.[11]

Salvation is in two parts: the saving work of Jesus completed to infinite perfection for all mankind and the saving work of God as accomplished when the sinner believes in Jesus; and includes redemption, reconciliation, propitiation, forgiveness, regeneration, justification, sanctification and glorification.[12]

Adam's sin is attached to the fallen race on the basis of original sin[13] and every descendant of Adam is prone to sin from birth but this evil station was judged by Jesus on the cross[14] never to be removed in this life. The believer receives triumphant power over death by the grace of God.[15] God's remedy for sin lies only in Jesus' atoning death both in prospect [16] or retrospect [17] which removes death, the penalty of sin. The unsaved will answer for their sin by punishment both on Earth and eternally in Gehenna. By walking in the law of the spirit in Christ Jesus makes one free from the law of sin and death.[18]

According to Christian theology, sincere personal faith in Jesus is all that is needed:

> "According to the grace of God which was given to me...as builder I have laid
> the foundation...another builds on it. But let each one take heed [how] he builds
> on it. " [19]

Notes, references and comments:
8 Luke 7:50, 1 Corinthians 1:30; 1:18; & 2 Corinthians 2:15. 9 1 Corinthians.1:2. 10 Ephesians 2:5-8. 11 Romans 29-30, 6:11, Galatians 2:19, 20; 2 Corinthians. 3:18, John 1:12. 11 Romans 6:11, 8:29, 13:11.12 John 3:16, 2 Corinthians 5:17, Colossians 2:10, Romans 6:13, 8:29, 1 Corinthians. 15:49, Romans 3:25. 13 Philippians 3:21.14 1 Corinthians 15:54-56, 1 John 3:2. 15 Romans 5:12-18. 16 Romans 6:10. 17 Romans 8:2, Galatians 5:16-25.18 1Corinthians 3:9-15, 1 Peter 2:24, 2 Corinthians 5:10, Ephesians 2:8-10, John 3:16, 36, 5:24, Romans 1:16, 5:1. 19 1 Corinthians 3:9-15, 1 Peter 2:24, 2 Corinthians 5:10, Ephesians 2:8-10, John 3:16, 36, 5:24, Romans 1:16, 5:1; by baptism sinner/believer is welcomed into the body of Jesus. purpose for mankind, Matthew 7:21.

12 God of People

Religion and faith are two different things. Religion is attached to ritual in the habitual attendance of church (Christian) or prayer several times a day at a mosque (Islam) and is not by itself an expression of faith; as one may *habitually* eat or be at a particular time in a particular place. The futility of religious ritual is mentioned in the Bible; [1] mock solemnity; [2] lip service; [3] or singing deceptive works.[4] Faith is the placing of trust in a particular super being with the belief that God is effective everywhere, can be worshiped anywhere and by anyone, and at any time. Universally most faiths carry the notion that higher powers consist of both gods and demons and there is no equality between them; and God being the good protector holding powers stronger than those of Satan. Some believe that we live in Satan's world managed by demons where God or gods play no role. Most Christians, as those of other faiths, believe that God cannot deliberately harm humans but that misfortunes are as a consequence of the individual's actions; while others believe that evil actions are motivated by demons posing as humans. Many cultures have lacked industrial development or literacy, but seemingly, none has been without a religion since the dawn of time.[5] However much religious faiths may differ in practice, their objective is to serve humanity, as expurgatory to individuals or communities, obedience to moral norms and, by some governments, as an instrument of social control. Believers humble and surrender themselves to invisible spiritual forces.

Sacredness is attached to most religions. Nearly everything on earth has been vested with sacredness by a variety of people. Things that are treated as sacred are usually natural and visible, such as hills, rivers or snakes. In India the River Ganges is regarded as holy where ashes of the dead are dispersed as a sanctified farewell but its waters must be highly polluted by all that is thrown into it. People living near the sea worship the sea and its

Notes, references and comments:
1 Amos 5:21-23. 2 Isaiah 58:4, 5. 3 Amos 5:26. 4 Jeremiah 7:4: turn to songs of Lamentation and Mourning. 5 A Lions Handbook: *The World's Religions*. Collins *Latin-English Dictionary,* and Readers Digest *Word Power Dictionary:* the Latin term *Religio* defines different beliefs as supernatural, superstition, reverence, sacred, among other generic connotations; and the belief in and worship of a superhuman controlling power, especially a personal God or gods usually complemented by some ritual based on an iconic human figure or iconic effigy or some invisible being. Since the nineteen sixties the idea of icons evolved to

superstars or celebrities who are considered by devotees as outstanding in their particular fields. Some become idolised seemingly eternally such as Elvis Presley and many others; and persons or things become icons to those who are impressed by them. As the Dalai Lama said: *"Human beings need more than material things – they need spiritual sustenance."* Quoted by N D Patel, historian: *"All traditions and cultures pre-date any known religion in the world."* Why are there so many different faiths in people created by one God? However much we may differ in the methods of worship but we are all subject to some immutable Divine Law or Law of Nature by which we all subconsciously abide by – in this lies proof of the equality of all humans and any differences are man-made. At the core of most faiths, is *belief in an invisible supreme being*, the manifestation of a single God of people.

creatures. Mountain dwellers have held certain rocks as sacred in the same way as the Hebrews viewed Mount Sinai. In the book of *Genesis* we are told that God created man in His own image thereby attaching Godliness to person and human attributes to God. According to this belief, God resembles not a snake, a hill or water but human and God. Religious differences also reflect cultural differences. Most people claim theirs to be the true faith hence to the true God. In one individual there is one point of view and there are as many different points of view in as many individuals. Why do people believe in religion? There are things which are beyond human understanding, such as death, particularly death of an infant or a child who has not lived life to the full. Religion may not answer inexplicable questions but it somewhat eases the situation to the believers; from the position of perplexity religion fills the vacuum. Human curiosity motivates the human mind to seek an explanation for the unknown.

Monotheistic Faiths are eschatological and promise the believer forgiveness of sin, resurrection, and eternal life traced to Abraham: Isaac, Judaism; Jesus, Christianity; and Ishmael, Islam, and the Baha'i Faith. Not all individuals share the *wish to live forever*, however, particularly those who believe in reincarnation within the majority of Indian religious tradition such as Hinduism, Jainism and Sikhism among others. To this day Judaism does not regard Jesus to be the Messiah - they are still waiting for the Messiah though they accept that Jesus is a Jew.

> *"It is not the logical substance of the Old Testament that [arrests] the mind of man but the sonorous strophes of the ancient bards and Prophets...[nor] is it the system of jurisprudence of the New Testament that melts his*

heart...but simply the poetical magic of the Sermon on the Mount...and the incomparable story of the Child in the Manger..." [6]

Seventh-day Adventist **is the Church that had extended faith and health around the world. Ellen Gould White (née Harmon, November 26, 1827 – July 16, 1915) was a prolific author and an American Christian pioneer. Along with other Sabbatarian Adventist leaders, such as Joseph Bates and Ellen's husband James White, formed what is now known as the Seventh Day Adventis Church.**

Messianic Fellowship is a Fellowship of Jacob's Ladder, a Congregation of Jews and Gentiles who believe in Yeshua. Their objective is vibrant and caring fellowship with mutual trust. [7]

Notes, references and comments:
6 J L Menckren, *Selected Prejudices* (see Bibliography). 7 Genesis 28:12, 13. Judaism generally regards Jesus as one of a number of Jewish Messiah claimants who have appeared throughout history, and Jesus as the most influential, hence damaging of all messiahs; and those Jews who follow the Messianic faith are not regarded as Jews by those who believe in Judaism, author's anecdotal testimony. It is generally understood that being Jewish means being a descendant of Reference 7 continued below...

Born Again Christianity also known as regeneration is a novel concept of Christianity that has become increasingly popular, particularly since the late 1980s. Discoursing with Nicodemus, Jesus says:
   "Except a man is born again he cannot see the kingdom of God."

Nicodemus is confused and asks:
   "...enter the womb and be born again?"

Jesus clarifies:
   "... born of water (baptism) and spirit ...born of flesh is flesh, of spirit is spirit." [8]

The phrase "born again" has raised some questions among scholars about its meaning and authenticity. Some say there has been a need for the renewal of Christ's mission and fulfilment of the Scriptures.[9] Born Again Christianity has been on rise in various modes of worship that differs markedly from traditional Christianity evolving to new charismatic churches. A good number of Born Again Christian organisation groups from non-European countries, particularly Africa, spread the message of Jesus to modern day European heathens. [10]

Notes, references and comments:

Reference 7 continued: Abraham, Isaac and Jacob and follower of Judaism. "Messianic" refers to anyone, Jew or Gentile who has chosen to follow the Messiah Yeshua (Jesus). Perhaps one could say "Messianic Fellowship" is a meeting point between Judaism and Christianity where members can keep Biblical *kashrut*, Kosher laws, the body of Jewish religious law as concerning suitability of foods, the use of ritual objects, and other customs freely without legalism, as a way to worship God. 8 John 3:1-21; Ephesians 5:18: *"Be filled with spirit,"* John 3:3-21. 9 9 Continued: 1 Corinthians 12:4, 30; It is said the person of the Holy Spirit is at work in co-equally, co-eternally and in co-existent as one unit: Father, executive, Son architect, and the Holy Spirit, contractor; and that gifts and power come through the Holy Spirit who is the Old Testament anointer. This kind of analysis is influenced by the earthly human government model: God = head of state; Son = crown prince; and Holy Spirit = prime minister? According to Bart E Ehrman, this confusion is because in Greek (the language of the gospel) the word *again* is ambiguous, it might mean *again* or a *second time* or *from above.* In the time of Jesus, when the Jews were speaking Aramaic. The rise of "born again" may be attributed to *change,* in the evolution of all things: change is inevitable because people who hold or lead "contemporary ideals" pass away and new ideals are born, regardless of whether or not they are based on a definite ideal in a contemporary setting. 10 In Born Again Christian worship the mode of prayer has changed from the traditional old hymns accompanied by organ music to pop-like hymns with a live band consisting of guitars and drums, accompanied by dancing, and some, include sensual dancing. Similar to the theme of traditional churches, the leaders seek to provide social services in fieldssuch as education, medical facilities, orphanages and other humanitarian services and general fellowship. And, there are also those who are in the business of vending God through Christ and do so well financially, not unlike some in traditional Christianity, particularly the mother of Christianity, the Roman Catholic Church.

In Islam the key beliefs are: oneness and the omnipotence of Allah, God; regard the world as good; see and feel God's presence everywhere:

> *"No vain discourse shall they hear therein...but only the cry, 'Peace!' Peace!'* [11]

Pope John Paul II who commends [Islam's] social justice, moral welfare, peace freedom for benefit of mankind and says of Islam:

"The Church also has a high regard for the Muslims, who worship one God ...as a result of their monotheism. Beautiful names in the human language are given to the God of the Koran ...but ultimately a God outside of the world, a God who is only Majesty, never 'Emmanuel, God with us...human rights and principle of religious freedom are...interpreted in a very one sided way ... freedom to impose on all citizens the "true religion." [12]

Jehovah Witnesses is a millenarian restoration Christian denomination with non-trinitarian beliefs distinct from mainstream Christianity.In 1870 Charles Taze Russell (1852-1916) and others formed a group in Pittsburgh, Pennsylvania to study the Bible. During the course of his ministry, Russell disputed many beliefs of mainstream Christianity including immortality of the soul, hell-fire, and that Jesus is not God but son of God. Jehovah Witnesses believe that Jesus was crucified on a stake and not on a cross. Elliott Kenan Kamwana Achirwa (c. 1872–1956) was a preacher in Nyasaland (now Malawi) who popularised the Watchtower movement into Southern Easterm and Central Africa, and subsequently created his own independent Church, the "Mlondo" meaning Watchman Mission.

The Baha'i Faith is a monotheistic religion that emphasises the spiritual unity of all mankind. The key beliefs are: there is one God who is the source of all creation; all major world religions come from the same spiritual source and the same God; among the revealers of the word of God (described as Manifestations of God) are Abraham, Krishna, Zoroaster, Moses, Buddha, Jesus, Muhammad and Baha'u'lla, who, from age to age, unfold the same spiritual truths plus new social teachings to meet the needs of humanity's evolving understanding of God's will and purpose.

Baha'u'llah says:
> *"The Bearers of the Trust of God are made manifest unto the peoples of the earth as the Exponents of a new Cause and the Revealers of a new Message. Inasmuch as these Birds of the celestial Throne are all sent*

Notes, references and comments:

11 Muhammad, as quoted by Baha'u'llah. 12 Pope John Paul II, *Crossing the*

Threshold of Hope, the imposition on all citizens of the true faith is not confined to Islam, the Catholic Church surpasses other religions in this aspect, author's observation.

> *down from the heaven of the Will of God, and as they all arise to proclaim His irresistible Faith, they, therefore, are regarded as one soul and the same person. For they all drink from the one Cup of the love of God, and all partake of the fruit of the same Tree of Oneness. "It is clear and evident to thee that all the Prophets areTemples of the Cause of God, who have appeared clothed in divers attire. If thou wilt observe with discriminating eyes, thou wilt behold them all abiding in the same tabernacle ..." 13*

The conviction that we belong to one human family is at the heart of the Baha'i Faith and the principle of oneness of humankind the pivot round which all the teachings of Baha'u'llah revolve, all humans having been created spiritually equal in the sight of God and the diversity of race and colour appreciated as making the world more beautiful. Baha'is strive to live a spiritually orientated life accompanied by deeds. Perhaps among prophets of non-Christian religions, Baha'u'llah surpasses in spreading the teachings of Jesus, as can be seen in the following quote from his writings:

> *"The Great Being saith: Blessed and happy is he that ariseth to promote the best interests of the peoples and kindreds of the earth. In another passage He hath proclaimed: It is not for him to pride himself who loveth his own country, but rather for him who loveth the whole world. The earth is but one country, and mankind its citizens.* 14

On life and death, the Baha'i teachings say that the purpose is to understand that life is not the changes and chances of this world, and its true significance is found in the development of the soul. True life, the life of the soul, occurs in this world for a brief time and continues eternally in other worlds of God.

Hinduism sees *everything* in terms of "godliness", carries a trinity of gods, who are manifestations of Brahma, the *One Creator* whose tear was the source of the sacred River Ganges. Hinduism replaced Buddhism in northern India by the eleventh century AD.[15]

Notes, references and comments:
13 Abbud, Mazra'ih and was succeeded by his son Abdu'l-Baha. The faith evolved from a single individual to an administrative order with both elected bodies and appointed individuals. Gail Marzieh, ed *Selections from the Writings of Abdu'l-Baha*. There are about five million Baha'is around the world in more than two hundred countries. Shrine of Bab and garden on Mount Carmel, Haifa, Israel, is the world centre of Baha'i Faith. Baha'u'llah: *"So powerful is the light of unity that it can illuminate the whole earth."* 14 Gleanings From the Writings of Bahá'u'lláh, Author: Bahá'u'lláh, Source: US Bahá'í Publishing Trust, 1990 pocket-size edition, Pages: 79-80: "God, the Creator, saith: There is no distinction whatsoever among the Bearers of My Message. They all have but one purpose; their secret is the same secret. To prefer one in honor to another, to exalt certain ones above the rest, is in no wise to be permitted. Every true Prophet hath regarded His Message as fundamentally the same as the Revelation of every other Prophet gone before Him. If any man, therefore, should fail to comprehend this truth, and should consequently indulge in vain and unseemly language, no one whose sight is keen and whose understanding is enlightened would ever allow such idle talk to cause him to waver in his belief."
Reference 15 continued below...

Behind the countless Hindu gods and goddesses (deities) lies Brahman, the supreme reality, infinite, impersonal, uncreated, unnameable; and buried beneath layers of egotism; and at the core of every human being is the divine spark, *Atman*. Worship and manifestations of Brahman: Brahma, the Creator. Siddhartha Gautama, defines certain self actions as enemies of the individual; such as sensual passions, discontent, hunger and thirst, craving, terror, uncertainty, hypocrisy, stubbornness; wrongfully gained: offerings, fame and status; self-praise and disparagement of others:

> *"Hatred does not cease by hatred but only by love."* [16]

Bhaktivedanta Swami Prabhpada who coined the phrase "Krsna Consciousness", held the teachings of Yeshua as similar to the Hindu; and other Hindu writers wrote about Christ Consciousness interchangeably with "Krsna Consciousness":

"Peace comes from within. Do not seek it without" - Buddha.

Reincarnation is at the heart of Hinduism, though other faiths believe in incarnation, which is the religious or philosophical concept that the soul or spirit, after biological death, begins a new life in a new body. This belief is also shared by other faiths or Indian religions and various ancient and modern **religions, such as Spiritism, Theosophy, and Eckankar, found in many tribal societies around the world, in places such as Siberia, West Africa, North America and Australia. These groups include Kabbalah, Cathars, Druze, and Rosicrucian, and others.**

Notes, references and comments:
Reference 15 continued: Gautama Buddha (title), `Enlightened One' or `Awakened One', founder of Buddism. (c.563-c483 BC), philosopher, teacher and religious leader. Buddhism could be regarded as a different expression of `monotheistic' faith. *"Judge not lest ye be judged".* This is the eternal rule of Hinduism, not dissimilar to the teachings of Yeshua: *"...the end sum of the law is love others as yourself".* There are extraordinary connections between Druidry and Hinduism which cancels the split between East and West, according to Gaius Plinius Secundus, 23/24-79 AD; the keywords are: Druidry, Hinduism, spirituality, common ancestry, East and West and Proto-Indo European Archaeological and genetic evidence support the theory of their common ancestry. There are similarities in beliefs, spiritual practices, myths, symbols, laws and customs. The Roman writer Pliny the Elder believed "Druid" to be a cognate with the Greek word "drus," meaning "an oak." "Dru-wid" combines the root words "oak" and "knowledge", "wid" means "to know" or "to see" - as in the Sanskrit languages. 16 The concept of rebirth or reincarnation is a belief held by historic figures such as Pythagoras, Plato and Socrates; Taliaferro, Charles, Draper, Paul, Quinn, Philip L: *A Companion to Philosophy of Religions*, John Wiley & Sons, 2010, page 640, Google Books. **Reincarnation research of Ian Stevenson, MD, involves children's past life memories that can be factually verified, ISIS.net published on May 21, 2013. Dr Smikiw also introduced the reincarnation case of Anne Frank/Barbro Karlen, child prodigy writer, much like Anne, who related her childhood past life memories of being Holocaust victim Anne Frank, who was persecuted as a Jew by the Nazis. Barbro was born into a Christian family in Sweden nine years after Anne's death.**

The historical relations between these sects and the beliefs about reincarnation, are characteristic of Neoplatonism,   Orphism, Hermeticism, Manicheanism and Gnosticism of the Roman era, though in modern times reincarnation is popular in America and at least half the world. The majority of sects of the Abrahamic

monotheistic religions do not believe in incarnation, though some do refer to it.

Mahatma Gandhi (a Hindu, 1869-1948) said Jesus was the greatest teacher humanity has ever had and to his believers he was God's only begotten son. Gandhi asks:

> *"If I do not accept this belief would it diminish its influence upon my life? I think not."*

He adorned the wall over his desk with a picture of Jesus and *The Sermon on the Mount* was a source of guidance and inspiration to him. He said to be a good Hindu meant that he would be a good Christian, no need for him to become a Christian to be a believer or try to follow the beauty of the teachings of Jesus. Of Jesus he said:

> *"Jesus' own life is the key to His nearness to God. He expressed, as no other*
> *could, the spirit and will of God."*

Yoga **places emphasis on spiritual values in self-realisation to become a high-souled being. The teachings of Yoga were mastered by Paramahansa Yogananda (1893-1993), fifth in line of Gurus since Bhagavan Krishna, great deity of later Hinduism worshipped as incarnation of Vishnu. On *karma,* the effects of past actions in this or a former life (from Sanskrit verb *kri, "to do"*) teaches that even one with the worst of karma loses the effects of past bad actions by constant meditation on God, the way to attain peace; and one who puts trust in God never perishes.** [17]

Confucianism **is the moral philosophy of Confucius/K'ung Fu'Tzu, a Chinese civil servant who became a teacher to whoever was willing to be taught, regardless of wealth or class.**

Notes, references and comments:

[17] **Paramansa Yogananda,** *Autobiography of a Yogi*: **Not unlike the teachings of Jesus. Yoga teaches that to serve mankind is one's larger Self,**

and to seek complete harmony and basic oneness of original Christianity as taught by Jesus Christ and original Yoga as taught by Bhagavan Krishna. According to Emerson, "all science is transcendental or passes away. Botany is now acquiring the right theory – the avatars of Brahma will presently be the textbooks of natural history", Paramansa, The wireless inventions of J C Bose, India's great scientist, ante-dated those of Marconi. The Lotus flower is an ancient divine symbol in India; its unfolding petals suggest the expansion of the soul in its pure beauty and from the mud of its origin holds a benign spiritual promise. Paramansa Yogananda, Self-Realisation Fellowship, hold that "no department of study, particularly in the humanities, in any major university can be fully equipped without a properly trained specialist in the Indic phases of its disciplines..."

> *"He who respects others will not be insulted;*
> *he who tolerates will win popular support;*
> *he who acts in good faith will be trusted by others;*
> *he who is diligent will succeed in his undertakings;*
> *he who is generous will make others work hard for*
> *him."*   - Confucius

Taoism and Confucianism, two of three faiths of China developed before contact with the rest of the world, unlike the monotheistic religions, which are religions with God at the centre. The Chinese Taoist philosophy is a holistic **discipline that combines the spiritual and the physical. Taoism is the closest thing to indigenous religion in China. Everything in the universe is in constant** state of change in the interplay of the great forces of the Cosmos in two symbolic principles of the egg/Yin and sperm/Yang, in the energetic dance of life and regeneration. [18]

Sikhism **originated in the fifteenth century AD amid conflicts between Muslims and Hindus in northern India. Offering a simple monotheism, it was intended as a peaceful middle way by its founder. Those faithful to Sikhism strive for union with Satguru, God, by adoring the Holy Name, through hard work and by being of service to others, especially their own family.**[19]

The Quakers, or Society of Friends', fundamental principle is "Freedom of Conscience". The English jury's right, according to their *conscience,* to bring in a verdict on the accused in a court of law, has its roots in the Quakers. The Quakers are opposed to wars or killing and are

Conscientious Objectors. Their motto of *"peace"* was taken from the Qur'an:

> *They who worship the Merciful One are they who walk on the earth gently and*
> *who, when fools speak to them, say "Peace".* [20]

Notes, references and comments:
18 Founded in the 6th century BC by the reclusive scholar and poet Lao Zi (Lao Tsu) 551-479 BCE. The Idea of Zi that became systems of social ethics which greatly influenced Chinese society after his death. Chinese religion is unique in that it first developed in isolation from the world's great religions. 19 Guru Nanak (1469-1539), Paul Carus (1852-1919) on Sikhism. 20 Quoran 25.64, Holy book of Islam revelation of Allah (God) to Mohammed (d. AD 632). Should a Christian be involved in police or military service? Paul says: *"If rulers serve well and justly they are God's ministers because they* **restrain evil,"** **Romans 13:2-7; soldiers were shot for defecting, though not any more, but society is continually evolving and the laws that govern it. George Fox could not accept the churches were presenting true followers of Jesus; he believed the divine spirit. is in every person and all have immediate : access to God & God to all. He taught that religion of love taught by Jesus, was a way of life which should embrace our daily life. William Penn and William Meade were charged at the Old Bailey for preaching in Green church Street. The jury refused to bring in a guilty verdict & the judge jailed them for contempt. The English jury's right to bring in a verdict `according to their conscience'**
Reference 20 continued below...

The Rosicrucian distinguishes Jesus from Christ: Jesus is a high Initiate of the human life wave evolving within the cycle of birth having a pure mind. Jesus is the immortal while Christ is buried in the heart. That Jesus was educated during his youth among the essences and thus prepared Himself for the greatest honour bestowed upon a human being. His highly evolved physical body had already been attuned to high vibration of the "Life Spirit", in the moment of the baptism, to the Christ for His earthly ministry. At the crucifixion the Christ was released from the body of Jesus that entered into the earth. [21]

Christian Science maintains that Jesus as a man on earth was not the exact equivalent to God, He thoroughly embodied the spiritual son of God having the nature of God; and that the Christ, or divine manifestation of God, continues infinitely to enlighten humanity and to destroy sickness, sin and death. [22]

The Church of Jesus Christ of Latter-day Saints, **also known as Mormonism, is just one example of the rise of many Christian denominations who had their own visions that led or lead to new Christian cults.** [23]

Since the advance of science **religion became increasingly seen as a "crank" idealism.** [24]

Notes, references and comments:

Reference 20 continued: has its roots in the Quakers who had a difficult passage in the freedom of faith & most emigrated to the colonies where the Puritans were more tolerant of their faith. William Penn founded Pennsylvania (USA) where Quaker principles could be practised in government; which was followed by 70 years of peace & stability; and most of its principles were embodied in the constitution of USA. Penn's treaty with Indians (1683) established peace, and Voltaire said: "...the only treaty never sworn to, never broken..." 21 Max Heindel, *The Rosicrucian Cosmo-Conception* (Part 111, Chapter XV), *Christ and his Mission.* 22 Founder Mary Baker Eddy (1821-1910). 23 Founded by Prophet Joseph Smith Jr (1805-1844), in New York in 1820. The church has its own Bible, though based on the Old and New Testaments *The Book of Mormon – Another Testament of Jesus Christ.* James 1:5. Affected by the great religious excitement around Manchester, New York, fourteen year old Joseph Smith went to a secluded wood and prayed for God's guidance where he met God and Jesus who told him not to join any of the churches. Thereafter, he claimed to have been visited by an angel named Moroni who told him of an ancient record on God's dealings with former inhabitants of the American continent. He translated the words by the gift of God, and the result was the Book of Mormon, published in 1830. The motto: *"You have got to learn how to be Gods yourselves, and to be kings and priests of God, the same as all Gods have done before you." The Journal of Discourses,* Vol. VI, page 4. The Mormon church places emphasis on code of dress. Most members of the Mormon Church met by the author, including other people's comments, and pictures of the founder, exhibit film star-like appearance as the early Hollywood film stars. 24 Particularly Richard Dawkins, *The God Delusion.* Who says those who believe in God are "ignorant, stupid or insane". One should be free to express belief without being ridiculed. Is the obsolescence by design of the natural function of male sperm and female ovum ethically acceptable? Does genetically modified (GM) food improve nutritious value? To some, playing God may not be acceptable, but all things are free - God denies us nothing but we take the consequences of our actions.

An inspiring statement is by McGrath:

> *"I had loved the natural sciences since I can remember loving anything...*
> *as a Christian theologian who believes it is essential to listen seriously...*
> *carefully to criticism of my discipline..."* [25]

There is a general tendency among some to regard the religions of Africa as mere superstitions but the basis of all human existence is *belief in the supernatural.* In African religions, amongst the hundreds of clans, there is not a single sacred book like the Bible or the Q'uoran. This is because of the lack of the art of writing. Chinua Achebe gives an account of a festival which takes place before the start of cultivation of crops.[26] In most African societies there is the belief, that at the origin of all things there is one *Supreme Being,* Cauta (God), also called Mulungu or *Namalenga,* the latter literally meaning "Creator" in most Bantu languages. Names of the long dead are perpetuated in new born babies of any era as a unifying force with ancestors; and the belief that the names carry them to infinity. [27] African religions worship the spirits of ancestors who dwell in the mysterious realm of the Supreme Being, and are more conversant with that realm. Islam (c. eighth century) and Christianity (eighteenth century) had a great impact on Africa but some still transmit traditional African faith into new faiths, and respect for ancestral spirits remains strong in family ties.

Animatism developed into **Animism**, the spirit-fearing religion of most isolated tribal people. People of certain cultures believe that animals, plants, and inanimate objects were endowed with certain powers, which were both impersonal and supernatural. [28]

Sathya Sai Baba Movement
A follower of Jesus, Sai Baba's primary teachings are: love for all creatures; service to others; curb one's desires; the world is an illusion (*maya*) only God is real; every person is God in form (though most do not experience this as reality); meditation; the acceptance of all religions as ways to the realisation of the one God; non-violence (*ahimsa*); peace (*shanthi*); right conduct and living in accord with natural truth. [29]

Zoroastricism, **an ancient semi-dualisticmonotheist religion of Greater Iran is much like the Roman religion for Rome, which was adopted in differing forms as the generally inclusive overarching state religion of the Achaemenid Empire and subsequent Parthian and Sasanin**

Notes, references and comments:

25 Alister Edgar McGrath, *Iustitia Dei: A History of the Christian Doctrine of Justification,* **pages 2 and 13.** 26 Chinua Achebe, *Things Fall Apart.* 27 Author's anecdotal evidence. **28 T**erm Animism was coined by English anthropologist R.R. Marett (1866–1943). **The channel of communication was religion between the living and the dead ancestors which gave a chance to the living to renew their social covenants and unity. 29 Sathya Sai Baba, 1926-2011, Saint, born in India, spiritual leader claimed to be reincarnation of Sai Baba, born Pathri, India – d.1918), author's enecdotal evidence by**

(or Sassanid empires),[30] lending it immense prestige in ancient times. Consequently, several aspects of Zoroastricism including messianism, either influenced or inherited contemporary and later religions including Second Temple Judaism, Gnosticism, Christianity and Islam. Zoroastricism gradually became marginalised and somehow absorbed by Islam from the 7th century with the decline of the Sasanian Empire. Currently Zoroastrians are estimated to be 2.6 million most in India and Iran. **Zoroastrianism has no major theological divisions though it is not uniform.**

The worship of Mammon may not be regarded as a religion but it is the god of money who has existed since the beginning of time though more and more worshiped by those who seek wealth in material things. Some Christians become wealthy by preaching as if God was a piece of merchandise to be vended. Jesus said:

"No one can serve two masters ...You cannot serve God and mammon." [31]
make friends for yourselves by unrighteous mammon, that when you fail,
they may receive you into an everlasting home."

Fanaticism in Religion is dangerous when people *impose* their beliefs upon others; or use religion to persecute those whose faith differs from theirs; or to control society; or engage in bad intentional acts, under the pretext of faith; or by looking for a lucrative means; and other reasons which are not for the common good.

Notes, Reference and Comments:
30 Also called Zarathustraism, Mazdaism or Magianism. Modern era influences have a significant impact on individual and local beliefs, practices, values and vocabulary. A good number of religions combine faith with health in varying degrees, for the good of humanity. J Hinnel, *The Penguin Dictionary, Penguin Books UK* (1997). The intention of most faiths is to serve and direct humanity. Faith of whatever kind should not be blamed but only those individuals or organisations who use their faith for bad intentional acts. It is not the kind of faith but in whose hands it is. Is science or religion put to good use? By 2010 it became possible for lesbian or gay couples to have a child carrying their blood lines aided by scientific technology. Some ask, if this is ethical, while others say "man playing God." 31 Matthew 6:24, Perhaps there is no other time Mammon has been so worshiped as in the first quarter of the twenty-first century. A church, mosque or any other place of worship reflects a particular kind of society as God is not only found in designated places of worship; not only prayer at a particular place of worship leads man to the path of righteousness but to *do no harm to any one.* A worshiper in any place of worship who carried out evil deeds could not be exonerated from such conduct because of attendance at a place of worship. Any conduct that causes suffering to anyone upsets the equilibrium and as such could not receive God's blessing. Nonetheless, every kind of faith has its opponents who present their own reasons for rejecting any faith and argue what they believe in is the "only truth". Many sacred writings in various religions are classed as Holy Scriptures. Faith is an aspect of 'ideology' and most ideologies once confirmed become self-existent entities – independently rolling on as the celestial bodies. And, the *Du Bartas syndrome* is apparent in most faiths because of the differing opinion of the teachers.

Fanatics of most religions claim their religion to represent the true God. Another difficulty with religion, as in science, is that religion is not always put to good use nor does religion promote peace all the time but promotes unity or solidarity only within limits.
Examples are India at the attainment of its independence (1947) split into India and Pakistan; Northern Ireland was divided on denominational differences; as the endless conflict between Israelites and Arabs over Palestine. The history of religion is written, not with ink, but with blood, particularly Christianity, Islam, and Judaism, for

inexplicable reasons. African traditional religion was never a source of conflict such as that found among Western and Eastern faiths though Africans were divided by tribalism.

Epilogue

In addition to Biblical Gospels, I have analysed the Coptic Gospel of Thomas, discovered in 1945 among the Gnostic texts at Nag Hammadi in Upper Egyp; and the writings of Ehrman on early Christianity based on his comprehensive, careful, and methodical researches. His account on Christianity is mind-opening on politics, power, and the clash of claims among Christians in the decades before one group came to see its views prevail. Modern archeology has recovered a number of key texts, and as Ehrman shows, these ostentatious finds reveal religious disparity that confirms much about the ways in which history gets written by the winners. It is worthy of note that not only those who claim to be Christians believe in Jesus, but also people of other faiths and the big question is:

" *After Jesus, the lead messenger, what has the Christian messenger, delivered*

   about the message the Bible holds?"

Faith is the belief in something for which there is no evidence. Individual perception of the world differs markedly, more so where faith is concerned, particularly in the interpretation and the understanding of the Bible. The Christian fath, as other faiths, is based on legacy over the centuries and no one is eye-witness to events that led or lead to the formation of beliefs. Any faith lies in hope in the individual mind. And, each individual has the right and freedom of spirit to hold a personal view on faith; and the views of others on faith deserve respect. Because of the lack of respect for the beliefs of others, the history of religion and faith has been written not with ink but with blood. Therefore, also analysed are the theory of Evolution, and, a few of the many religions that exist in our world – to keep an 'open mind'. Insular and encumbered as we are by gravity and self-centred by our false sense of importance rooted in the ego of the present, Christianity conditioned followers to believe that Planet Earth was the only place where humans were in God's universe. There may be other beings on other planets far more intelligent and compassionate than we are or worse.

But one can only ask more questions: Where did we come from? Some other planet to planet Earth? Why are we here? To be schooled or perfected? Where are we going from here? Are we to end up in heaven, hell or another planet to the sum of our deeds on planet Earth? And, the big question is: "*Is the promise of eternal life 'reserved' for only Christians? "*

The evidence about the coming and ministry of Jesus: The Bible; the Works of Flavius Josephus; Ian Wilson's book, which is well supported by archaeology - logical, historical, and other evidence; and other historical writings, indicate that the story of Yeshua is true. The "Sermon on the Mount" surpasses in moral standards, and teaches that love, truth, peace and charity are eternal and indestructible values. Among the great messengers of God's word chronologically before Jesus were Abraham, Krishna, Zoroaster, Moses, and Buddha. After Jesus were Muhammad, Baha'u'llah, Sai Baba, and others. Though the universal spread of Christianity was backed by imperial power, it is less than likely that writers of the New Testament of the Bible, writers of Jewish history, such as Flavius Josephus, who was a contemporary of Jesus, could have been complicit in recording Jesus as sinless. As one commentator on the Gospel of Thomas says:

> "...the living Jesus: probably not the resurrected Christ as commonly
> understood, but rather Jesus who lives through his sayings."

Faith is the substance of hope and the eternal light that lives in almost every heart and in the hope that we shall meet our loved ones including innocent infants in mortality; for it is hard to think that we can be happy in heaven if we have the thought that those we loved and who loved us on earth would not be present. One's awareness is among those who strive for love, truth, peace and charity now and in the hereafter. Revelation 21:4 tells us:

> "He will wipe every tear from their eyes. There will be no more death or

mourning or crying or pain, for the old order of things has passed away."

Book of Revelation reveals previously unknown secrets and the vision given to John, the Evangelist, during his exile in Patmos (c. 95-96 AD close to the reign of Domitian). A communication from Jesus in His glorified state said to have been given by God - Father to the Son, according to Christianity. The *Book of Revelation* is the climax to the preceding Books of the Bible and is written by John, to the Seven Churches of Asia signified by the seven golden candlesticks; and for the purpose of this book is about Past, Present and Future (Revelation 1:19):

The Almighty holds a blue print for each one of us, regardless of the circumstances of our birth, or how we die, even the aborted foetus (by design) or the miscarried foetus – such is the sanctity of the human being, God's beautiful ornament. And, although all of us have sinned in varying degrees, mercy is not beyond our reach, for *mercy overrides judgment* – the Cherubim at the entrance to the Garden of Eden represent mercy.

Testament: The Revelation of Yeshua Messiah = Jesus Christ – The Apocalypse stands in the closest affinity to the Gospel of John:

"The Son has everything the Father has and yet has nothing but what He has

of the Father."

God is the *Testator* through Yeshua whose testament took force after His death: The *Beneficiary* is the Believer in Yeshua and the *Bible* is the *witness* document recorded by God-inspired writers. The difference between the testament by a human, whereby the beneficiary benefits during life on Earth after the death of the testator, and the Biblical *Testament*, the Beneficiary/Believer benefits only after his or her own death – for the Believer follows Yeshua the way to God as all things are from God. And, there are some who have never been exposed to Christianity but 'believe' as evidenced by their actions, they too are children of the promise.

Given all the blood shed by the Jews and Arabs upon the Promised Land, for centuries to the present, is Palestine/Israel the Promised Land? Or is it symbolic to the heavenly Promised Land? Jesus said to the apostles but addressed to each one of us:

"I am with you always, until the end of age...Be not afraid".

BIBLICAL GLOSSARY OF WORDS

Glossary – interpretations taken from the *Oxford English Dictionary and Readers Digest Word Power.*

Adam – Hebrew – made from *adamah* earth, male meaning man, male or female not just male.

Advent - the first and second coming of Jesus.

Ark – Latin - Chest, or Noah' ship to save his family and animals from the Flood; Ark of the Covenant containing the Ten Commandments or ancient Scrolls kept in the Synagogue of the Hebrew.

Calvary Hill - Representation of place of Crucifixion, Roman Catholic church.

Christian orthodoxy- holding generally correct or currently held or accepted opinion: Eastern or Greek Church separated from Western Church, recognising Patriarch of Constantinople as head of national Churches or Russia, Romania and Greece; other: conforming to traditional/general belief as authoritatively established.

Chromosome - Threadlike structure found in the nuclei of most living cells carrying genetic information in the form of genes.

Clairvoyance - Exceptional insight or prediction opposed to Biblical prophesy.

Covenant – Latin *convenire* = come together a blood compact or solemn commitment between God and Israelites otherwise moral obligation or contract under seal.

Creation - act of creating especially the world of biological species to special creation not to evolution.

Currency - in spiritual terms the binding covenant otherwise commodity used as medium of exchange/money in the banking system of a country.

Decalogue - The Ten Commandments collectively.

Deify - make into or worship as a god.

Deity - divine status.

Dispensation - divine providence in management of people or community; other distribute, or imanage without.

Dogma - an inflexible principle or set of principles established by authority, doctrine or ideology.

Ecumenical - representing the whole Christian world.

Enlightenment, the - European intellectual movement of the late 17th and 18th centuries emphasising reason and individualism rather than tradition also collectively known as "founding fathers" of that era in modern thought. Also Nirvarna Buddhist state of enlightenment.

Enzyme - substance produced by a living organism and acting as a catalyst to promote a specific biochemical reaction, particularly in conception of life.

Eschatological - promise of life after death and resurrection.

Evolution - process by which different kinds of living organism are believed to have
developed from earlier forms especially by natural selection, or gradual development as opposed to Creation.

Exodus – the ancient departure of the Israelite from Egyptian bondage; mass departure of people especially emigrants.

Fanaticism - narrow minded or biased.

Galactic dust - relating to Galaxy or galaxies of the stars.

Gentile -person who is not Jew.

Griot – Portuguese *criado* - human archive in oral testimony or story teller, applying to societies without the art of writing.

Hades - dark underworld or abode of the spirits of the dead, Greek or *Sheol* in Hebrew.

Hallelujah – Hebrew: Hail YAHWEH - praise to God, Roman Catholic Church part of mass.

Hartlot - prostitute or promiscuous woman.

Holistic - tendency in nature to form wholes.

Indoctrination - teach, instruct or imbue with an idea or opinion.

Infinite - boundless, endless, continue indefinitely.

Laissez-faire - non interference policy of government in commerce, liberal in allowing free action.

Messianic - inspired hope or belief in a deliverer.

Magneto - electric generator using permanent magnets especially for ignition In internal combustion engines producing the required intermittent high tension current independently of a battery.

Metamorphosis - transformation of the body by resurrection.

Miscegenation - interbreeding of races particularly of whites and non-whites.

Monotheistic - belief that there is only one God.

Mortal - subject to death, especially human being and other organisms.

Omni – having jurisdiction in all things, all ways.

Omnipotent - having infinite absolute power.

Organism - organised body with interdependent parts sharing common life.

Ovum - female germ-cell capable of developing into individual organism when fertilised by male sperm.

Pater – Latin legal father – Biblical: Joseph legal father of Yeshua.

Pathology - science of bodily diseases.

Pentecost - Jewish harvest festival on 5th day after the 2nd day of Passover,
Leviticus 23:15, 16. In Hebrew Synagogue anniversary of giving law on Mount Sinai. In Christianity Whit Sunday after Easter commemorating descent of Holy Spirit at Pentecost, Acts 2.

Pharisee - member of ancient Jewish sect noted for their strict observance of traditional and written law, also a self-righteous person.

Plebeian or for short pleb - commoner in ancient Rome - person of the lower classes.

Prophet - person who predicts or foretells the future in a philosophical sense.

Prophesy - prediction of future Biblical events opposed to clairvoyancy.

Publican – owner/manager of a place where alcohol is consumed.

Redemption - deliverance from sin/ damnation in the atonement of Jesus.

Rent - to tear upwards or downwards, example: a veil or curtain.

Resurrection - rising of Jesus from the grave, rising again of dead before the last judgment.

Revelation - last Book of the New Testament which reveals the prophesies.

Sanction - penalty for disobedience or reward for obedience usually attached to law.

Scribe - ancient Jewish maker/keeper of records, person who can write or an ancient clerk.

Sinai – triangular pensula linking Africa with Asia, area: 61,000 square km; mountain place where Moses received the Ten Commandments.

Spermatozoon, spermatozoa singular - sperm in science or seed in Biblical understanding of organisms.

Tabernacle - tent, portable or temporary house – temporary temple or house of God.

Tares - injurious corn weed.

Theanthropic – Greek - both divine and human embodying deity in human form, Greek god-man.

Typological – Greek *tupos* - Biblical type.

Underdog - loser of a fight or one in a state of inferiority or subjection.

Usurpation - encroach or assume power or throne wrongfully.

Usury – Biblical sin of lending money for interest.

Veil - to separate from something, particularly separation of the general area and the sanctuary of a Jewish temple or tabernacle, other: disguise.

Vicarious - deputed or delegated, acting or done for another: the suffering of Yeshua for sinners.

Postscript

A wooden object known as *Ngoma Lungundu* claimed to be a replica of the *Ark of Covenant* went on display in 2010 at Harare Museum, Zimbabwe, Africa. It belongs to the Lemba people, black Africans who claim Jewish ancestry (BBC World Service/Africa 18/02/10).

The origin of the connection with the Lemba people is said to be Menelik, the son of King Solomon and Queen of Sheba, but there are conflicting accounts. The Hebraic account is that Solomon and Sheba were mere fellow monarchs engaged in the affairs of state.

Josephus records that the "queen of Egypt and Ethiopia" visited King Solomon. One account is that Queen Candace of Ethiopia visited Solomon, but Solomon could have been visited by many queens at the peak of his power and affluence.

The imperial family of Ethiopia claimed its origin directly from Menelik. One half of Ethiopians followed the law of Moses and the other half worshipped pagan gods. With few interruptions, the dynasty of Ethiopia lasted for close to three thousand years, next to China the oldest in the world – 225 generations, and the dynasty ended with the fall of Emperor Haile Selassie in 1974.

On the tabernacle and ark of covenant:

"The innermost chamber measured 30 feet and was similarly separated by a curtain from the outer part. Nothing at all was kept in it, it was unapproachable, inviolable, and invisible to all, and was called the *"Holy of the Holies"* - Book V, Chp. V 5: Williamson, page 304.

"The post-exilic temple apparently contained no Ark - *The Wars of the Jews, Book Five* - Josephus, the Jewish historian who lived in the time of Yeshua.

Sources:

Bibliography

Main references and most information have been selected from the following and applied to relevant chapters and quoted at the bottom of each page of the text. Most chapters contain only Biblical references as quoted:

THE HOLY BIBLE: *King James Authorised Version, The Spirit Filled Bible KJV* and *New King James Authorised Version.* To mark the 400th anniversary of the KJV publication in 1570 James Naughtie (BBC/Radio4 from 03/01/11, for seven days) told the story of how and why King James VI of Scotland, who later became James I of England, commissioned a new translation of the Bible. William Tyndale (c.1494-1536) made the first translation of the Bible into English directly from Hebrew and Greek at Oxford. The translators drew heavily on his work. Tyndale did so much for posterity in his translation of the non-English versions of the Bible. He was executed by the Belgian government when he attempted to translate the Bible without permission of the Church.

CROSSING THE THRESHOLD OF HOPE, a book by Pope John Paul II, written with humility and generosity sixteen years into his Papacy and on the eve of the Millennium; his message, quoting Jesus, is simply *"Be not afraid."* Published by Alfred A Knopf, New York 1994, edited by Vittorio Messori, translated from Italian by Jenny McPhee and Martha McPhee. In October 1993 Pope John Paul II, at the request of the Italian radio and television was interviewed by the Press Secretary for the Holy See, Dr Joaquin Navarro-Valls, a very competent ex Spanish psychiatrist who became a journalist.

JOSEPHUS, Flavius, *The Complete Works of Flavius Josephus.* 4 volumes to which are added Three Dissertations concerning Jesus Christ, John the Baptist, James the Just, God's Command to Abraham, with a complete Index (contained in Volume 4) to the whole translated by William Whiston, A M. London, William Tegg & Co. Cheapside, MDCCXLV111; Oxford printed by D A Talboys, commentary by Paul L Maier 1999 (English). Kregel Publications, Inc, P O Box 2607, Grand Rapids MI49501.

NEIL,William, *One Volume Bible Commentary*, Hodder and Stoughton Ltd. 1962.

PARAMAHANSA YOGANANDA, Autobiography of a Yogi, Self-Realisation Fellowship, founded 1920.

THE TIMES HISTORY OF THE WORLD, New Edition 2001, ISBN 0 7250 08949.

PAAS, Steven, *Christianity in Eurafrica,* published by New Academia Publishing, Washington DC; republication of the book in Wellington (South Africa in 2016, obtainable from Amazon.

UNGER, Merrill F, *Unger's Survey of the Bible*, particularly on chapters, 4, 6, 7, 8, 9, 10 and 12), Tyndale House, 1974. *Concise Bible Dictionary*, 1985, 1987, 1989, reprints by Baker Book House, USA.

WILSON, Ian, *Jesus: The Evidence*, 1984, Harper Collins Publishers, East 53rd Street, New York, NY10022. First published in Great Britain in 1996 under the same title by George Weidenfeld & Nicolson Ltd. This is one of most well-documented books on Jesus, supported by archaeological and historical evidence.

PART ONE -

Chapter 1: The Holy Bible -

DURANT, Will, *History of the King James Version of the Bible.*

Good News, page 3: *The Sinaiticus Codex* (Latin for Book) which was discovered by a German Scholar Tischendorf in 1844 at St Catherine's Monastery in the Sinai Peninsular in Egypt.

MEYER, Marvin, *The Gospel of Thomas, The Hidden Sayings of Jesus,* Interpretation by Harold Bloom; Harper Collins Publishers, New York 100022; ISBN 0-06065581-X.

NEIL, William, ditto.

STAGG, Evelyn and Frank, *Woman in the World of Jesus.* Philadelphia Westminster Press, 1978.

The Good News, November-December 2009.

UNGER, *Major Themes of the Bible.*

VEITH, Walter, *Battle of the Bible, Changing the Word*, CD's Parts 1, 2 and 3.

Chapter 2:

The 6 Covenants:

Abrahamic Covenant:

Father of nations, promise of land for the Israelite, A glimpse of

the Tabernacle: Isaac and first altar of the tabernacle.

HOSEN, Imran, *The Religion of Abraham & The State of Israel.*

Edenic Covenant:

Creation, genealogy of man.

Creation or Evolution?

BRECHT, Bertolt, *The Life of Galileo.*

CANN, Rebecca L, Mark Stoneking & Allan C Wilson, *Mitochondrial Eve, Mitochondrial DNA and Human Evolution*, Department of Genetics, University of Hawaii, Honolulu, Hawaii 96822; Durand, Michigan, *Ask a Scientist*, General Biology, 7 May 2005, *The Out of Africa theory;* and *Times History of the World*, Out of Africa second major dispersal of homo sapiens.

DAWKINS, Richard, presenter of *The Genius of Darwin*, TV Channel 4 programme, 04 August 2008 (in two sessions).

READERS DIGEST, *Facts at Your Fingertips,* Published by The Reader's Digest Association Limited, London, New York, Sydney, Montreal.

SYKES, Bryan, *The Seven Daughters of Eve,* 2001, ISBN-0-393-02018-5.

DAWKINS, Richard, ditto.

DEBUS, Allen G *Man and Nature in the Renaissance.*

FLETCHER, Richard, *The Conversion of Europe from Paganism To Christianity,* 371-1386 AD, Harper Collins Publishers, 1996.

KOESTLER, A1959 - *The Sleepwalkers: A History of Man's Changing Vision of the Universe.*

HARMAN, *The Scientific Revolution*, Ch. 9 of The New Cambridge Modern History, Vol.13 (Companion Volume).

JOSEPHUS, Flavius ditto.

Unger's Survey of the Bible.

WILSON, Ian ditto.

Further reading on the theory of evolution:

ATKINS, Peter William, *Creation Revisited*. 1993, W H Freeman & Co. Ltd. Special: Book Sources/0716745003.

AUST, Jerold, *The Good News,* November-December 2009 – *Creation or Evolution – Which is Believable?* P28.

BAKER, Paul T,1966 – *Human Biological Variation as an Adaptive Response to the Environment. Euginics Quarterly*, 13:81 – 91 *Mendel, His Work, and His Place in History. In: Proceedings of the American Philosophical Society,*

Vol.109, No 4 (Commemoration of the publication of Gregor Mendel's pioneer experiments in Genetics), August 18, Philadelphia: American Philosophical Society.

BODMER, W F and L Cavalli-Sforza, 1976, *Genetics, Evolution and Man.* San Francisco: W H Freeman and Company.

DARWIN, Charles, 1859 – *On the Origin of Species*. A Facsimile of the First Edition, Cambridge, Mass. Harvard University Press 1964.

DAWKINS, Richard, *The God Delusion,* Oxford University Press, New York. 1976.

The Good News, November-December 2009.

DUNN, L C, 1965. Lowenberg, Bert James, 1959, *Darwin, Wallace and the Theory of Natural Selection,* Cambridge, Mass. Arlington Books. Jensen, Karen & The Editors of US News Books, 1957, *Reproduction – The Cycle of Life.*

ENNS, Paul, *The Moody Handbook of Theology.*

HISLOP, Alexander, *The Two Babylons,* 1957, pp 97-98.

KELSO, A J 1974 – *Physical Anthropology* (2nd Ed.) New York: B Lippincott Co.

LINUS, Paulin 1974 – *Molecular Basis of Biological Specificity, Nature,* 248 (No. 5451): 769, 771.

LIVINGSTONE, Frank B, 1980 – *Natural Selection and the Origin of Maintenance of Standard Genetic Marker Systems. Yearbook of Physical Anthropology, 1980, 23: 25-42.*

MAWR, Bryn, Classical Review 2010.03.25, Berlin/New York: Walter de Gruyter, 2009. Pp. xiii, 476; 4 p. of plates. ISBN 9783110208085.

MAYR, Ernst and Provine, William B (eds) Cambridge, Mass. Harvard University Press 1980, *The Gene Machine;* ditto *The Evolutionary Synthesis.*

MORPHET, C, G*alileo and Copernican Astronomy* – A Scientific World View.

OLBY, Robert, 1974 - *The Path to the Double Helix,* Seattle, University of Washington Press; ditto *Origins of Mendelism* (1996), New York, Basic Books, Inc.

ROBERTS, D F 1973 – *Climate and Human Variability.* An Addison Wesley Module in Anthropology, No 34, Reading, Mass., Addison Wesley. Eukaryotic cell.

WATSON, James D 1968 – *The Double Helix,* New York, Atheneum.
Adamic Covenant:

Fall of man and the promise.
Noahic Covenant:
The flood, human government & blessing of animals.

Mosaic Covenant:
Ten Commandments, Sabbath, Passover, and the Tabernacle.
Davidic and Land Edict:
Confirmation of land promise and coming of Messiah.
Chapter 3: Prophesy -
BENITE, Zvi Ben-Dor, *The Ten Lost Tribes: A World History,* Oxford University Press 2009, ISBN 978-019-530733-7, Review by Bob Goldfarb.

BROWN, Dan, *The da Vinci Code*, Transworld Publishers, 2003.
BULLINGER, *The Companion Bible*, Appx. 162.
EUROPE IN PROPHESY – *The Unfolding of End Times,* 1987. Thomas Nelson Inc Publishers.
KENNEDY, Paul, *The Rise and Fall of the Great Powers*, 1987.
McCALLUM, Dennis and DE LASHMUTT, Gary, *The New Testament Definitions of the Church from the Introductory Study Guide.*
NEIL, William ditto
POPE JOHN PAUL II, ditto pages 28-53.
The Good News, January-February 2010, pages 9-11.
The Good News, November-December 2009.
The Times History of the World ditto.
UNGER, *Major Themes of the Bible,* ditto. *Unger's Survey of the Bible.*
VEITH, Walter, *Battle of the Bible, Changing the Word*,   CD's Part 1, 2 and 3.
WEINLAND, Roland, *2008, God's Final Witnesses,* ISBN 978-0- 9753240-6-6 (hard cover), 978-0-9753240-7-3 (soft cover). Chapters 1, 3, 8 and 12 contain only Biblical references.
WILSON, Ian ditto.

PART 2 -
Chapter 4: Who is Jesus?
BROWN, Peter, The Rise of Christendom, 2nd edition (Oxford, Blackwell Publishing, 2003).

CAROL, Warren H., *The Building of Christendom*,1987, Special: Book Sources/0931888247.
HANSON, R P C (1988). T & T Clark. pp.318–381.
HODGKIN, Thomas, The Dynasty Of Theodosius: Or Eighty Years' Struggle With The Barbarians. Kessinger Publishing, LLC, 2007. ISBN 978-0548239995.
HOOKER, Richard, *World Civilizations.*
KELLY, J N D,*The Creed of Nicea* in *Early Christian Creeds,* 1982.
McMULLAN, Ramsay, Christianizing the Roman Empire A.D 100-400 Yale University Press, 1986, ISBN 978-0300036428.
POPE JOHN PAUL II, ditto.
READER'S DIGEST, ditto.
The Good News, November-December 2009, page 3.
The Interpreter's Dictionary of the Bible
WIENLAND, Ronald ditto.
WILLIAMS, Rowan, *Arius: Heresy and Tradition* - Revised Edition, 1987, 2001 – Synopsis.
WILSON, Ian ditto.

Chapter 5: Is the existence of God a figment of the imagination of the human mind?

Chapter 6: Genealogy of Yeshua -

BART, D Ehrman, *How Jesus Became God: The Exaltation of a Jewish Preacher from Galilee;* Harper One, An Imprint of Harper Collins, Publishers, ISBN 978-0-6-177 818-6.

DAWKINS, Richard, *The Selfish Gene,* 1976, Oxford University Press, Walton Street, Oxford, OX2 6DP.

GIBRON, Khalil, *The Broken Wings,* 1912.

GRAYS ANATOMY, *The Anatomical Basis of Clinical Practice,* Ed in Chief.

POPE JOHN PAUL II, Crossing the Threshold of Hope, pages 28-53.

SINGH, Indibir, *Introduction to Human Embryology for Medical Students* 1978.1973 – *Principles of Human Genetics,* (3rd Ed.). San Francisco: W H Freeman and Company.

STANDING, Susan, 39th Ed. ISBN Main edition 0443 071683.

VAN DE GRAAF, Kent, *Concept of Human Anatomy and Physiology,* Graaf, McGraw Hill Companies, p. 962.

VELLACOTT, Jane and SIDE, Sarah, *Understanding Advanced Human Biology,* Hodder & Stoughton, 1998, Eukaryotic Cell, page 8; pp.81, 97, blood cells.

WALKER, Richard, *Guide to the Human Body,* Philips, division of Octopus Publishing Group Ltd,2-4 Heron Quays, London E14 4JP, pp.67,102-104, et al.

PART THREE -

Chapter 7: Ministry of Yeshua

Baha'u'llah, Reachings from *Reflections on the Life of the Spirit, Life and Death* page 35, Ruhi Institute, Book 1. Baha'i Books UK, 5 Station Approach, Oakham LE15 6QW.

BART, D Ehrman, *Lost Christianities, Books That Did Not Make It Into The New **Testament,* Oxford University Press, 2003**

HOOKER, Richard, *World Civilizations* ditto.

KING, Karen L, The Gospel of Mary of Magdala: Jesus and the First Woman Apostle, Polebridge Press, Santa Rosa, California, 2003). Written in Greek and Coptic, *The Gospel of Mary,* codex is dated to the 3rd (Greek) and 5th (Coptic) centuries A.D.

MALACHI, Tau, *The Gnostic Gospel of St Thomas, Mediation on Mystical Teachings,*
Llewellyn Worldwide Ltd, 2004.

MEYER, Marvin, *The Gospel of Thomas: The Hidden Sayings of Jesus,* Deckle Edge publishing, 2004.

NEIL, William ditto

PAGELS, Elaine, *Beyond Belief:The Secret Gospel of Thomas,* Random House, 2004.

TANNER, Stephen L (classicist), *Women in Literature of the Old Testament,* University of Idaho, 1975. ERIC ED112422.

THE COLUMBIA ENCYCLOPAEDIA, 6th edition, 2008, Encyclopaedia.com, 29 May 2009.

THE LOST YEARS OF JESUS, Elizabeth Clare Prophet

THE LOST YEARS OF JESUS: THE LIFE OF SAINT ISSA, Translation by Notovitch. THE URANTIA BOOK, published by Urantia Foundation in 1955 sometimes called the Urantia Papers or The Fifth Epochal Revelation is a spiritual and philosophical book that originated in Chicago between 1924 and 1955. The authors introduced the word 'Urantia' as the name of planet Earth with the intent to an all-embracing concept of religion, science and philosophy, besides the meaning and origin of life, humankind's place in the universe, the relationship between God and people, and the life of Jesus.

Chapter 8: Arrest, Trial, and Crucifixion.

Chapter 9: Core of Redemption

The New Covenant and Fullness Times

McCALLUM, Dennis and DE LASHMUTT, Gary, ditto. and *The Good News,* November-December 2009.

Newsweek, 5 Sept. 2005.

UNGER, Merrill F ditto

PART FOUR -

Chapter 10: Assumed Divine Mandate

BRODD, Jefferey (2003) World Religions, Winona, MN: Saint Mary's Press, ISBN 978-0-88480-725-5.

NATHAN, Peter, *The Original View of Originsl Sin*

PREAMBLE AND ARTICLES OF FAITH V SIN, Original and Personal, Church of the NAZARENE.

BROWN, Dan ditto.

BART, D Ehrman, *Lost Christianities: The Battles for Scripture and The Faiths We Never Knew;* Oxford University Press Inc. Publishers; ISBN-13: 978-0-19-514183-2; ISBN-10: 0-19-514183-0.

DICKENS, Charles, *Oliver Twist,* published by Richard Bentley in 1838.

EDIE, Kate, *Nobody's Child, 2005, Hodder & Stoughton.*

ENCYCLOPAEDIA BRITTANICA, 11th Edition, Vol.14, p.273.

FLETCHER, ditto.

GREER, Germane, The *Female Eunuch*, Flamingo an imprint of Harper Collins (1991).

GRINDLE, Gilbert (1892) *The Destruction of paganism in the Roman Empire,* **pp 29-30.**

HISLOP, Alexander, *The Two Babylons,* 1957, pp 97-98.

HYERS, M. Conrad. *The meaning of creation: Genesis and modern science.* Westminster John Knox Press, 1984, p.3. special: Book Sources/-9780804201.

O'GORMAN, Colm, *Beyond Belief,* 2009, Hodder and Stoughton, Hardback ISBN 9780 34092505 8, Trade Paperback ISBN 278 0 340 92505 5: pages 19, 105, 129, 217, 244, 253-56 and 294.

ROBINSON, B.A. The status of women in the Bible and in early Christianity. Ontario Consultants on Religious Tolerance, 2010.

ROUTERY, Michael (1997), *The Serapeum of Alexandria, The First Missionay War. The Church take over of the Roman Empire.*

WEINLAND, Ronald ditto.

ZWIERLEIN, Otto, *Peter in Rome.* The literature with a critical edition of the martyrdom of Peter and Paul on the basis of a new manuscript. Series: Studies on ancient literature and history in 1996, Berlin, published by de *Gruyter, 2009, ISBN 978-3-11-020808-5, Vol. XIII 476.*

Chapter 11: The New Covenant and Administration of the Church

KIRSCH, P, *St. Peter, Prince of the Apostles*, "Catholic Encyclopedia".

McCULLOGH, Colleen, *The First Man in Rome*, Random Century Group 1990.

Chapter 12: The Palestinian Covenant on Messianic Administration

UNGER, Merrill F ditto.

WARREN, Dr. Lee B.A., D.D. (c) 1999 PLIM REPORT, Vol. 8, No. 5.

New Covenant & Administration of Fullness Times:

Chapter 13: God of People

Monotheistic and Other Faiths.

ADIELE EBERECHUKWU AFIGBO, Robin H. Palmer,*The Making of Modern Africa: The Twentieth Century*, 1986 Elliot Kenan Kamwana and African Watchtower The largest movement expressing rejection of white domination in religions ... between 1908 and 1909 by Elliot Kenan Kamwana.

ACHEBE, Chinua, *Things Fall Apart*, 1958, William Heinemann Ltd.

A LIONS HANDBOOK, *The World's Religions,* ISBN 07459 3720. A most useful book on the subject with more than fifty authors' contributions from faiths of many countries.

ARULMEYAM, Durai, The Gospel of Shirdi Sai Baba, A Holy Spiritual Path, New Delhi, Sterling, 2008, ISBN 978-81-207-3997-0.

BAKER EDDY, Mary (1821-1910), *Christian Science,* author of Science and Health with a key to the Scriptures.

CARUS, Paul (1852-1919). *The Gospel of Buddha* was an 1894 book modelled on the New Testament and tells the story of Buddha through parables. 1 KB (147 words) - 13:52, 11 April 2008.

DEEDAT, Sheikh Ahmed, *What The Bible Says About Muhammad,* Published and distributed by I.D.C.I – Islamic Dawah Centre International, Freepost, Birmingham, B8 1BR (UK).

GHANDI, Mohandas Karamchand, *What Jesus Means to Me,* Compiled by Prabhu Navajivan Publishing House, Ahmadabad, 1959, pp 9 and 10.

HEINDEL, Max, The Rosicrucian Cosmo-Conception, Part 111, Chapter XV, *Christ and His Mission*, 1909, ISBN-0-911274-34-0.

HINE, Reginald L, pamphlet *Meet the Quakers, Society of Friends,* London (1984).

LIU WU-CHI, *A Short History of Confucian Philosophy*; Pelican Books published by Penguin Books Ltd. Harmondsworth, Middlesex, UK, 1955, a most useful book on Confucius, China's greatest philosopher.

MARZIEN, Gail, ed Selections from the Writings of Abdu'l-baha (1978), Wilmette, Illinois, US, Baha'i Publishing Trust ISBN 0-85398-084-5.

McCULLOGH,Colleen, *The First Man in Rome*, Random Century Group 1990.

McGRATH, Alister Edgar, *Iustitia Dei: A History of the Christian Doctrine of Justification* (1986) Special: Book Sources/0521624266.

MENCKREN, J L, *Selected Prejudices,* The Travellers Library, reprinted 1928, Jonathan Cape, 50 Bedford Square, London, England.

PARAMAHANSA YOGANANDA, Autobiography of a Yogi, Authorised by the International Publications Council of Self-Realisation Fellowship, founded 1920, 3880 San Rafael Avenue, Los Angeles, California 90065, USA. Library of Congress Catalog Card No: 78-151319, ISBN 0-87612-079-6. Printed in the United States of America 10425-9876. Translated into 18 languages.

TALIAFERRO, Charles, DRAPER, Paul; QUINN, Philip L: *A Companion to Philosophy of Religions*, John Wiley and Sons, 2010, Google Books.

URANTIA BOOK, author unknown, first published by Urantia Foundation in 1955, a US-based non-profit group; others (since becoming public domain) in 2001.

www.ingramcontent.com/pod-product-compliance
Lightning Source LLC
Chambersburg PA
CBHW072003090426
42740CB00011B/2070